# LAW'S RELIGION

## Religious Difference and the Claims of Constitutionalism

Prevailing stories about law and religion place great faith in the capacity of legal multiculturalism, rights-based toleration, and conceptions of the secular to manage issues raised by religious difference. Yet the relationship between law and religion consistently proves more fraught than such accounts suggest. In *Law's Religion*, Benjamin L. Berger knocks law from its perch above culture, arguing that liberal constitutionalism is an aspect of, not an answer to, the challenges of cultural pluralism. Berger urges an approach to the study of law and religion that focuses on the experience of law as a potent cultural force.

Based on a close reading of Canadian jurisprudence, but relevant to all liberal legal orders, this book explores the nature and limits of legal tolerance and shows how constitutional law's understanding of religion shapes religious freedom. Rather than calling for legal reform, *Law's Religion* invites us to rethink the ethics, virtues, and practices of adjudication in matters of religious difference.

BENJAMIN L. BERGER is an associate professor at Osgoode Hall Law School at York University.

# Law's Religion

*Religious Difference and the Claims of Constitutionalism*

BENJAMIN L. BERGER

UNIVERSITY OF TORONTO PRESS
Toronto Buffalo London

© University of Toronto Press 2015
Toronto Buffalo London
www.utppublishing.com

ISBN 978-1-4426-4357-4 (cloth)    ISBN 978-1-4426-1206-8 (paper)

---

**Library and Archives Canada Cataloguing in Publication**

Berger, Benjamin L., 1977–, author
Law's religion : religious difference and the claims of constitutionalism /
Benjamin L. Berger.

Includes bibliographical references and index.
ISBN 978-1-4426-4357-4 (bound). – ISBN 978-1-4426-1206-8 (paperback)

1. Constitutional law – Religious aspects. 2. Religion and law. I. Title.

K3280.B47 2015    342.08′52    C2015-905233-5

---

University of Toronto Press acknowledges the financial assistance to its
publishing program of the Canada Council for the Arts and the Ontario
Arts Council, an agency of the Government of Ontario.

Canada Council    Conseil des Arts
for the Arts       du Canada

ONTARIO ARTS COUNCIL
CONSEIL DES ARTS DE L'ONTARIO
an Ontario government agency
un organisme du gouvernement de l'Ontario

Funded by the    Financé par le
Government   gouvernement
of Canada      du Canada

*For my mother and father*

# Contents

# Acknowledgments

When I began the research that would lead to this book, I could not have imagined the way in which the scholarly study of law and religion would grow, both in law schools and as a topic for interdisciplinary inquiry. Although the social disputes and tensions that occasioned this growth have not always been welcome, the development of this field has generated singularly valuable avenues of insight into the character of law and the nature of modern religious life. My hope is that this book contributes to the understanding of both.

During the period leading to this book, I was very fortunate to have the support of two outstanding law schools, Osgoode Hall Law School and the Faculty of Law, University of Victoria. Both are institutions animated by a rich, critical, and socially sensitive posture towards the study of law, as well as a keen appreciation for the fruits of interdisciplinary and socio-legal inquiry. These institutions, and the outstanding scholars that inhabit and give life to them, have been centrally important to my ongoing development as a scholar and teacher. The many friends and colleagues who have been generous, provocative, and supportive conversation partners over these years are too numerous to name. Among that wonderful group, a special thank you to my friends and colleagues Carys Craig, Sonia Lawrence, and Lorne Sossin, at Osgoode Hall Law School, and Gillian Calder, Gerry Ferguson, Hamar Foster, Andrew Newcombe, Hester Lessard, and Andrew Petter, from my time at the University of Victoria, for their friendship and personal support. Among my friends outside the academy who have supported me along the way, a particular thank you to Eliott Behar for the depth and constancy of his friendship and encouragement.

I owe a special debt of thanks to Paul Kahn. Through our conversations over the years, he not only helped me to explore and develop the ideas that led to this book, but taught me broader lessons about the creative heart of the scholarly enterprise and the possibilities for what legal scholarship can be. I am fortunate to have had a wonderful community of friends and scholars specifically interested in issues of law and religion. Thank you to John Borrows, Paul Bramadat, Avigail Eisenberg, John McLaren, Dick Moon, Winnifred Sullivan, Shauna Van Praagh, and Jeremy Webber for their generosity, insight, and for many enjoyable and rich conversations. I have learned a great deal from each of you.

Over the course of this book's development, I had the benefit of the outstanding work of an exceptional group of student research assistants. Thank you in particular to those who helped as the manuscript has come to publication: Hannah Askew, Amy Brubacher, Rachel Devon, Geneviève Murray, and Anthony Sangiuliano.

I had an excellent experience publishing this book with the University of Toronto Press. I am enormously grateful to Daniel Quinlan, my acquisitions editor, for his sage advice, insightful comments, patience, and guidance along the way. One could not ask for a better editor. Thank you to Wayne Herrington, my managing editor, who steered the book to production with an expert hand. Thanks also to Ian MacKenzie, who copy-edited the book, and to UTP's marketing and production groups.

I gratefully acknowledge the financial support of the Social Sciences and Humanities Research Council, which aided in the production of this book and my research and publication in the years leading to it. A portion of chapter 1 is drawn from a piece published as "The Aesthetics of Religious Freedom" in Winnifred Fallers Sullivan & Lori G Beaman, eds, *Varieties of Religious Establishments* (Surrey: Ashgate, 2013) 33. Versions of chapter 2 were previously published as "Law's Religion: Rendering Culture" in (2007) 45:2 Osgoode Hall LJ 277, and in Richard Moon, ed, *Law and Religious Pluralism in Canada* (Vancouver: UBC Press, 2008) 264, and a version of chapter 3 appeared as "The Cultural Limits of Legal Tolerance" in (2008) 21:2 Can JL & Jur 245, and in Courtney Bender & Pamela E Klassen, eds, *After Pluralism: Reimagining Religious Engagement* (New York: Columbia University Press, 2010) 98. Thank you to the editors and publishers who supported the early versions of this work.

Two important acknowledgments remain. First, I am grateful for the superb students that I have had the honour of teaching over my years as a professor in the Faculty of Law, University of Victoria, and Osgoode Hall Law School. The diversity, insight, and creativity of my students is a constant source of energy and inspiration. Teaching – in its variety of forms – is the heart of what we do as professors and I am very fortunate to have been exposed to such exceptional students. My ideas about the issues discussed in this book have been shaped, challenged, and improved through engagement with my students, particularly those in my Law and Religion seminars.

Finally, a loving thank you to my first and wisest editor and conversation partner, my father.

LAW'S RELIGION

Religious Difference and the Claims of Constitutionalism

# Introduction

In the fall of 1875 there was an election approaching in the County of Charlevoix, Quebec. This federal by-election pitted a Liberal candidate, Pierre-Alexis Tremblay, against a father of Confederation and a trusted senior minister in Sir John A. Macdonald's Conservative governments, Hector-Louis Langevin. Langevin had been politically bruised by the 1873 scandal surrounding the construction of the Canadian Pacific Railway but was returning to federal politics at the urging of the Conservatives and with the prospect of a safe seat in Charlevoix. He enjoyed the support of the Catholic Church, which regarded this election with much interest.

Starting in the mid-nineteenth century the ultramontane movement in Roman Catholicism gained a substantial foothold in Quebec and a sympathetic ear among Conservatives. Ultramontanism translated papal supremacy and infallibility into a claim about the relationship between church and state. Inferior to the church in origin and nature, the state was beholden and should accede to the positions, directions, and interests of the church. On this view, there was no principled basis for drawing a sharp line between the theological and the political, with the church's authority serving as the controlling principle for both. The Liberal party of the time resisted such claims, seeking to limit the privileges and powers of the church in the affairs of state.

On September 22, 1875, the bishops of the ecclesiastical province responsible for the County of Charlevoix, Quebec, issued a pastoral letter and directed that it be read and published at all churches, chapels, and missions in the county. The letter explained sharply and clearly what, for the church, was at stake in this election: a dangerous claim about the separation of religion and politics.

Men bent upon deceiving you, Our Dearly Beloved Brethren, incessantly repeat that religion has nothing to do with politics; that no attention should be paid to religious principles in the discussion of public affairs; that the clergy has duties to fulfil, but in the Church and the sacristy; and that in politics the people should practice moral independence!

Monstrous errors, O.D.B.B, and woe to the country wherein they should take root! By excluding the clergy they exclude the Church, and by throwing the Church aside they deprive themselves of all the salutary and immutable principles she contains, God, morals, justice, truth; and when they have destroyed everything else, nothing is left them but force to rely upon![1]

The bishops instructed the curés of the county to direct their parishioners not to vote for Mr Tremblay, declaring "that to vote on such a side is a sin, that to do such an act makes [one] liable to the censures of the Church."[2]

The record shows that the clergy, called to action by this dispatch, complied with enthusiasm and fervour, appealing forcefully to the political and spiritual consciences of their parishioners. In a speech delivered on the Sunday before the election, the Rev Mr Sirois, priest and curé of St Paul's Bay, instructed his parishioners to "bind yourselves to the Holy Church, to the salutary teachings which she gives you through the voice of her pastors, if you wish to escape the woes which the false prophets of our day prepare for us."[3] He assured them that they could not err by following the guidance of the church and that they should be "deeply impressed with the truths set forth in the last pastoral letter (*mandement*) of our Bishops, on the Constitution of the Church, on Catholic Liberalism, and on the office which the clergy is to fulfil in the time of elections."[4] Rev Sirois explained that the bishops' instructions had not been made "for the United States, but for the Province of Québec"[5] and that the risks of which they warned were very real, indeed. The bishops "do not wish to warn you against phantoms, but, indeed, against Liberalism and its partizans," he explained, and he cautioned the congregation not to be deceived by those who would

---

1 Quoted in *Brassard v Langevin* (1877), 1 SCR 145 at 153 [*Brassard*].
2 *Ibid* at 156.
3 *Ibid* at 160.
4 *Ibid*.
5 *Ibid*.

suggest "that there is no Liberalism in our country."[6] Having thus set the political scene, Rev Sirois framed the coming election in terms that would resonate deeply with his parishioners:

> You shall see men having outward appearances of piety and religion allow themselves to be fascinated without suspecting it, by the deceitful words of the serpent Catholic Liberal. You know in what manner the serpent found his way into the terrestrial paradise, with what cunning he succeeded in convincing Eve that she should not die, nor Adam either, by eating of the forbidden fruit. You all know what took place; the serpent was the cause of the misfortunes that are weighing upon us. In the same manner Catholic Liberalism wishes to find its way into the paradise of the Church to lead her children to fall. Be firm, my brethren, our Bishops tells [sic] us that it is no longer permitted to be conscientiously a Catholic Liberal; be careful never to taste the fruit of the tree Catholic Liberal.[7]

Rev Sirois admonished the congregation to obey him: "I am here as your legitimate pastor," he advised them, and "if you despise my word, you despise the word of your Bishop, then of the Pope, and even thereby the word of our Lord who hath sent us."[8] Yet the curé would be even more explicit, emphasizing the importance of the vote and reminding his congregation that "one day God shall ask you to give an account of it before His formidable tribunal."[9] He pointedly asked if it were "not true that on your death-bed you would reproach yourselves bitterly if your conscience should upbraid you for having contributed, by your vote, to the election of men who wish to separate the Church from the State?"[10]

Rev Sirois' sermon was not an isolated exhortation. In the parish at St Hilairion, the Rev Mr Langlais echoed these directives and warnings. "Liberalism," he reminded his congregation, "is condemned by our Holy Father, the Pope."[11] The implications of that condemnation on the parishioners' conduct were clear: "The Church condemns only what is evil;

---

6 *Ibid*.
7 *Ibid* at 160–1.
8 *Ibid* at 161.
9 *Ibid* at 160.
10 *Ibid*.
11 *Ibid* at 163.

now Liberalism is condemned, then Liberalism is bad, and, therefore, you ought not to give your vote to a Liberal, your bishops declare it openly."[12] In no uncertain terms, Rev Langlais told his congregation that "if you know that [the candidate] is a Liberal, you cannot conscientiously give him your vote," because "you are sinning by favouring a man who supports principles condemned by the Church, and you assume the responsibility of the evil which that candidate may do in the application of the dangerous principles which he professes."[13] Like Rev Sirois, Rev Langlais reminded his parishioners of the link between their current duty and their ultimate fate:

> Remember, my dear children, that you shall have to render to God an account of the vote you will cast this week. Tell me on what side would you prefer to be at the hour of your death? Is it on the side of the Church, of your Sovereign Pontiff and your Bishops? or on the side of Victor Emmanuel and Garibaldi?[14] Consider, and decide like men and not like children.
>
> The act which you are going to perform has, perhaps, more importance than you could imagine.[15]

In the pastoral letter, the bishops assured the clergy that they had not only the authority but the duty to use their offices to influence this political decision. "The Church," the bishops held, "is not only independent of civil society, but is superior to her by her origin, by her comprehensiveness, and by her end."[16] The letter explained that civil society originated in the will of God, and that God wished that men would live in civil society, but that, unlike civil society, the church had an atemporal and mythic foundation: "[T]he forms of civil society vary with times and places; the Church was born on Calvary of the blood of a God, from His lips She has directly received her immutable constitution, and no power on earth can alter the form thereof."[17] This origin

---

12 *Ibid*.

13 *Ibid*.

14 Earlier in his sermon, the curé reminded the congregation of the evils committed against the church by Victor Emmanuel and Garibaldi, even though they were Catholics, just as Mr Tremblay, the Liberal candidate, was a Catholic.

15 *Brassard, supra* note 1 at 164.

16 *Ibid* at 152.

17 *Ibid*.

story imposed an affirmative obligation to augment not only one's private life, but also politics with the goods found in the church. The bishops explained in their letter,

> Whoever has his salvation at heart should regulate his actions according to the divine law, of which religion is the expression and the guardian. Who does not understand how justice and rectitude would everywhere prevail, did rulers and people never lose sight of this divine law, which is equity itself, nor of the formidable judgment they shall have, one day, to undergo before Him whose look and strong arm nobody can escape. The people have, therefore, no greater enemies than those men who want to banish religion from politics, for under the pretence of freeing the people from what they call *priest tyranny, priest's undue influence*, they are preparing, for the same people, the heaviest chains, and the most difficult to throw off: they put might above right, and they take from the civil power the only moral restraint which can stop it from degenerating into despotism and tyranny![18]

On January 22, 1876, the Liberal candidate was defeated, and the Honourable Hector L. Langevin was elected to the House of Commons. But a supporter of Mr Tremblay brought a petition to the courts, alleging that the *Dominion Controverted Elections Act, 1874*, had been offended by the "undue influence" exerted by the clergy.[19] The respondents resisted the claim, arguing in part that freedom of religion entailed the church's immunity from such limits.[20] The Liberal

---

18 *Ibid* at 153–4 [emphasis in original].

19 Section 95 of the *Dominion Controverted Elections Act, 1874*, SC 1874, c 10, provided as follows: "Every person who, directly or indirectly, by himself or by any other person on his behalf, makes use of, or threatens to make use of any force, violence or restraint, or inflicts or threatens the infliction, by himself, or by or through any other person, of any injury, damage, harm or loss, or in any manner practices intimidation upon or against any person, in order to induce or compel such person to vote or refrain from voting, or on account of such person having voted or refrained from voting at any election, or who, by abduction, duress or any fraudulent device or contrivance, impedes, prevents or otherwise interferes with the free exercise of the franchise of any voter, or thereby compels, induces or prevails upon any voter to give or refrain from giving his vote at any election, shall be deemed to have committed the offence of undue influence."

20 Ian Bushnell, *The Captive Court: A Study of the Supreme Court of Canada* (Montreal & Kingston: McGill-Queen's University Press, 1992) at 78.

supporters lost at first instance, with Justice Routhier holding that "spiritual influence" was not prohibited by the Act. The case made its way to the Supreme Court of Canada, which had been established just months before, in 1875.

The Supreme Court unanimously overturned the lower court decision, annulling the election on the basis that it had been spoiled by "undue spiritual influence."

Justice Taschereau – brother of the archbishop of Quebec at the time, Elzéar-Alexandre Taschereau – began his reasons by reflecting on "the difficulty of the position in which I, together with one of my colleagues upon this Bench, am placed as a Catholic" by virtue of the issues raised in the case.[21] Nevertheless, he found that "[t]he law expressly forbids all undue influence, from whatever source it may arise, and without any distinction."[22] He found that these sermons evoked in the electors of the county "a serious dread of committing a grievous sin, and that of being deprived of the sacraments."[23] The evidence showed that "a general system of intimidation was practiced [and] that as a consequence undue influence was exercised."[24] Indeed, he characterized this as "undue influence of the worst kind," because the declarations came from priests and

---

21  *Brassard, supra* note 1 at 189. The colleague to whom Justice Taschereau was referring was Justice Fournier. See Bushnell, *ibid* at 80. Bushnell reports that Archbishop Taschereau "was not in complete sympathy with the ultramontane position and the court's decision did not offend him," though it did upset the bishops of the province. Indeed, "[a]s a result of the stand taken by the Taschereau brothers, they were denounced and their religious faith questioned by the strong ultramontane forces in the province."

22  *Brassard, supra* note 1 at 199. Rejecting the notion of ecclesiastical immunity that Justice Routhier relied upon in the court below, Justice Taschereau reasoned that "the minister who so far forgets himself in the pulpit as to revile or defame any person, does not speak of religion, does not define doctrine or discipline, but puts aside his sacred character, and is considered like any other man as satisfying his personal revenge, or as acting through interest, and, in consequence, he is not held to be in the exercise of his spiritual functions" (198–9). In another fascinating passage rejecting the respondent's argument that this matter could be judged only by an ecclesiastical tribunal, Justice Taschereau reasoned that no such tribunal existed and "it would be only in the form of a conventional arbitration, which would be binding on no one but the parties themselves" (197).

23  *Ibid* at 194.

24  *Ibid* at 195.

were aimed at an unlearned community committed to following the counsel of their clergy.[25]

Justice Ritchie agreed, arguing that "the combined effects of the bishop's pastoral and the denunciations of the clergy so permeated the county as to make it impossible for [him] to say that there was a free election."[26] Most striking about Justice Ritchie's opinion is his consideration of whether, owing to the special protections afforded the Roman Catholic Church in the *Treaty of Paris* and other early imperial acts, the clergy were not subject to the jurisdiction of the courts. On this topic, he stated,

> Thus we see that under these Acts the free exercise of the religion of the Church of Rome is guaranteed to the inhabitants of Quebec as far as the laws of Great Britain permit, subject to the King's supremacy. But while the members of that Church thus have a perfect right to the full and free exercise of their religion in as full and ample a manner as any other Church or denomination in the Dominion, every member of that Church, like every member of every other Church, is subordinate to the law. There is no man in this Dominion so great as to be above the law, and none so humble as to be beneath its notice. So long as a man, whether clerical or lay, lives under the Queen's protection in the Queen's dominion, he must obey the laws of the land, and if he infringes them he is amenable to the legal tribunals of the country – the Queen's Courts of Justice.[27]

His rejection of the contention that the church was above the law was unequivocal. He adopted the language in *O'Keefe v Cardinal Cullen*,[28]

---

25 *Ibid* at 194. Justice Taschereau explained, "I can conceive that these sermons may have had no influence whatever on the intelligent and instructed portion of the hearers; nevertheless, I have no doubt but these sermons must have influenced the majority of persons void of instruction, notwithstanding that by reason of the secrecy in voting by ballot it has not been possible to point out more than six or eight voters as having been influenced to the extent of affecting their will. According to the testimony of over fifteen witnesses, a very large number changed their opinion in consequence of this undue influence. I may here state, that, in like cases to annul an election, a large number of cases of undue influence by a candidate or an agent is not required, and that one single case well proved, suffices, although the candidate availing himself of it may have had an overwhelming majority" (194–5).

26 *Ibid* at 229.

27 *Ibid* at 220.

28 [1873] 7 IR CL 319, Fitzgerald J.

in which Justice Fitzgerald explained, "No church, no community, no public body, no individual in the realm, can be in the least above the law, or exempted from the authority of its civil or criminal tribunals. The law of the land is supreme, and we recognize no authority as superior or equal to it. Such ever has been and is, and I hope will ever continue to be, a principle of our Constitution."[29] For Justice Ritchie, the controversy in this case was not "at all a religious question";[30] rather, electoral law involved statutory civil rights "pure and simple" and the issue raised in this case was, therefore, "simply a constitutional legal question"[31] for the courts to determine. This question had been decided – the priests had exerted undue spiritual influence over the constituents – and the election was annulled.

The judgment was rendered on February 26, 1877. The Honourable Hector Louis Langevin was re-elected on March 23, 1877, and served as a Conservative member of Parliament until 1896.

One view of this late nineteenth-century case is that it merely reflects an early phase in the development of Canadian constitutionalism, in which the relationship between religion and the legal structure had not yet been settled. The country had been established only a decade earlier, and the constitutional compromise (as it is sometimes referred to) was marked by a much more complex legal status for religion in Canada than a clear separation of church and state.[32] From this perspective, the tensions at play in *Brassard v Langevin* would simply have to await a "right accommodation" of religion into Canadian constitutionalism or a perfected understanding of pluralism and secularism. This is the kind of reading of the case that fits within the prevailing story about law and religion, one that finds hope for a denouement in Canada's modern

---

29 *Ibid* at 371.
30 *Brassard, supra* note 1 at 215.
31 *Ibid.*
32 In addition to the early Acts guaranteeing to the people of Quebec the freedom of the church and of their Roman Catholic faith, with the *British North America Act, 1867*, Roman Catholic schools gained constitutional protection outside of Quebec, as did Protestant schools within Quebec. For discussions of this history, see Janet Epp Buckingham, *Fighting over God: A Legal and Political History of Religious Freedom in Canada* (Montreal & Kingston: McGill-Queen's University Press, 2014); MH Ogilvie, *Religious Institutions and the Law in Canada*, 3rd ed (Toronto: Irwin Law, 2010).

policies of multiculturalism and its commitment to rights-based legal tolerance. This reading of *Brassard v Langevin* casts the case as simply an initial stage in what the Supreme Court of Canada has referred to as Canada's "evolutionary tolerance for diversity and pluralism" – an early stop on a "journey [that] has included a growing appreciation for multiculturalism, including the recognition that ethnic, religious or cultural differences will be acknowledged and respected."[33]

This interpretation rests on a particular way of imagining and portraying the character of law – understood in this volume as self-described "secular" state law[34] – in contrast to religion. It leans on a specific way of configuring the cultural location of law that is as influential today as it was at the time of *Brassard v Langevin*. A distance of so many years and the openness of the language of the litigants provide a clear line of sight onto this configuration. It is a line of sight that offers a picture of things that could form the basis for a more complicated, subtle, and fraught understanding of the dynamics reflected by this case and still extant in the endlessly productive interaction between law and religion.

Consider the building blocks that form each position. The pastoral letter and sermons admit of no ambiguity about their source of authority: legitimacy and authority flow in an unbroken chain from God, through the pope and the church, and are finally vested in the pastor. This authority is transcendent and, therefore, supreme over any earthly institution. The church's authority is timeless: "The forms of civil society vary with times and places; the Church was born on Calvary of the blood of a God, from His lips She has directly received her immutable constitution."[35] The implications of this electoral event are not contained within the political or juridical moment; rather, they ripple into the afterlife. The significance of the election is attributable, in part, to its impact upon the eternal soul of the voter. As the religious leaders explain, "[O]ne day God shall ask you to give an account of it before His formidable tribunal."[36] In this, the pastoral letter and sermons assert the utter indivisibility of the religious and political self and, with it, the public and private aspects of subjectivity. The religious position in this case is saturated with the particular – with elements of

---

33  *Bruker v Marcovitz*, 2007 SCC 54 at para 1, [2007] 3 SCR 607, Abella J.
34  See Winnifred Fallers Sullivan, Robert A Yelle & Mateo Taussig-Rubbo, eds, *After Secular Law* (Stanford, Cal: Stanford University Press, 2011).
35  *Brassard*, *supra* note 1 at 153.
36  *Ibid* at 160.

belief, claims about time and the self, and positions about authority that we recognize as specific to a given world view and way of life and, accordingly, assign to the realm of "culture."

The essential response from the legal side is that it sits above and is separate from such particular claims. It is apart from the realm of culture, such that Justice Ritchie was able to characterize the problem before the Court as a constitutional question "pure and simple."[37] The conceptions of subjectivity, of authority, of temporality, etc., reflected in the religious position are all tacitly refuted in the legal position and, indeed, law substitutes its own peculiar framing commitments and intuitions on each point. Indeed, as this case makes wonderfully clear, law *must* have such competing conceptions (and must reject the religious positions) to arrive at the substantive result that it does in the case. But that competition is effaced by the legal response; taking the ground of constitutional law "pure and simple" is ascending above the realm of the particular, rising above culture.

This way of imaging the nature and location of law in relation to religion remains as central to the prevailing contemporary account of the interaction of religion and Canadian constitutionalism as it was in the *Brassard v Langevin* case. This account has held that, in a society characterized by deep pluralism, the role of the law is to operationalize a political commitment to multiculturalism by serving as custodian and wielder of the twin key tools of tolerance and accommodation. In the context of religious difference in Canada, this commitment has translated into a prevailing juridical wisdom that freedom of religion is a hallmark of the liberal constitutional order and that the mechanism by which such cultural differences can be harmonized with the state is through the rights-based use of these legal tools. The tacit starting proposition of this commitment to legal multiculturalism and rights-based toleration is that law is a means of managing or adjudicating cultural difference but enjoys a strong form of autonomy from culture.[38] In a case addressing whether a witness should be able to wear a face covering – a niqab – while testifying, Justice LeBel offered but one particularly clear reflection of this orthodox understanding; he explained that religious multiculturalism is an important part of Canadian constitutional life,

---

37 *Ibid* at 215.
38 Wendy Brown, *Regulating Aversion: Tolerance in the Age of Identity and Empire* (Princeton, NJ: Princeton University Press, 2006) at 166ff.

but noted that "at the same time, however, the recognition of multiculturalism takes place *in the environment of the Constitution itself*, and is rooted in its political and legal traditions."[39] The cultural pluralism imagined by legal multiculturalism never includes the constitutional rule of law itself; rather, law sits in a managerial role above the realm of culture. Law is the curator – rather than a component – of cultural pluralism. This positioning of law as a structure above and apart from the particularly and contingently cultural is essential to prevailing public stories about the interaction of law and religion; it is the defining feature of what I will refer to as the "conventional story" or "conventional account" of the interaction of law and religion. Examining, troubling, and offering an alternative to that account is the subject of this book.

**The Trouble with the Conventional Story**

In the summer of 2003, Canada was again faced with the Roman Catholic Church seeking to formally and directly influence political affairs. On June 2, 2003, in the wake of Cabinet's decision to introduce legislation in Parliament that would legalize same-sex marriage, the Congregation for the Doctrine of the Faith, under the prefecture of Cardinal Joseph Ratzinger (later Pope Benedict XVI) and with the approval of Pope John Paul II, published a document that condemned same-sex marriage.[40] But mimicking the basic facts of the 125-year-old *Brassard v Langevin* case, the document went further and asserted, "When legislation in favour of the recognition of homosexual unions is proposed for the first time in a legislative assembly, the Catholic law-maker has a moral duty to express his opposition clearly and publicly and to vote against it. To vote in favour of a law so harmful to the common good is gravely immoral."[41] Some Canadians applauded this intervention,

---

39  *R v NS*, 2012 SCC 72 at para 72, [2012] 3 SCR 726 [emphasis added].
40  Congregation for the Doctrine of the Faith, *Considerations regarding Proposals to Give Legal Recognition to Unions between Homosexual Persons* (Nairobi: Pauline Publications Africa, 2003). "Congregation for the Doctrine of the Faith" is the modern name for the oldest of the congregations of the Roman Curia, once infamously active under the name "Holy Office of the Inquisition."
41  *Ibid* at 15. The document goes on, at 15, to admonish that "[w]hen legislation in favour of the recognition of homosexual unions is already in force, the Catholic politician must oppose it in the ways that are possible for him and make his opposition known; it is his duty to witness to the truth."

while many condemned it. As it was in the 1877 case, the discussion was again about the imagined respective positions of religion and constitutional law.

And in 2013–14, attention would again focus on the relationship between religion and "secular" state law in Quebec, with a public debate inaugurated by the sovereigntist Parti Québécois government's introduction of Bill 60,[42] the so-called Charter of Secularism. The bill sought to establish a distinctive form of secularism in Quebec, one whose most contentious feature was the prohibition that it would place on those discharging public duties from wearing conspicuous religious symbols, including kippahs, turbans, and hijabs. The more contemporary roots of this fiercely contested bill could be found in a series of prominent cases of religious accommodation that took place over the prior twenty years, cases that stirred the controversy leading to the 2008 Bouchard-Taylor Commission, which was tasked with inquiring into practices of accommodation and religious toleration in Quebec.[43] The commission report offered the language of "interculturalism" as a version of legal multiculturalism more appropriate to the particularities of Quebec, and urged the idea of "open secularism" as the most attractive legal and political response to religious difference. Yet Bill 60's response to this report, to the broader public debate, and to the many causes célèbres that provoked both, was to seek the establishment of a form of laïcité heretofore foreign to Quebec, one that would roll back forms of religious inclusion and accommodation that fit the narrative of "evolutionary tolerance for diversity and pluralism" offered by the Supreme Court of Canada. Although the issue would move to the political backburner with the defeat of the Parti Québécois in the next provincial election, the debate over Bill 60 marked a crisis in the relationship

---

42  *Charter affirming the values of State secularism and religious neutrality and of equality between women and men, and providing a framework for accommodation requests*, 1st Sess, 40th Leg, Quebec, 2013.

43  Gérard Bouchard & Charles Taylor, *Building the Future, a Time for Reconciliation: Report* (Quebec: Commission de consultation sur les pratiques d'accommodement reliées aux différences culturelles, 2008). For important discussions of religion and the duty of reasonable accommodation in Canada, see José Woehrling, "L'obligation d'accommodement raisonnable et l'adaptation de la société à la diversité religieuse" (1998) 43 McGill LJ 325; Avigail Eisenberg, "Rights in the Age of Identity Politics" (2013) 50 Osgoode Hall LJ 609.

between law and religion as pronounced as any in the history of the country.

Those dedicated to finding a "right accommodation" or perfecting a notion of pluralism or secularism should find the persistence of these fundamental structural tensions between law and religion in Canada deeply uncomfortable. The continuity in the experience of the law's relationship to religious difference – the durable instability of that relationship – belies the story that the better management of religion by law is what is at stake in the encounter of law and religion, now as then. Over 135 years have passed since *Brassard v Langevin*, over which time Canadian constitutionalism has matured and developed. Canada has adopted an explicit policy of multiculturalism, notions of secularism and tolerance have been debated and refined, human rights acts have been enacted, and the *Charter of Rights and Freedoms*[44] has since been entrenched. And yet the tensions between law and religion have not abated. On the contrary, they have gathered energy, replicating patterns and reposing questions, and in increasingly difficult form. Legal multiculturalism and rights-based toleration seem to have largely preserved, rather than disrupted, the fundamental tensions generated by the complex interaction of religion and law. This is the one way in which the conventional account fails us: the faith in the progressive realization of the promise of the constitutional management of religious diversity that is folded into prevailing stories seems maladapted to the reality of the durably fraught political experience of the meeting of law and religion. There is more going on than the evolution of an increasingly sensitive and refined legal doctrine or the working pure of the concept of the secular.

The prevailing political and juridical story also fails to offer a satisfying explanation for the anxiety, dissatisfaction, and deep contestation that is such a salient aspect of the contemporary experience of the interaction of religion and the constitutional rule of law. Within the terms of the conventional story, it is difficult to account for the fact that religious communities and commentators are expressing dissatisfaction with what they feel to be the oppressive force of secular law. Describing this phenomenon, Winnifred Sullivan writes of a "growing disjunction between the expectation of both these fissiparous communities

---

44 *Canadian Charter of Rights and Freedoms*, s 2(b), Part I of the *Constitution Act, 1982*, being Schedule B to the *Canada Act 1982* (UK), 1982, c 11 [*Charter*].

and their members with respect to their right to self-determination as *religious* communities and the realities of legal regulation."[45] Although she is describing the facts on the ground in the United States, the same is true in Canada.

The same-sex marriage dispute, for example, became both a lightning rod, attracting the pointed arguments of those who would see an utter severance of religion's appearance in the public sphere, and a moment for the expression of resentment of certain religious communities at their felt exclusion from Canadian public debate. Religious communities in various parts of the country have spoken out about their sense of marginalization brought about by legal decisions surrounding public education. As in other parts of the world, representatives of elements of the Muslim community have complained of an abiding social and legal intolerance of Islam, with an attendant sense of social marginalization that has only deepened since 9/11. Organizations representing communities that are disenchanted by the felt marginalization of religious culture and arguing for the increased presence of religion in public life, have become increasingly vocal, growing active politically and intervening in cases before the courts.

In spite of the palliative rhetoric of Canada's commitment to religious multiculturalism and legal toleration of religion, one finds discontent in many quarters on the state of this relationship and a sense that the experience of legal regulation is not as benignly curatorial as the orthodox political and juridical stories would suggest. This experience of management at the hands of the law should matter to us; and yet the pacific image of a rights-based tolerance and accommodation deployed by a basically autonomous legal order sitting above the realm of culture has great difficulty accounting for that experience of law's rule. This is another descriptive shortfall in the conventional account.

The character and experience of the relationship between law and religion in Canada is not adequately reflected by the account that we have at hand. This relationship repeatedly proves to be far more fraught, far more agonal, and far more durably so, than the story that the law tells about its encounter with religion – indeed, the picture given by most liberal theory that treats this issue – would suggest. Unable to account for the durability of the structural tensions, unable to explain

---

45 Winnifred Fallers Sullivan, *The Impossibility of Religious Freedom* (Princeton, NJ: Princeton University Press, 2005) at 153 [emphasis in original].

the felt force of law's rule, our prevailing stories fail to capture salient dimensions of the social, historical, and political experience of the interaction of religion and the constitutional rule of law. And if our account is flawed, so too is our appreciation of the character and stakes – for law and religion alike – of this relationship. That is the trouble with the conventional story.

**In Search of a New Account**

In this book I turn away from this conventional account and look afresh at the character of the interaction of law and religion as it shows itself in the modern rights-based management of religious diversity. The analysis that I offer yields a story about the contemporary relationship of law and religion that denies us the comfort of law's conceit of its distance and autonomy from culture. Generated from a close reading of the jurisprudence arising from religious freedom claims in Canada, the account urged in these pages insists that the constitutional rule of law is an engaged and forceful actor within the domain of culture, which is traditionally cast as the object of law's concern in models of multiculturalism, interculturalism, or secular legalism. The argument advanced in the chapters that follow seeks to knock law from its managerial or curatorial perch, from where it administers and assesses cultural claims, and to understand it, instead, as itself a cultural form – that is, an interpretive horizon composed of sets of commitments, practices, and categories of thought, that both frames experience and is experienced as such. It is inevitable that the legal framework will shape the debate about, and set the limits of, religious freedom and equality; viewing law as a cultural form will not alter this. The goal, instead, is to make the culture of constitutionalism, with its symbolic, behavioural, and aesthetic claims, visible as an object of inquiry in the analysis of the interaction of law and religion.

Viewed in this way, this book is about repositioning law in our understanding of the challenges posed by religious difference. Law is more edifyingly approached as one complex cultural system among others. Levelling law and religion in this way brings the force of law's culture into clear view while disturbing much in conventional assumptions about the nature of the constitutional rule of law. In so doing, the account offered in this book also generates difficult questions about the quality and ethics of constitutional adjudication, questions to which I turn in the latter portions of this volume. This reimagining of the cultural location of law reflects the unsettling truth that, in the modern liberal state, the constitutional rule of law is an aspect of – not an answer to – the challenges of cultural pluralism. The meeting of law and religion is not, at heart, a juridical or technical problem to be addressed through better laws; rather, it is profitably understood as an instance of cross-cultural interaction and, as such, endlessly unstable and provocative. Though it agitates, this way of understanding better captures salient dimensions of law's meeting with religion that are left unaccounted for by prevailing juridical and political stories.

Approaching the interaction of law and religion in contemporary constitutional life in this fashion raises certain issues about how one thinks about the academic study of law and how one imagines the constitutional rule of law itself. Chapter 1 prepares the ground for the analysis offered in this volume by taking up these framing questions. I point to the limits of prevailing approaches to the study of law and religion in the legal academic literature, approaches that tend either to focus on the exposition and interpretation of legal doctrine or to ascend to the realm of ideal or comprehensive theory. I argue for a kind of phenomenological turn in the study of law, one that gives explanatory and analytic priority to understanding the experience of law. When it comes to accounting for the complex relationship between law and religion in Canada, beginning with the "experience of law" in this phenomenological sense means focusing on how Canadian constitutionalism serves as a particular means of framing and conditioning law's experience of religion and is, in this particularity, something that is experienced by religious communities and claimants as a cultural force.

To some, speaking of the "experience of law" or "law's understanding" of religion flirts with a reification of law that would hide the human actors and relationships that actually constitute law. Indeed, the very title of this book might raise concerns of this nature. To be sure, one sees certain things about the nature and character of law when one concentrates on the individual decisions and personal interactions that produce law. Yet this volume proceeds from the idea that a different and valuable set of insights can be generated by taking seriously the way in which, at points when religion becomes the object of scrutiny and stories about legal tolerance and multiculturalism are deployed, law indeed presents itself and is commonly experienced in this somewhat reified form. Speaking of law in this way thus captures something real about the modern institutionalized interaction of religion and the constitutional rule of law; it is a heuristic move, one that can afford a different appreciation of the character of the legal engagement with religious difference.

There are analytic burdens that come with employing the concept of "culture" as I do in this volume. I argue that it is both useful and edifying to understand the political and juridical experience of the relationship between constitutionalism and religious difference in terms of cultural interaction; however, to lean on that volatile concept as freely as I do in this book will rightly generate in many thoughtful readers the desire to specify what it is that I mean by "culture." Chapter 1 is therefore also concerned with explaining and defending the understanding of culture that underwrites the account that emerges from my analysis. The latter portion of the chapter offers a sustained example of the rewards of thinking about the constitutional rule of law as a cultural form that shapes the experience of phenomena.

Chapter 2 descends into the jurisprudence to explore and explain the way in which the Canadian culture of law's rule fashions religion as a political and social phenomenon. The chapter shows the way in which law always encounters religion within the pre-existing frame of law's basic intuitions and commitments. In this sense, quite apart from the results and doctrinal analysis in each case, the jurisprudence discloses the extent to which, in addressing issues of religious difference, equality, and freedom, law fashions religion in its own cultural image and likeness. Otherwise put, religion is not only what the law imagines it to be.[46] Appreciating the effect that this has on the shape of the relationship between law and religion in Canada is crucial to the account that I seek in this book.

Chapter 3 focuses on one such effect: the picture thereby disclosed about the character of legal toleration. Whereas chapter 2 explores the way that the culture of law's rule shapes law's experience of religion, in chapter 3 I turn the issue in our hands by asking what this means for the way that the culture of law's rule is experienced by religious actors and communities. Analysing the juridical practices of legal toleration of religion as a mode of cross-cultural interaction disturbs prevailing wisdom about the nature and limits of legal tolerance, showing it to be a more complex and ambivalent concept than our political and legal rhetoric would suggest.

---

46  See Sullivan, *supra* note 45.

The account that emerges from these chapters captures aspects of the experience of the relationship between religion and the constitutional rule of law left in the shadows by the conventional account. In this, it allows us to see better. It does not, however, yield the kind of prescriptive solutions to which we are accustomed in legal scholarship. Generating a new or refined doctrinal scheme that could resolve those tensions and paradoxes is not the goal or purpose of this book; indeed, the approach and animating ethic of this volume stand against an orientation towards such legal or theoretical "solutions." Yet this book does arrive at a kind of prescription born of this different account. Other paths and lessons are open to us when we see better, no matter how unruly that new way of understanding might be. Chapter 4 explores those paths and lessons, suggesting what seizing this new account might offer for the way we live and reason together and, specifically, what it might suggest about the ethics and practices of adjudication in a world of deep religious and normative difference.

Throughout this book I draw from the history, jurisprudence, and debates generated out of the Canadian constitutional experience of religious difference. There is a resulting specificity to the claims that I make in these pages: the immediate purpose is to offer a more satisfying account of the interaction between constitutional law and religion in Canada. And yet many of these claims also speak to features of Canadian constitutionalism that are shared with other liberal legal orders. As such, in identifying the partial (in both senses of the word) character of law's understanding of religion, the limits of legal toleration, and the analytical and political challenges posed by the adjudication of religious freedom, there is every reason to think that this account will expose patterns and dynamics that will be useful to the broader and comparative study of law, religion, and politics in contemporary constitutionalism. In particular, the heart of this book is a critical scepticism about the impulse to use tidy stories about law and religion to hide the abidingly unstable and unruly relationship between religious difference and modern constitutionalism, stories that overwhelmingly depend on the conceit of law's autonomy from culture, history, and politics. As I first explain in chapter 1, the paragon of this impulse is over-reliance on the concept of secularism. I argue that such appeals to the descriptive and prescriptive power of "secularism" confound our understanding of the interaction of law and religion. The Conclusion returns to this theme, explores some of these broader lessons, and charts avenues for further inquiry in the study of law, religion, and the politics of religious freedom that are opened up by the account that I offer in this book.

To claim that issues raised by the interaction of law and religion can be understood as legal questions "pure and simple" or that there is anything about this interaction that can described as posing "simply a constitutional legal question" is as plainly unsatisfying today as it was when Justice Ritchie so characterized the issue that came before the court in *Brassard v Langevin* in 1877. In spite of the juridical and political appetite to describe the relationship between law and religion in just these terms, experience tells us that it is not so – that describing the relationship in this way conceals more than it reveals. Worse than misleading, this way of understanding the interaction of religion and the constitutional rule of law in contemporary liberal democracies weakens our capacity to critically examine and assess the exercises of power, the durable salience of history, and the limits of – and opportunities for – cultural understanding at work in the relationship between law and religion. This is why we need a new account.

# Chapter 1

# Studying Law and Religion: Where to Begin?

... prescription begins when curiosity breaks down.

Adam Phillips, *Terrors and Experts*[1]

The problem to which this book responds is that there is something abidingly unsatisfying about the authoritative ways that we tell the story about – and, hence, understand – the interaction of law and religion in Canada. Despite the appeal and purchase of prevailing public accounts of legal multiculturalism, interculturalism, or legally mediated "open secularism,"[2] there seems to be a gap between the role imagined for law in these models and the experience of the legal regulation of religion. This experiential gap is found on both sides of the interaction: on one hand, religious communities and individuals experience the legal management of religion in far more political and less pacific terms than these conventional narratives allow; on the other, from the perspective of law and constitutional authority, there seems to be much more at stake in these encounters than simply a regulatory problem of sorting out, for example, the boundary between the public and private. The challenge is strangely durable and distinctively unruly. There is, in short, a troubling experiential residue left after the prevailing accounts of the interaction of

---

1 Adam Phillips, *Terrors and Experts* (Cambridge, Mass: Harvard University Press, 1996) at 104.
2 The latter two terms were offered by the Bouchard-Taylor Commission in its report on religious diversity and accommodation in the Province of Quebec. See Gérard Bouchard & Charles Taylor, *Building the Future, a Time for Reconciliation: Report* (Quebec: Commission de consultation sur les pratiques d'accommodement reliées aux différences culturelles, 2008).

law and religion exhaust their explanatory efforts. If this is the problem to which this book responds, the burden of this book is to show that one can see differently – can see better – if the interaction between law and religion is approached with a different orienting story in hand.

The heart of the offering in the chapters that follow is that by understanding the contemporary Canadian constitutional rule of law as a culture, we gain access to a different and more satisfying account, and thereby a more complete appreciation, of what is happening when law and religion interact. The goal of this book is to aggravate and disrupt settled understandings about the challenges that are generated by the modern constitutional experience of religious diversity. And so tacit in this project is a critique of the way that legal scholarship and theory have framed and approached the analysis of religious diversity as a constitutional problem. This chapter explores the nature of this critique and draws out the theoretical approach that informs the balance of the book, that of understanding the constitutional rule of law as a cultural form. Ultimately, the argument will be for something of a phenomenological turn in the study of legal problems generally, and in the analysis of law and religion more specifically: an orientation that privileges the experience of law as the ground and starting point for analysis. In our pursuit of a better account of the nature of the interaction between law and religion, the constitutional rule of law can be profitably analysed as both a peculiar context for framing the experience of phenomena and, in its very specificity, something that can itself be experienced – two senses of what it means to begin with the "experience of law." This chapter is concerned with explaining how one might understand such a suggestion to study the interaction of the law and religion in this way. It traces streams of methodological inspiration for such an approach and turns, in the latter half, to a focused study of foundational ways in which the culture of Canadian constitutionalism shapes and frames its relationship with religious difference through basic understandings of space and time, what I describe as the "aesthetics of religious freedom." First, however, I want to be clear about what I am writing against: habits or styles of analysis that, whatever their merits and utility, have obscured important dimensions of the interaction of law and religion, dimensions that I am eager to recover.

## A Tale of Two Starting Points

If there is an explanatory deficit in the extant legal scholarship on the interaction of law and religion in Canada (as I say there is), this problem can be traced to a question of starting points. What is the ground or starting point – the analytic touchstone – for understanding the contemporary interaction of religion and the constitutional rule of law? The two prevailing answers mirror broader trends in legal scholarship and political theory, trends and habits of thought that others have explored and critiqued. These two starting points have visited themselves on the study of law and religion in ways that have harmed our understanding of the nature of this interaction.

## Beginning with Law

Unsurprisingly, the overwhelming habit of legal scholarship is to frame social and political issues as problems to be analysed using the authoritative categories and organizing tools of legal thought. On this approach, the world of law and the conventions of legal reasoning offer themselves as the authoritative frames of reference, a kind of fixed point in a turning world wherein, no matter how contested the debate, the terms of that debate are the terms offered by the legal system itself. The contemporary role of social and political rights is crucial here. In this body of scholarship, contested social issues present first and foremost as issues to be interpreted in the framework of legal rights, with any legitimate analysis to be anchored in the authority of those rights. Raymond Geuss describes this powerful analytic tendency in the following way: "[I]t has come to seem perfectly natural to us to assume that the basic framework for thinking about politics is a set of properly constituted rights, either legal rights or some more vaguely envisaged 'human' rights."[3] To be sure, the scope of possible analysis within this framing is substantial and the outcomes are important: one can and will have scholarly debates about how to interpret the law, about the scope of legal rights, and about the analytic priority of certain rights over others. Note, however, that the constant in these important debates is that they all take place within the conventions and terms of the rule of law itself. Having begun by framing a political, social, or cultural issue in legal terms, the natural destination is an argument for an improved or more appealing legal interpretation. As Paul Kahn describes it in his critique of legal scholarship, this is a kind of analysis in which "[t]he

---

3 Raymond Geuss, *Philosophy and Real Politics* (Princeton, NJ: Princeton University Press, 2008) at 60.

grounds of law's legitimacy provide a ground for interpretation and thus a critique of what the law is or should be."[4] This kind of "auto-theory," as he calls it, "provides the content for the research agenda of the modern law school."[5]

What is changed or distorted in our understandings when legal categories are taken as analytic starting points? The first, and crucial, observation is that framing matters in terms of legal categories effaces the processes of contestation and exercises of power that went into the constitution of those categories in the first place. Indeed, this framing conceals the fact that the decision to cast matters in legal terms itself affirms and consolidates certain distributions of social and political power. To frame an issue as one of competing rights over property, for example, is to begin where a set of political and social battles about the very category of property and law's role in protecting it left off. This is not to suggest that all legal analysis must be historical, invariably putting into question the categories of law; it is just to point out that to choose a legal framing is to choose to obscure those lines of inquiry. Using law as a starting point highlights certain lines of inquiry while discouraging or distracting from others. In this vein, complaining of the distorting effects of Robert Nozick's insistence that the starting points for political philosophy is the existence of certain rights, Geuss observes that "by presenting 'rights' as the self-evident basis for thinking about politics, [Nozick] actively distracts people from asking other, highly relevant questions."[6] One of those other, highly relevant questions is about the experience of law itself as a way of organizing social and political relations, complete with its own exercises of power. Law cannot be both the terms of the debate and the object of study. This is how I understand Kahn when he states that "by accepting auto-theory as the limit of its self-construction, the law school is not studying law: it is doing it."[7]

A second loss occasioned by taking legal categories as the starting point for analysis is the limited view that it gives of life itself. With the invocation of legal categories comes a raft of relevancies and irrelevancies. The range of social life revealed through legal categories is

---

4 Paul W Kahn, *The Cultural Study of Law: Reconstructing Legal Scholarship* (Chicago: University of Chicago Press, 1999) at 86 [Kahn, *The Cultural Study of Law*].
5 *Ibid* at 87.
6 Geuss, *supra* note 3 at 69.
7 Kahn, *The Cultural Study of Law, supra* note 4 at 87.

narrow, indeed. Again, this is not a critique of law but, rather, an honest recognition of what it requires to function. Legal analysis depends on the flattening of complexity, on the selection of material dimensions of experience and the deemed irrelevance of others. Legal doctrine is a deposit left after life takes place. There is much truth in Bruno Latour's felicitous image of attempting to access knowledge of life through the language of law: that doing so is "like trying to fax a pizza."[8]

Finally, there is the drive to prescription. When the terms of legal analysis are taken as starting points, the natural stopping point is a normative claim about the best interpretation or about what the law should be. There is nothing wrong, of course, with normative prescription, and the health of a legal system depends on good constructive analysis and proposals for reform. When trying to understand a social issue, however, the drive to prescription is limiting, foreclosing potentially revealing outcomes: for example, that there is no legal solution to a given problem or that the terms of law are not suited to understanding what is at stake in a given issue. Those are, of course, conclusions never available once the terms of law are already taken as authoritative and guiding. A court can never conclude that there is simply no answer, and legal scholarship seems no less loath to do so. Yet there is a certain tyranny of insistence on constructive solutions: it tends to limit the range of possible criticism and is, in this sense, deeply conservative. Again, Geuss puts it well:

> [A]ny society has a tendency to try to mobilise human inertia in order to protect itself as much as possible from radical change, and one main way in which this can be done is through the effort to impose the requirement of "positivity" or "constructiveness" on potential critics: you can't criticize the police system, the system of labour law, the organization of the health services, etc., unless you have a completely elaborated, positive alternative to propose. I reject this line of argument completely: to accept it is to allow the existing social formation to dictate the terms on which it can be criticised, and to allow it to impose a theoretically unwarranted burden of positive proof on any potential critic.[9]

---

8 Bruno Latour, *The Making of Law: An Ethnography of the Conseil d'Etat* (Cambridge, UK: Polity Press, 2010) at 268.

9 Geuss, *supra* note 3 at 96.

Taking legal categories as the starting point for analysis of social issues tends to set one on the path to prescription, with this associated risk of loss of critical imagination.

The tendency to "begin with law" has visited itself powerfully on the study of the interaction of law and religion. Its chief expression is the translation of the subject of "law and religion" into the topic of "freedom of religion," giving priority to a legal framing of a much more complicated historical and contemporary interaction. This propensity is evident in the U.S. scholarship, in which the study of law and religion in law schools is heavily focused on the study of the byzantine law of the First Amendment, guided by the legal concepts of "nonestablishment" and "free exercise." But one finds this impulse in the Canadian study of law and religion too, with the scholarship centred on questions of the meaning and content of the *Charter*'s section 2(a) protection of freedom of religion and the section 15 guarantee of religious equality. The imprint of this framing can be seen in the central discussions that define this literature: having begun with the problem as one of legal rights, nestled in the terms and tools of the legal system itself, the focus of the scholarship naturally takes on a certain doctrinarism, sorting through possible approaches to conflicting right and debates about whether there are hierarchies of rights; working out the nature of the balancing appropriate when justifying limits on religious freedom or equality; and battling about the scope and interpretation of these rights themselves.[10]

Important though these discussions and interventions are from the perspective of legal practice, they exhibit the imaginative and critical limitations that come with law as the starting point of analysis, complete with the drive to prescription that characterizes the genre. This is largely auto-theory, however sophisticated, with the authority and terms of law serving as the orienting frame for understanding, rather than themselves objects of study. With the presuppositions of legal culture already taken as given, analysis of religion takes on a Procrustean

---

10 An example of an approach that begins and ends within the logic of rights can be seen in Christopher L Eisgruber & Lawrence G Sager, *Religious Freedom and the Constitution* (Cambridge, Mass: Harvard University Press, 2007). The orienting question of this very interesting and insightful work is whether a right of equality and liberty can do the work that a constitutional privileging of religion (problematically, in their view) purports to do. Provocative and challenging though this work is, the various effacements that concern me here are patent in that framing.

character, trimming and shaping life in a way that is the central concern of chapter 2. Starting with law means effacing the history and politics at play in the workings of law, including (as chapter 3 explores) those involved in the power-saturated concept of toleration, one of the natural tools of the legal management of religion. The result is that a highly salient – perhaps the most phenomenologically significant – aspect of the interaction of law and religion drops out of the frame of concern and attention. And as chapter 4 explains, the need for prescription occludes other morals to the story of religion's interaction with law, emphasizing certain ethical and political virtues at the expense of others. These combined effects, put into motion by taking law as the starting point for analysis, generate the experiential residue – and the explanatory gap – with which this book is concerned.

Perhaps a corrective is to be found by turning away from the world of law and ascending to the heights of theory.

*Beginning with Theory*

If one tendency in legal scholarship is towards a limiting doctrinarism occasioned by framing social and political issues within the terms of law, an enticing alternative is to move in the other direction, taking the world of abstract, ideal, or transcendental theory as the starting point for inquiry. This orientation to legal and political issues serves as the other pole for legal scholarship. Sloughing off the details and shaping concepts indigenous to a given legal order, this approach seeks an abstract philosophical frame for analysis, one that, through sufficient definition and elaboration, can make sense of the messiness of legal and political life. The appeal of this move is its offer of explanatory range, a promise achieved by framing inquiry in terms of moral intuitions or needs that have a universal or self-sufficient character. The pathologies of this ascent to this style of theory are Geuss's preoccupation, though this approach to thinking about social and political issues has also attracted sustained criticism from Amartya Sen.[11]

---

11 Amartya Sen, *The Idea of Justice* (Cambridge, Mass: Belknap Press of Harvard University Press, 2009). Sen describes this approach as one of "transcendental theory," which he opposes to his "comparative" approach. See especially chapter 4, "Voice and Social Choice."

For both Geuss and Sen, the immediate target of criticism is John Rawls and his theory based on justice as a freestanding social ideal.[12] The concern is, again, with starting points; one begins with a theoretical construct rather than "with a substantive account of human nature and its exigencies, of the demands that collective action imposes on us, or of purportedly basic or historically constituted human social and political institutions."[13] But Rawls is, of course, just an exemplar of a more general orientation to the analysis of social and legal problems. Geuss regards Rawls as simply an example of "a strong Kantian strand in contemporary political philosophy,"[14] where Kant is a placeholder for the desire to treat theoretical intuition as the point of departure for understanding the complexities and demands of the social world. Indeed, appeal to moral intuitions is just one way in which this ascent to abstract theory as a starting point finds expression in the scholarship. As an alternative to framing matters in terms of legal concepts, Geuss provides a more general description of this analytic orientation: "Another way is to develop a full political theory by picking a single purported political 'virtue' from among the many human excellences and aspects of politics or society that are admirable; one tries to give an abstract 'conceptual analysis' of 'our' conception of that virtue without taking account of the social context in which it is instantiated or its history, and then constructs an idealized theory of what a society would have to look like if it were to instantiate that virtue fully."[15] "Virtue," here, is a broad concept. It should be taken as not only ethical virtues generated from intuitions, but also abstract features of a good society, as well as broad claims about larger social-historical process. The heart of this approach is to base one's analysis in some general "aspects of politics or society that are admirable," and, having done so, to proceed with the features of that virtue as the authoritative touchstone for political, legal, or social inquiry. In this respect, the fashion of Kantian or Hegelian reflection on legal issues[16]

---

12 John Rawls, *A Theory of Justice*, revised ed (Cambridge, Mass: Belknap Press of Harvard University Press, 1999).

13 Geuss, *supra* note 3 at 70.

14 *Ibid* at 89.

15 *Ibid* at 59.

16 See e.g. Alan Brudner, *Punishment and Freedom: A Liberal Theory of Penal Justice* (New York: Oxford University Press, 2009); Ernest J Weinrib, *The Idea of Private Law*, revised ed (Oxford: Oxford University Press, 2012).

is no different in kind from the industry of law and economics[17] and its aspiration to offer a comprehensive model of social analysis grounded in the logic of efficiency.

If one turns to consider the imaginative losses and distortions of understanding that happen when this style of theory is taken as the starting point for the analysis of social and political themes, a notable echo emerges. Although "beginning with law" and "beginning with theory" present as alternative points of departure, they can visit similar effects on the way that social problems are framed. Similar to the framing of matters in terms of legal categories, one of the most potent effects of the ascent to pure theory is that it tends to conceal the question of power and the history of its exercise. When based on moral intuitions, these theoretical starting points present instincts about justice, fairness, or equality as natural, rather than as intuitions that only seem intuitive on a path of common sense that has been, and is continually, cleared by substantial exercises of power. Indeed, this is Geuss's chief criticism of Rawls: "To think that an appropriate point of departure for understanding our political world is *our* intuitions of what is 'just,' *without* reflecting on where those intuitions come from, how they are maintained, and what interests they might serve, seems to exclude from the beginning the very possibility that these intuitions might themselves be 'ideological.'"[18] When this theoretical starting point is based on broad claims about social-historical processes, such as the march towards reason or the juridification of the life world,[19] the concealment of power happens by effacing the struggle, conflict, and suppression that sit behind any such grand historical themes. Otherwise put, analysing social and political issues from theory down obscures the fact that we have not just reasoned our way to our theories, but fought and struggled over them. This is not to simplistically oppose the ideal and the real, for as Martha Nussbaum reminds us, "Ideals are real: they direct

---

17  See e.g. Richard A Posner, *The Economics of Justice* (Cambridge, Mass: Harvard University Press, 1981); Steven Shavell, *Foundations of Economic Analysis of Law* (Cambridge, Mass: Belknap Press of Harvard University Press, 2004).

18  Geuss, *supra* note 3 at 90 [emphasis in original].

19  Jürgen Habermas, *The Theory of Communicative Action*, translated by Thomas McCarthy, vol 2 (Boston: Beacon Press, 1987); Gunther Teubner & Firenze Bremen, "Juridification: Concepts, Aspects, Limits, Solutions" in Gunther Teubner, ed, *Juridification of Social Spheres: A Comparative Analysis in the Areas of Labor, Corporate, Antitrust, and Social Welfare Law* (Berlin: De Gruyter, 1987) 3.

our striving, our plans, our legal processes."[20] Nor is the claim that this kind of theory cannot be insightful, instructive, or positively illuminating. Rather, the concern is that, unless such exercises are tethered to the gritty, restive nature of political and social life, this edification may come at the expense of attention to history and the experience of power, doing mischief to the stories that we will end up telling.[21]

Theory of this form also tends towards the same flattening effect that is seen when one takes the concepts and categories of law as the starting point for analysis. Although the effect is similar, it is achieved through different means. If relevance is the mechanism for the flattening or trimming of the legal view of life, abstraction is the engine that drives the process when one begins with this style of theory. Indeed, theory of this sort thrives – it subsists – on the suppression of existential detail. Bernard Williams critiqued Kantian forms of moral philosophy on just this basis, contending that "it is not involved enough; it is governed by a dream of a community of reason that is too far removed, as Hegel first said it was, from social and historical reality and from any concrete sense of a particular ethical life."[22] When a theory holds out the promise of broad explanatory appeal, its aspiration towards the universal tends to pull it away from the particular. This is true to the extent that historical texture is sacrificed in favour of broad sociological trends or when, as in Rawls, claims about "our" intuitions conceal the empirical complexity of motivations, attitudes, and experiences. This is an unsurprising observation and not necessarily a criticism of this style of theoretical inquiry; indeed, "[e]mpirical abstemiousness and systematicity are two of the major virtues to which 'ideal' theories of this kind aspire."[23] Again, the point is simply that if insight into the texture and messiness of

---

20  Martha C Nussbaum, *Political Emotions: Why Love Matters for Justice* (Cambridge, Mass: Belknap Press of Harvard University Press, 2013) at 383. Nussbaum further observes that "the real also contains the ideal. Real people aspire. They imagine possibilities better than the world they know, and they try to actualize them … so any political thinker who rejects ideal theory rejects a lot of reality" (384).

21  Geuss, *supra* note 3 at 94, makes an even stronger claim: "A theoretical approach with no place for a theory of power is not merely deeply deficient but actively pernicious, because mystifying."

22  Bernard Williams, *Ethics and the Limits of Philosophy* (London: Routledge, 2006) at 197. Evocatively, Williams goes on, explaining that this style of moral philosophy is "farther removed from those things, in some ways, than the religion it replaced."

23  Geuss, *supra* note 3 at 7.

experience is one's aspiration, starting with theory of this sort would be a curious choice to make.

Finally, the drive to prescription also afflicts the use of this brand of theory as a starting point for political or social analysis. This effect is arguably less pronounced when one begins with theory than when one begins within the framing terms of law and rights. Indeed, the traditional knock against such theory is that it fails to answer the "so what?" Yet for certain styles of theoretical inquiry, framing matters in terms of broad social trends or the logic of moral intuitions ultimately tends to call quite powerfully for conclusions or solutions. Prescription is often precisely the hoped-for outcome of inquiries that begin in ideal or transcendental theory, as it is for the Kantian-style inquiry that concerns Geuss or the Rawlsian inquiry into the demands of a freestanding conception of justice. In such cases, perhaps the impulse to prescription is an artefact of the other two observations: perhaps it is a predictable feature of theories based on the universality or naturalness of certain moral and political intuitions and on the concealment of particularity. Both features are congenial to prescription. And, as explained above, whenever prescription is the presumed outcome, there is basis to worry that the range of critical insights has already been limited.

The study of the interaction of law and religion has strongly felt the influence of adopting abstract theory as a starting point for analysis. Most famous, no doubt, has been Rawls's imprint on the way in which religion is imagined to fit into a theory of political liberalism. Rawls was, in fact, centrally interested in how one should manage deep normative diversity, and the problem of the interaction between legal institutions and religious difference featured prominently in his animating concerns. His choice to ground his analysis in an idea of justice as a freestanding virtue shaped both his understanding and his prescriptions in particular ways. This choice led famously to the claim that comprehensive doctrines could not form a part of public reason; with this, Geuss's concerns about a Rawlsian-style approach to political analysis were realized in the analysis of law, politics, and religious difference.[24] It was arguably the extent to which this influential thesis concealed the experience of power and exclusion, as well as the imperatives of

---

24 Seen most clearly in John Rawls, *Political Liberalism* (New York: Columbia University Press, 1996).

democratic life viewed in finer detail, that impelled Rawls to introduce a proviso to this general theory, just as it led Habermas to revise his early positions on religion and public life.[25] The point is a more general one, however: that this style of analysis has produced, in the scholarship, certain ways of understanding and approaches to the "problem" of religious diversity within the contemporary constitutional rule of law, while foreclosing other, perhaps more "realistic" accounts. Most influentially, as I explore in chapter 3, beginning with the commitments of liberal theory hides certain realities about the interaction of law and religion.

Yet it is the focus on explicating a concept of secularism, and what it demands, that has left the most consequential and distorting imprint of this use of broad theory as a starting point for understanding the contemporary interaction of law and religion. The instinct to reason about the relationship of law and religion from the historical fact or philosophical nature of secularism is prevalent in the scholarship, with substantial debates focused on the proper definition of secularism and what it implies for the management of religious diversity. Yet such analysis, whose point of departure is an ideal of "the secular," ultimately hides more than it illuminates. It is not just that the content and implications of the concept are deeply contested, meaning that tires can quickly begin to spin, though that is true. The more troubling effects are the distortions that I have described as resulting from taking theory as a starting point. An important effect of the focus on secularism has been its tendency to strip away lived experience. What a general claim about the nature of secularism achieves in prescriptive and explanatory breadth, it achieves at the expense of regard for the messy details of wrestling with the relationships between religion, law, and politics.[26] As a number of those writing from the fields of religious studies, anthropology, and sociology have shown, there is no single phenomenon of secularism but, rather, "secularisms," suffused with local history and ethnographic complexity,

25  For his mature view, see Jürgen Habermas, "Religion in the Public Sphere" (2006) 14:1 European Journal of Philosophy 1.

26  For an illuminating examination of secularism as a mode of governance and its structuring effects on U.S. foreign policy and international relations, see Elizabeth Shakman Hurd, *The Politics of Secularism in International Relations* (Princeton, NJ: Princeton University Press, 2008).

and manifesting wide variation.[27] Even within one national tradition, the conceptual blanket of secularism can cover up what is of most interest and, indeed, relevance to truly understanding the fraught interactions of law, politics, and religion. John Bowen's work, for example, shows that beneath the powerful claims about French *laïcité* – what many would take as a comparatively stable and well-defined local conception of secularism – is a rich associational life that belies the republican ideal.[28]

The uses of secularism also illustrate the way in which ascent to theory and broad historical claims conceals power and privilege, and does so at the cost of our understanding of what is at stake in the interaction of law and religion. As local and lived experiences are stripped away in favour of explanatory capaciousness, so too is the way in which history and struggle have themselves constituted the concept of the secular, and the way in which appeal to such concepts sustains and entrenches those relations of power. The local shape of the secular has more to do with the particularities of political history than the purity of principle.[29] Talal Asad's excavation of the genealogy of European secularism, and the relationship between Christianity and a particular understanding of that concept, should be a powerful prophylactic to bullishness about the character of secularism or what it requires.[30] The 2013 proposal for a "Charter of Quebec Values" was an example of the temptations and dangers of prescription

---

27  See e.g. Janet R Jakobsen & Ann Pellegrini, eds, *Secularisms* (Durham, NC: Duke University Press, 2008); Michael Warner, Jonathan VanAntwerpen & Craig Calhoun, eds, *Varieties of Secularism in a Secular Age* (Cambridge, Mass: Harvard University Press, 2010).

28  See John R Bowen, *Can Islam Be French?: Pluralism and Pragmatism in a Secularist State* (Princeton, NJ: Princeton University Press, 2010); Pierre Rosanvallon, *The Demands of Liberty: Civil Society in France since the Revolution*, translated by Arthur Goldhammer (Cambridge, Mass: Harvard University Press, 2007).

29  See e.g. Ahmet T Kuru, *Secularism and State Policies toward Religion: The United States, France, and Turkey* (New York: Cambridge University Press, 2009), in which Kuru emphasizes the influence of political history and reactions to an ancien régime in the development of approaches to realizing secularism. As William Connolly puts it, "[S]ecularism is a political settlement rather than an uncontestable dictate of public discourse itself." William E Connolly, *Why I Am Not a Secularist* (Minneapolis: University of Minnesota Press, 1999) at 36.

30  Talal Asad, *Formations of the Secular: Christianity, Islam, Modernity* (Stanford, Cal: Stanford University Press, 2003).

when an abstracted conception of secularism is used as the foundation for understanding the political, legal, and social issues that constellate around the fact of religious difference. Cumulatively, these effects have meant that using secularism as a point of analytic departure has done more to limit rather than enrich our stories about religious diversity within the constitutional rule of law; in so doing, it illustrates the way in which a certain kind of reliance on theory can generate the kinds of experiential elisions and unsatisfying accounts that are the concern of this book.

Legal analysis and ideal theory have their place. We should be, however, very aware of the gaps left by both, gaps that are found most crucially in their regard for lived realities, the experience of power, and law's role in both. If we want our stories to account for those features, we need to choose a different starting point.

## Approaching Law as Culture: A Phenomenological Turn

There are, of course, perils associated with invoking the term *culture* in the analytically central way entailed by the argument of this book. The term has a winding etymological and political history that allows it to bear a wide range of meanings and to be put to a dizzying variety of analytical ends.[31] The capaciousness of the term – its unruliness – can make reference to *culture* seem like an analytic sleight of hand, too vague to be useful but too loaded to be mere verbiage.[32] Clifford Geertz, to whose thought I will return soon, helpfully described the anxiety around the use of the term *culture*: "It is fugitive, unsteady, encyclopedic, and normatively charged, and there are those, especially those for whom only the really real is really real, who think it vacuous altogether,

---

31 See Raymond Williams, *Culture* (Glasgow: Fontana Paperbacks, 1981).
32 Stephen Greenblatt writes that "[l]ike 'ideology' ... 'culture' is a term that is repeatedly used without meaning much of anything at all, a vague gesture toward a dimly perceived ethos." Stephen Greenblatt, "Culture" in Frank Lentricchia & Thomas McLaughlin, eds, *Critical Terms for Literary Study* (Chicago: University of Chicago Press, 1990) 225 at 225.

or even dangerous, and would ban it from the serious discourse of serious persons."[33]

But as Pierre Legrand has observed, the indeterminacy of the notion of *culture* should be an impediment only for those engaged in a positive project aimed at instrumental or technical ends; it should not trouble a project whose goal, rather, is to "awaken assumptions."[34] In a study concerned with awakening and uncovering assumptions in the interaction of constitutional law and religion, the wisdom of reliance on the idea of culture should not turn on whether one can attract consensus around the definition of the term but, rather, whether the particular use to which the term is put helps us to see better – the degree to which it illuminates something real but not otherwise sharply apprehended. In this sense, the concept of *culture* used in these pages is unapologetically stipulative.

The invitation to understand Canadian constitutionalism as a culture is intended to designate a different starting point in the study of religion's contemporary interaction with law. It is a way of approaching law that begins with the experience of living within the constitutional rule of law. *Culture* is thus a marker for a kind of phenomenological turn in the study of law and religion, one that seeks to privilege experience of the law as the analytic starting point, rather than legal concepts or ideal forms of theory.[35] There are, of course, many ways that one may go about privileging and accessing lived experience. One might engage

---

33  Clifford Geertz, *Available Light: Anthropological Reflections on Philosophical Topics* (Princeton: Princeton University Press, 2000) at 11 [Geertz, *Available Light*]. For an account of the debate about the utility of the concept of culture within anthropological circles, see Robert Brightman, "Forget Culture: Replacement, Transcendence, Relexification" (1995) 10 Cultural Anthropology 509.

34  Pierre Legrand, Book Review of *Comparing Legal Cultures* by David Nelken, ed, (1997) 56 Cambridge LJ 646 at 647. James Clifford, in *The Predicament of Culture* (Cambridge, Mass: Harvard University Press, 1988), describes culture as "a deeply compromised idea I cannot yet do without" (10).

35  David Schneiderman has developed and employed – to illuminating effect – a different understanding of "constitutional culture." See David Schneiderman, "Property Rights and Regulatory Innovation: Comparing Constitutional Cultures" (2006) 4:2 International Journal of Constitutional Law 371. His concept of "constitutional culture" is more particularly descriptive of the "dominant 'social consensus' on pressing questions reflective of basic rules" (376). For different approaches to the salience of culture to constitutional analysis, see e.g. Menachem Mautner, *Law and the Culture of Israel* (Oxford: Oxford University Press, 2011); Robert C Post, "Foreword: Fashioning the Legal Constitution: Culture, Courts, and Law" (2003) 117 Harv L Rev 4.

in detailed ethnography or turn to empirical and qualitative research. (Either could be extremely edifying, as Bruno Latour's ethnography of the Conseil d'Etat has shown.[36]) The approach taken here – that signalled by the use of the term *culture* – inheres in asking a different set of questions when analysing the points of interaction between law and religion, questions about how law digests the experience of religion and about how religious individuals and communities experience the force of such legal understandings. This is what it means for me to talk about understanding the constitutional rule of law as a cultural form: it is a way of positioning law as an object of inquiry, one that takes as its primary focus the particular way that law shapes and gives meaning to experience and, given that particularity, the way that it can itself be experienced.

This more phenomenological approach to the study of law and religion, and the understanding of culture on which it is based, draws a certain inspiration from – or is sympathetic to – a methodological posture found in the world of cultural anthropology. It does so both in the analytic precedence that it gives to lived experience and in the idea that culture is found in those practices, habits of thought, and organizing commitments that frame that experience and make it meaningful. Mary Douglas stakes out this anthropological position in her illuminating (and still very relevant) study, *Purity and Danger*, when she describes her guiding understanding of culture. "Culture," she explains, "in the sense of the public, standardized values of a community, mediates the experience of individuals. It provides in advance some basic categories, a positive pattern in which ideas and values are tidily ordered."[37] One sees in this definition both the idea that experience is the ground for analysis, and that culture serves a framing role, offering basic categories through which that experience takes place – through which it is ordered, arranged, and understood. Whether that "positive pattern" is, in fact, "tidy," or whether it simply aspires to that tidiness is another matter. Cultural systems are always under pressure from the unruliness of experience.

Clifford Geertz describes the central commitments of his interpretive anthropology, including the idea of culture that underwrites it, in

---

36  Latour, *supra* note 8.
37  Mary Douglas, *Purity and Danger: An Analysis of Concepts of Pollution and Taboo* (London: Routledge, 2002) at 48.

similar terms. In his early work, Geertz wrote about culture in terms of "patterns of meaning," or a "system of symbols," and invoked Weber in describing culture as the "webs of significance" in which the human animal is suspended.[38] When, late in his career, he reflected on the basic commitment at the core of his body of work, he offered a helpful account of the animating methodological insight that organized his work; Geertz explained, "To discover who people think they are, what they think they are doing, and to what end they think they are doing it, it is necessary to gain a working familiarity with the frames of meaning within which they enact their lives."[39] There is much to be cautious about in Geertz's approach to culture: it appears overly propositional at points and seems to imagine (as does Douglas's understanding of the concept) too high a degree of coherence, stability, and unity within culture.[40] Yet the heart of the approach remains instructive, insisting as it does that experience is always framed and that the study of these frames is the study of something usefully called "culture."[41]

The idea conveyed by Geertz, Douglas, and other modern cultural anthropologists is that, in studying culture, one is studying the foundational and often otherwise diaphanous structures of thought and habit that shape experience. As Pierre Legrand puts it, culture is something like the "framework of intangibles within which an interpretive community operates."[42] Tomoko Masuzawa observes that, on this approach, cultures are imagined both "as an object *and* context of interpretation"

---

38  Clifford Geertz, *The Interpretation of Cultures* (New York: Basic Books, 1973) at 5 [Geertz, *The Interpretation of Cultures*].

39  Geertz, *Available Light, supra* note 33 at 16.

40  Nothing about the approach that I am urging here requires that kind of commitment to the homogeneity or stability. Culture, in the sense used here, can be contested and dynamic, yet also have sufficient unity and coherence to serve as a heuristically useful category.

41  In this sense, although Bourdieu would discard the word *culture*, my understanding shares much with his preferred concept of the habitus, which he describes as "a system of acquired dispositions, functioning on the practical level as categories of perception and assessment or as classificatory principles as well as being the organizing principles of action." Pierre Bourdieu, *In Other Words: Essays Towards a Reflexive Sociology* (Stanford, Cal: Stanford University Press, 1990) at 13.

42  Legrand, *supra* note 34 at 646. Legrand's full definition is as follows: "I understand the notion of 'culture' to mean the framework of intangibles within which an interpretive community operates, which has normative force for this community (even though not completely and coherently instantiated), and which determines the identity of a community *as community*" [emphasis in original].

and that this "renders the anthropological study of culture analogous to the study of a work of art or literature in its most typically hermeneutical formulation."[43] (Both Legrand and Masuzawa gesture to the influence of another body of thought, to which I will return in chapter 4, namely philosophical hermeneutics.) In these attitudes towards the study of culture, one finds a resonance between this starting point found in cultural anthropology and the starting point urged in this work.

In many ways, Paul Kahn has plotted the course for this kind of inquiry. His influence on this book will be felt in a number of places, not least in the final section of this chapter. In his volume *The Cultural Study of Law: Reconstructing Legal Scholarship* Kahn made explicit the methodological call that is implicit in his work generally, namely the insistence that the rule of law must be analysed as "a way of being in the world,"[44] one that "structures our understanding of space and time, self and community,"[45] and one that "must compete with other forms of social and political perception."[46] Kahn's core provocation in urging a cultural study of law is that "law's claim upon us is not a product of law's truth but of our own imagination – our imagining its meanings and our failure to imagine alternatives."[47] Much of his work is dedicated to exploring the architecture of those imaginative structures and tracing their genealogy, understanding how they came to exert the imaginative force that they do, as well as the alternatives that they have more or less successfully displaced.[48] To insist on experience of law as the ground of analysis for the contemporary interaction of law and religion in Canada is a way of accepting Kahn's challenge to approach law as a form of social and political perception – one that competes with others – and to heed his call to study the places where we find friction between law and these alternative frames of perception.

The chapters that follow are concerned with two larger questions about the way in which the culture of Canadian constitutionalism

---

43  Tomoko Masuzawa, "Culture" in Mark C Taylor, ed, *Critical Terms for Religious Studies* (Chicago: University of Chicago Press, 1998) 70 at 80 [emphasis in original].

44  Kahn, *The Cultural Study of Law, supra* note 4 at 36.

45  *Ibid* at 86.

46  *Ibid* at 84.

47  *Ibid* at 39.

48  See e.g. Paul W Kahn, *Political Theology: Four New Chapters on the Concept of Sovereignty* (New York: Columbia University Press, 2011); Paul W Kahn, *Finding Ourselves at the Movies: Philosophy for a New Generation* (New York: Columbia University Press, 2013).

shapes the experience of the interaction of law and religion. Chapter 2 asks how Canadian constitutional law understands and processes religion, and chapter 3 inquires into the way in which law's "management" of religion through tools of legal toleration is experienced as a mode of cross-cultural interaction. Addressing these questions will yield essential elements in a retelling of the story of law and religion in Canada.

But as a form of social and political perception, law's role in the framing of the experience of religious difference – its phenomenological force – begins prior to the analysis of constitutional rights and legal tools. Understanding law in the terms that I have urged in this chapter involves addressing the way in which it has more foundational, elemental effects on our political and social perception. As Kahn suggests, a cultural understanding of law involves thinking about the way in which it "structures our understanding of space and time, self and community."[49]

In *An Essay on Man*, Ernst Cassirer argued, "Space and time are the framework in which all reality is concerned. We cannot conceive any real thing except under the conditions of space and time."[50] Cassirer's project was to develop a philosophy of human culture by exposing its "architectural structure."[51] In pursuit of that project, one that was itself inflected by a certain anthropological sensibility, an exploration of these formative categories of space and time would be indispensable. "To describe the specific character which space and time assume in human experience," Cassirer explained, "is one of the most appealing and important tasks of an anthropological philosophy."[52] If the methodological heart of this book is to turn to a more cultural, phenomenological understanding of the interaction of law and religious difference, then such an account should inquire into the ways in which these fundamental conditions of thought and perception fashion the framework for the interaction of religion and the constitutional rule of law. Before turning, then, in chapters 2 and 3 to the larger questions of how religion is perceived through the law and how legal tolerance is experienced within the culture of Canadian constitutionalism, the remaining portion of this chapter takes up this imaginative scaffolding within which the dynamics of religious freedom take place – what I refer to as the "aesthetics of religious freedom."

---

49  Kahn, *The Cultural Study of Law, supra* note 4 at 86.
50  Ernst Cassirer, *An Essay on Man: An Introduction to a Philosophy of Human Culture* (New Haven, Conn: Yale University Press, 1944) at 42.
51  *Ibid* at 36.
52  *Ibid* at 42.

## The Aesthetics of Religious Freedom

A reader coming to a discussion of the aesthetics of religious freedom might reasonably anticipate a treatment of any number of possible topics. A substantial body of work has centred its consideration of law and aesthetics on an understanding of aesthetics as the historical or philosophical study of the artistic, or of judgments about the beautiful.[53] Other scholars concerned with law and aesthetics have been focused on the relationship between legal imagery and the authority of law.[54] And, of course, a number of contemporary debates about religious freedom concern "aesthetics" in the more conventional sense of appearances and representations, such as the French and Québécois concern with "conspicuous religious symbols" or the Canadian debate about the niqab and the law's desire to see the face of the witness.[55] Although these topics are both important and interesting, they engage a different and less basic sense of the aesthetic than concerns us here.

To characterize an inquiry into the framing influence of relationships to time and space as an *aesthetic* inquiry is to appeal to the etymology of the term, in which the word *aesthetic* refers to the basic elements of sense or perception.[56] This is the sense of aesthetics that Kant used when he argued that our perceptions of the world come to us already shaped by basic intuitions about space and time, a set of intuitions that he called the "transcendental aesthetic."[57] The transcendental aesthetic gives form and order to our experience of all phenomena and, for

---

53  See e.g. Daniel J Boorstin, *The Mysterious Science of the Law: An Essay on Blackstone's Commentaries* (Gloucester: Peter Smith, 1973); Adam Geary, *Law and Aesthetics* (Oxford: Hart, 2001).

54  See e.g. Costas Douzinas, Shaun McVeigh & Ronnie Warrington, "The Alta(e)rs of Law: The Judgement of Legal Aesthetics" (1992) 9:4 Theory, Culture & Society 93; Costas Douzinas & Lynda Neal, eds, *Law and the Image: The Authority of Art and the Aesthetics of Law* (Chicago: University of Chicago Press, 1999).

55  See *R v NS*, 2012 SCC 72, [2012] 3 SCR 726.

56  Pierre Schlag makes this etymological move in his piece "The Aesthetics of American Law" (2002) 115:4 Harv L Rev 1047.

57  These intuitions serve a purpose very much like Heidegger's "forestructure of understanding," a congruity that underscores the phenomenological heart of this kind of approach. Martin Heidegger, *Being and Time* (New York: Harper & Row, 1962) at 193. For an exploration of Heidegger's phenomenological reading of Kant, see Martin Weatherston, *Heidegger's Interpretation of Kant: Categories, Imagination and Temporality* (New York: Palgrave Macmillan, 2002).

Kant (as it was for Cassirer), space and time are the essential aesthetic ingredients – the frame in which all experience occurs.[58] To take that insight and inquire into the variety of ways in which different cultural forms orient to space and time is to take Kant in a decidedly un-Kantian turn, pluralizing the idea and therefore at odds with the universalist ambition that drove Kant.[59] But if we understand the constitutional rule of law as one way of encountering the world, as one system of symbols and meanings that comprise a "way of being in the world,"[60] as a form of social and political perception – as, in Cassirer's sense, a cultural form – then a phenomenologically grounded inquiry into the interaction of law and religion should examine these framing aesthetics of space and time. The claim explored below, then, is that religious freedom within the culture of Canadian constitutionalism is, in interesting and formative ways, a matter of aesthetics.

*Space and the Aesthetics of Religious Freedom*

> They thought they could go back
> to find the same marked squirrels
> nesting in the walnut trees
> and that there would be some work
> to do, something useful
> and hard, and that they might please
>
> their own need to be doing.
> You know what they found. They found
> themselves standing in your yard
> awed by the gladiolus
> and the absence of something
> they knew. This had been free land,

---

58  As Kant explained, "[W]e find existing in the mind *a priori*, the pure form of sensuous intuitions in general, in which all the manifold content of the phenomenal world is arranged and viewed under certain relations." Immanuel Kant, *Critique of Pure Reason*, translated by JMD Meiklejohn (New York: Dutton, 1934) at 42.

59  I am aware of elements in the philosophical literature on Kant that suggest a more pluralist reading of his ethics. See e.g. Thomas E Hill Jr, "Kantian Pluralism" (1992) 102:4 Ethics 743; Dermot Moran, "Hilary Putnam and Immanuel Kant: Two 'Internal Realists'?" (2000) 123:1 Synthèse 65, in which Moran describes Hilary Putnam's account of the "glimmerings of 'conceptual relativity' and 'pluralism'" (83) in Kant's ethical thought.

60  Kahn, *The Cultural Study of Law*, *supra* note 4 at 36.

they said, but now it was yours
who went in to call the law.[61]

The City of Outremont, a vibrant part of Montreal, is home to a large
Orthodox Jewish population. On Shabbat, the weekly day of rest that
is also the holiest day of the year, a piece of rabbinic wisdom rings in
the ears of Orthodox Jews: "The Jews did not preserve the Shabbas; the
Shabbas preserved the Jews." It is a day with deep temporal significance, marking off sacred time from the everyday business of the week,
but the key admonition against work on Shabbat has profound implications for how Orthodox Jews move in the world. One can draw this
sense of Shabbat being both a temporal and spatial event from the word
used for observing Shabbat – one is *shomer* Shabbas. *Shomer* comes from
the root "to guard." One guards Shabbat.

The home is the sacred space of Shabbat. The injunction against work
includes a prohibition against carrying items outside one's home. In a
modern urban life, this prohibition poses certain serious limitations –
one would be prevented from pushing a stroller, from carrying medica-
tion, or even from bringing keys outside the home in order to lock the
door when one goes to synagogue on Shabbat or another Jewish holiday. The eruv has served as the solution to this Halachic (legal) conun-
drum. The eruv is a barely visible wire erected in Jewish communities
to symbolically enlarge the special space of the home across lanes and
sidewalks, common areas, and public spaces, turning them into a meta-
phorical extension of the home.[62] The space bounded by the eruv is
transformed into part of one's home, allowing movement through the
community on the holy days. The word *eruv* means "to mix or join";
the eruv mixes the home and the public, breaking down the distinction
in service of sacrality and in recognition of the day of rest, a day that
brings into each week the memory of the end of God's creation of the
world.

The City of Outremont began dismantling the system of eruvin in
2000, objecting to their presence across city streets and public spaces.
The city took these steps pursuant to its "duty to maintain the public

---

61 Philip Levine, "Possession" in *Not This Pig: Poems* (Middletown, Conn: Wesleyan
   University Press, 1968) 31. Reprinted by permission of Wesleyan University Press.
62 For a description of the technical features of the eruv, see Roger W Stump,
   *Geography of Religion: Faith, Place and Space* (Lanham, Md: Rowman & Littlefield,
   2008) at 3.

domain accessible to all residents of Outremont on the same basis and without distinction."[63] One argument made by the parties supporting the removal of the eruvin was that "the erection of eruvin involuntarily place non-members of the Orthodox Jewish faith within what amounts to a religious enclave with which they do not wish to be associated."[64] To allow the eruvin "would inevitably create what amounts to an officially recognized religious territory."[65] A group of petitioners from the Jewish community sought relief from the Quebec Superior Court in 2001, claiming that the actions of the city interfered with their constitutionally protected right of religious freedom. The Court found that the city had a supervening public authority to regulate the erection of the eruv but that this should be done in a way that gave reasonable room for the members of the religious community to observe their private commitments.

Some years before, also in Montreal, a number of Jewish members of a condominium association, the Syndicat Northcrest, erected a temporary booth, called a succah, for the eight-day festival of Succoth. Jewish law and tradition require that one eat meals and dwell as much as possible in the succah for the duration of this holiday. The very basic structures, covered with foliage but open enough that one can see the stars at night, are reminders of the fragile homes in which Israelites lived as they made that most crucial of territorial journeys over the span of forty years, from slavery in Egypt, to their homes in *Eretz Israel*, the land of Israel. The succah is a compendious reminder of this journey, of the space of freedom, of the sacrality of home, and of the promise of a homeland.

A number of residents of the Syndicat Northcrest built their succahs on their balconies, considered common space under the condominium bylaws. These bylaws prohibited alterations to the external appearance of the building and the erection of structures in the communal spaces of the condominium. A negotiation between the Jewish residents and the building management ensued, with a compromise found for many of the residents: a single communal succah would be built on the grounds of the condominium. Certain of the residents could not agree to this, however, convinced as they were that each of them was under

---

63 *Rosenberg v Outremont (City)*, [2001] RJQ 1556 at para 14 (CS).
64 *Ibid* at para 18.
65 *Ibid*.

an obligation to have a personal succah and unsatisfied with a common succah that would require them to carry items through common space during the holiday in order to use this structure. Despite having signed the condominium bylaws when they purchased their units, Moïse Amselem and three other Jewish residents insisted on the religious freedom to build their own succahs on their balconies. The case eventually found its way to the Supreme Court of Canada, where the Court held that, properly circumscribed, the applicants' private religious beliefs could be accommodated within the regime of collective property rights.[66]

When such events come before the bar of the law, to what spatial aesthetic are they subject? The question matters because, as Kant and Cassirer suggest, space is one of those framing intuitions that conditions the manner in which a culture will receive and respond to phenomena. The critical geographical literature has similarly emphasized the role of spatial understandings and metaphors as foundational aspects of how both individuals and cultures interpret and understand their worlds and themselves.[67] One can "see through" spatial metaphors and territorial conceptions, understanding them "as implicating and being implicated in ways of thinking, acting, and being in the world – ways of world-making informed by beliefs, desires and culturally and historically contingent ways of knowing."[68] In this sense, these conceptions of space "are significant cultural artifacts of a rather special kind."[69] As Delaney writes, "One might go so far as to say that a cultural formation or social order is unintelligible without reference ... to how it is territorially expressed."[70] One should expect, then, to find the liberal rule of law – a particularly salient modern cultural formation – informed

---

66  *Syndicat Northcrest v Amselem*, 2004 SCC 47, [2004] 2 SCR 551 [*Amselem*]. The *Amselem* decision is considered in greater detail in chapter 2.

67  David Delaney, *Territory: A Short Introduction* (Oxford: Blackwell, 2005). See also Nicholas K Blomley, *Law, Space and the Geographies of Power* (New York: Guilford Press, 1994); Wesley Pue, "Wrestling with Law: (Geographical) Specificity v (Legal) Abstraction" (1990) 11 Urban Geography 566; Kal Raustiala, "The Geography of Justice" (2005) 73 Fordham L Rev 2501.

68  Delaney, *supra* note 67 at 12.

69  *Ibid* at 10.

70  *Ibid*.

by and expressed in a sense of space and territoriality. And as a component of the legal way of "world-making," the imprint of this spatial logic will also be seen in the law's treatment of religion and claims of religious freedom, an imprint that I am describing as one aspect of the aesthetics of religious freedom.

"Morality," Kahn writes, "may be without borders, but law's rule begins only with the imagination of jurisdiction."[71] Jurisdiction is the guiding metaphor for law's understanding of space, serving as the conceptual means of "mapping" authorities within the legal world. As Valverde puts it, "[T]he governance of legal governance is the work of jurisdiction."[72] Although the concept of "jurisdiction" is not solely spatial – organizing, as it does, authority over objects, relationships, persons, and topics – its function in organizing and interpreting territorial or spatial relations is what interests me here. Jurisdiction is "a way of speaking and understanding the social world,"[73] one that does so by charting the boundaries of the legitimate exercise of authority. The experience of the social space of the law is one of moving within multiple domains of authority. Space matters to the law inasmuch as it is called upon to answer the question, who has authority or jurisdiction here and over what?

Some articulations of this jurisdictional way of organizing space closely mirror the cartographic. National and international borders are emphatically and obviously a matter of territory and the reach of political authority. These borders are not just (or even principally) physical; rather, they are aspects of the legal imagination that make territory as much an ethical as a geographical matter. Cases concerning the extraterritorial reach of even our most fundamental legal principles – in Canada, the extraterritorial impact of the *Charter*[74] – are such fraught questions precisely because the legal system is not solely a moral system, but also a jurisdictionally ordered social world. The same play of space and authority can be seen in Canada's internal federal organization. The constitution (in all senses of the word)

---

71  Kahn, *The Cultural Study of Law, supra* note 4 at 55.
72  Mariana Valverde, "Jurisdiction and Scale: Legal 'Technicalities' as Resources for Theory" (2009) 18 Soc & Leg Stud 139 at 141.
73  Richard T Ford, "Law's Territory (A History of Jurisdiction)" (1999) 97 Mich L Rev 843 at 855.
74  See e.g. *R v Hape*, 2007 SCC 26, [2007] 2 SCR 292; *Canada (Justice) v Khadr*, 2008 SCC 28, [2008] 2 SCR 125.

of the political community in Canada is based on the jurisdictional arrangement of competing legal authorities. The great spatial question of federalism is whether a matter is *intra vires* a province or a matter of federal regulation. Again, the lines on the political map of Canada are symbolic markers for the boundaries of legitimate authority. This is not to say that these lines are not real; it is, instead, to emphasize that, as Ford puts it, "they are constantly being *made* real"[75] through the range of practices of authority that take place within the culture of law's rule.

Yet some of the most influential aspects of the spatial intuitions of the law are not so literal, cartographic, and largely writ. Indeed, as Delaney observes, "[T]he micro-territories of everyday life may be more significant – or at least more noticeable, than the macro-territories of global politics,"[76] and the legal imagination has much to say about these "micro-territories." Like all other territorial imaginations, legal space "is as much a metaphysical phenomenon as a material one,"[77] implicating basic ontological questions that help to constitute political and social relations within the culture of law. Perhaps the most potent example of this ontological and social work done by legal mappings of space is the law of property, one of the building blocks of Western legal culture. "Within the ongoing practice of law's rule, any particular space appears first of all as property."[78] Property law is precisely the framing of space into competing authorities. It involves the legal parcelling of authority over space and objects in space. Whether one has a fee simple interest in land or merely a lease-hold is a legal distinction about space that shapes one's rights and entitlements within that sphere and, with this, one's social relations with other subjects. To interpret and negotiate space through the legal idea of property involves internalizing a particular range of power relations and distinctive ways of imagining the subject's relationship to the world and to other subjects; this is one respect in which the law does not merely act upon the world but "makes the world, helping to constitute the understandings and beliefs that make the world unfold *this* way, rather than *that* way," providing "hegemonic categories

---

75  Ford, *supra* note 73 at 856 [emphasis in original].
76  Delaney, *supra* note 67 at 5.
77  *Ibid* at 12.
78  Kahn, *The Cultural Study of Law, supra* note 4 at 63.

through which social life is ordered."[79] As scholars of Indigenous legal traditions have suggested, cultural understandings of space that differ from those found in the Western legal tradition can engender very different social relations and political formations.[80] The jurisdictions of everyday life created through the legal metaphysics of property are an important aspect of the way in which law, as a cultural formation, uses spatial and territorial conceptions to constitute a social and political world.

Within the social and political world constituted by the spatial intuitions of legal culture, the division of the world into private and public domains is of utmost importance. This distinction is, of course, "[o]ne of the most consequential of categorical boundaries relating to the spatial order of property,"[81] dividing the world into two spheres of ownership: public and private. Much ink has been spilled on the centrality of this division to the liberal rule of law, and some of it has explored the way in which this manner of dividing up the world distorts or fails to reflect the experience of those subject to law's rule. Yet law's fealty to a manageable and real distinction between the private and public is deep, an artefact of the contemporary constitutional rule of law's relationship to liberal political culture; as Blomley puts it, this distinction is "one of the crucial axes of liberal legalism."[82] The personal or private is protected space, the space in which interest and preference can guide conduct and, most crucially, the space over which the state has the weakest claim to authority. The public, by contrast, is the domain of state power and, concomitantly, governed by the demands of public reason over personal interest or preference. The influence of this ontological distinction is felt throughout the culture of law's rule, shaping constitutional principles as much as it does property relations. One need go no further than the law of search and seizure to find a pristine expression of this way of carving up space; the state has a claim of authority over

---

79  Nicholas Blomley, "Flowers in the Bathtub: Boundary Crossings at the Public-Private Divide" (2005) 36 Geoforum 281 at 282 [Blomley, "Flowers in the Bathtub"] [emphasis in original].

80  See e.g. Paul Nadasdy, "'Property' and Aboriginal Land Claims in the Canadian Subarctic: Some Theoretical Considerations" (2002) 104 American Anthropologist 247; James (Sákéj) Youngblood Henderson, "Postcolonial Indigenous Legal Consciousness" (2002) 1 Indigenous LJ 1; John Borrows, *Recovering Canada: The Resurgence of Indigenous Law* (Toronto: University of Toronto Press, 2002), especially 29–55.

81  Blomley, "Flowers in the Bathtub," *supra* note 79 at 283.

82  *Ibid* at 283.

what is left in public space or available for public observation that is at odds with the privacy enjoyed in one's personal space – be it the hyper-private space of the body or the hallowed territory of the home.[83] Even when it comes to the exercise of fundamental rights and freedoms, not all space is treated equally. The ambit of freedom of expression will differ vastly as between one's home, a public school, a private school, a park, a legislature, and an airport. These differences can all be traced to varying conceptions of the nature and locus of authority exercised in each of these spaces. Otherwise put, when the expressive event appears before the law, it appears subject to and within a preconception of space in which the salient and instinctive question is, who has what legitimate authority in this space? The accretion of these private/public distinctions does more than just formal legal work; it provides "a pervasive vocabulary through which the socio-spatial world is rendered intelligible."[84] The resulting and complex maps of private and public spaces, and their political and social implications, are an important part of the "micro-territories of everyday life"[85] lived under the rule of law.

These peculiar spatial intuitions in the culture of the rule of law imprint on the management and analysis of issues of religious freedom. In this way it is possible to speak of a spatial aesthetics of religious freedom. In supporting this assertion, one temptation would be simply to invoke broad claims about the nature of space in religion and to show an inherent conflict between "religious ways" of imagining space and what I have thus far described about the law. One might, for example, invoke Eliade and claim that, for religion, space is understood in terms of the sacred and the profane,[86] a meaningful way of dividing up the world that is simply missed if law approaches space as a matter of jurisdictional authority. It is no doubt true that many religions will find the sacred/profane division more true to their sense of movement through space. Where this is so, there might be a fundamental misunderstanding when law and religion meet on an issue that involves questions of space. Yet such sweeping claims on the religious

---

83  See e.g. *R v Feeney*, [1997] 2 SCR 13, on the powers of the police to enter into a home; *R v Patrick*, 2009 SCC 17, [2009] 1 SCR 579, on search, seizure and privacy rights on the borders between the home and public space.

84  Blomley, "Flowers in the Bathtub," *supra* note 79 at 284.

85  Delaney, *supra* note 67 at 5.

86  Mircea Eliade, *Sacred and the Profane: The Nature of Religion* (New York: Harcourt, Brace & World, 1959).

side are not, ultimately, terribly edifying. My purpose is instead to suggest that the law of religious freedom has an aesthetic component peculiar to it that – quite apart from any particular doctrinal development or argument about the just in a given case – shapes the way in which such issues will be experienced and discussed, and draws out particular terms as the salient terms for discussing freedom of religion. One ignores law's intuitions about space and jurisdiction at one's peril when advancing or analysing claims of religious freedom made within a liberal culture of law's rule.

Consider the cases explored at the outset of this section. The eruv was a problem for the law (and for the City of Outremont) because it sought to destabilize the border between the private space of the home and the space subject to public authority. In disrupting this border, the eruv challenged the liberal commitment to the privatization of religion, by evidencing a spilling-over of private religion into public spaces. In her assessment of debates about the eruv in one London neighbourhood, Davina Cooper traces community hostility to the fact that the eruv "flaunted minority beliefs, practices and loyalties in a way that provocatively disregarded the liberal public/private divide."[87] In transgressing the private/public border, the eruv not only symbolically privatized public space, it "was seen … as also transgressing the divide by bringing inappropriate expressions of religious faith into the public domain."[88] The eruv "mixed" or "joined" the public and the private and, in this sense, was "an affront to ontological ordering principles."[89] Within the range of distinctive religious beliefs and practices within this community, the eruv became a contested site precisely because it came into conflict with the law's orienting spatial intuitions. This is the influence of law's aesthetics at play in the interaction of law and religion, framing the experience of the world, viewed from law's perspective. The limit of a court's ability to reconcile a religious practice within legal space turns out to be one boundary of religious freedom.

---

87 Davina Cooper, *Governing Out of Order: Space, Law and the Politics of Belonging* (London: Rivers Oram Press, 1998) at 141.

88 *Ibid* at 130. Interestingly, while transgressing the legally understood boundary between public and private, the eruv was, in its own way, accepting and sharing the salience of the spatial distinction, but seeking to expand the realm of the public.

89 Blomley, "Flowers in the Bathtub," *supra* note 79 at 284.

*Amselem*, the case regarding the erection of a succah on a condominium balcony discussed above,[90] displays a similar dynamic. Quite simply, the matter would not have been of constitutional or legal moment were it not for the transgression of law's spatial aesthetics. Had Mr Amselem enjoyed a fee simple property interest in his balcony, the matter could not appear as a question of religious freedom – there would have been no legal issue because Mr Amselem's religious expression would have conformed to the spatial categories imagined by the constitutional rule of law. As a purely private expression, there would be no issue of religious freedom. The fact that the balcony had a public (or, at least, communal) quality is what lent the erection of the succah spatial relevance for the law, creating a constitutional issue. Again, one sees the contribution of ideas about space to the way that the culture of the constitutional rule of law packages, organizes, and presents the world; one sees law as something that frames experience and, as a consequence, is experienced by religious communities.

The case of *Chamberlain v Surrey School District No 36*[91] is a final example of the imprint of these spatial framings on the interaction of law and religion. *Chamberlain* concerned a school board's decision, based on religious objections of parents in the community, to prohibit the use of three books depicting same-sex parented families for use in a kindergarten/grade one curriculum. The Supreme Court of Canada quashed this decision on the ground that the school board had failed to comply with the admonition in the legislation that all public schools be administered on "strictly secular and non-sectarian principles."[92] This decision can be fruitfully analysed as a case about the concept of the secular and the demands of public reason, and this aspect of the case will be explored in chapter 2. Yet one might well understand the case in somewhat different terms: that prior to either of these questions, the issue engaged a spatial intuition suffusing law's interaction with religion.

The events in *Chamberlain* appeared to the law within the grid of competing authorities that shape its spatial intuitions. At the core of the question raised by this case was the potent spatial fact that the events at issue were concerned with what happened in a public school. Had the books been suggested for use in a family's home, it would not appear as

---

90  *Amselem, supra* note 66.
91  2002 SCC 86, [2002] 4 SCR 710.
92  *School Act*, RSBC 1996, c 412, s 76.

a legal event. Had the books been banned for use in a religious school, the doctrinal shape of the questions asked about religious freedom would have been manifestly different. This spatial distinction might not have mattered one whit to the religiously motivated participants in the discussion. Indeed, the tensions and passions provoked by this case may well have been inflamed by the mismatch between the way in which space mattered for the law and its relevance – or lack thereof – for those arguing that the books ought to be banned. Yet the spatial reception of these events – the aesthetics of religious freedom – set the frame of relevance and the terms for debate for this case.

## Time and the Aesthetics of Religious Freedom

Time present and time past
Are both perhaps present in time future,
And time future contained in time past.
If all time is eternally present
All time is unredeemable.[93]

In 1763 the military hostilities between the British and French in what would later become Canada ceased with the signing of the *Treaty of Paris*.[94] That treaty guaranteed the right of Roman Catholics in French Canada to carry on the practice of their religion. *The Quebec Act* of 1774,[95] another crucial legal step in the development of the Canadian state, included similar provisions providing special protections and rights for the Roman Catholic Church. With Confederation in 1867, the modern Canadian state took form. The nation's first constitution, the *British North America Act*,[96] provided for the basic structures of government in Canada, defining the legislative, executive, and judicial powers, and instituted the particular brand of Canadian federalism with the division of legislative authority between the federal government and the provinces. Also included in the *British North America Act* (which would

---

93 TS Eliot, "Burnt Norton" in *Four Quartets* (New York: Harcourt, Brace, and Company, 1943) 3 at 3. Reprinted by permission of Houghton Mifflin Harcourt Publishing Company. All rights reserved.
94 *Definitive Treaty of Peace and Friendship between Great Britain and the United States*, 3 September 1783, 48 CTS 487 (entered into force 12 May 1784).
95 *The Quebec Act, 1774* (UK), 14 Geo III, c 83.
96 *British North America Act, 1867* (UK), 30 & 31 Vict, c 3.

later be renamed the *Constitution Act, 1867*) was section 93, a provision that gave authority to the provinces to legislate in respect of education. Yet this provision also carried forward the tradition of affording legally distinct status to religious education, reflecting the history of Protestant and Catholic minorities in French and English Canada, respectively, by protecting the rights and privileges of Protestant and Catholic minority schools.

In the mid-1980s the Ontario government sought to introduce a bill providing for full funding of Roman Catholic high schools in Ontario. Despite the recent introduction of the *Charter of Rights and Freedoms*, the bill did not extend similar funding or protection to denominational schools of other traditions. The constitutionality of this bill was put to the courts, and one of the questions posed was whether the privileging of Roman Catholic schools was consistent with *Charter* protections of freedom of religion, which also prohibited state endorsement of religion,[97] and the equality of treatment on grounds of religion.

In its judgment on the constitutionality of the schools bill, the Supreme Court of Canada discussed the nature and import of section 93 of the *Constitution Act, 1867*, describing it as "part of a solemn pact resulting from the bargaining which made Confederation possible."[98] The Court explained that "[t]he protection of minority religious rights was a major preoccupation during the negotiations leading to Confederation because of the perceived danger of leaving the religious minorities in both Canada East and Canada West at the mercy of overwhelming majorities."[99] In spite of the apparent conflict between such specific protection of a given religion's educational interests over those of others, and the seeming awkwardness of holding this set of privileges together with the recently affirmed *Charter* commitment to the equal treatment of religious groups, Justice Wilson, writing for a majority of the Court, held that this privileging of Roman Catholic education was immune from *Charter* scrutiny. Section 93, "which represented a fundamental part of the Confederation compromise,"[100] was not subject to the claims of freedom of religion.

---

97  *R v Big M Drug Mart Ltd*, [1985] 1 SCR 295.
98  *Reference Re Bill 30*, [1987] 1 SCR 1148 at 1173.
99  *Ibid*.
100  *Ibid* at 1197–8.

This matter came back before the Supreme Court when a group of Jewish parents and a group of non-Catholic Christian parents sought a declaration that the failure to provide funding for Jewish and other Christian schools directly offended their section 15(1) equality rights and freedom of religion, guaranteed by section 2(a) of the *Charter*. Rather than seeking to declare the funding of Roman Catholic schools in Ontario unconstitutional, these parents sought the expansion of the funding regime – equal funding of their schools, the litigants argued, would protect their religious freedom in the same manner as Roman Catholic education protected Catholicism in the province. The majority of the Court confirmed that section 93 of the *Constitution Act, 1867*, served "to entrench constitutionally a special status for such classes of persons, granting them rights which are denied to others."[101] Yet when attention shifted to whether this offended the guarantee of freedom of religion, the Court again answered with an emphatic "no." "Without this 'solemn pact,' this 'cardinal term' of Union, there would have been no Confederation,"[102] Justice Iacobucci reasoned. "As a child born of historical exigency, section 93 does not represent a guarantee of fundamental freedoms,"[103] but, rather, was "the product of an historical compromise which was a crucial step along the road leading to Confederation."[104] This status immunized it from the logic of freedom of religion; section 2(a) simply did not apply.

While this case was being decided, Mr Arieh Hollis Waldman, the father of two Jewish children enrolled in a private day school in Ontario, brought a similar claim before the UN Human Rights Committee.[105] He argued that Ontario's policy of funding separate Roman Catholic schools violated religious freedom and equality guarantees found in the *International Covenant on Civil and Political Rights*. The tribunal took account of the reasoning in the *Bill C-30* case and the *Adler* decision, noting the special constitutional status of Roman Catholic education

---

101  *Adler v Ontario*, [1996] 3 SCR 609 at para 25.
102  *Ibid* at para 29.
103  *Ibid* at para 30.
104  *Ibid* at para 29. I discuss this case, and the "two logics" that it points to in the structure of Canadian constitutionalism, in Benjamin L Berger, "Children of Two Logics: A Way into Canadian Constitutional Culture" (2013) 11:2 International Journal of Constitutional Law 319.
105  *Waldman v Canada*, HCROR, 67th Sess, Annex, Communication No 694/1996 (1996) [*Waldman*].

reflected in section 93 of the *Constitution Act, 1867*. Yet it reasoned that "the fact that a distinction is enshrined in the Constitution does not render it reasonable and objective."[106] "In the instant case, the distinction was made in 1867 to protect the Roman Catholics in Ontario. The material before the Committee does not show that members of the Roman Catholic community or any identifiable section of that community are now in a disadvantaged position compared to those members of the Jewish Community that wish to secure the education of their children in religious schools. Accordingly, the Committee rejects the State party's argument that the preferential treatment of Roman Catholic schools is nondiscriminatory because of its Constitutional obligation."[107] The Human Rights Committee of the United Nations found Canada in violation of Article 26 of the *International Covenant on Civil and Political Rights*.

Kant privileged time in his transcendental aesthetics, stating, "In it alone is all reality of phenomena possible."[108] "Time," wrote Kant, "is the formal condition *a priori* of all phenomena whatsoever."[109] If time is that which frames and gives form and order to all that is perceived, all sensation of or reflection on phenomena, can anything be said about the way in which distinctive framings of time condition the way that phenomena are understood and dealt with in the law? In particular, are there any ways in which such framings might shape the interaction of constitutional law and religion?

One way that temporality may come to shape and structure issues of religious freedom is at points of substantial divergence between religious conceptions of time and secular legal understandings. To be sure, religion and the law may have fundamentally different framings of the relevance of time, a mismatch that can produce miscommunications that afflict the law of religious freedom. In those cases one sees very clearly the import of accounting for a tacit temporal aesthetic shaping law's experience of religious difference. In such cases, the limits

---

106 *Ibid* at para 10.4.
107 *Ibid*.
108 Kant, *supra* note 58 at 48.
109 *Ibid* at 50.

of religious accommodation may be traceable in certain instances to a basic aesthetic dissonance.

Consider the case of *AC*.[110] The case concerned an almost-fifteen-year-old girl suffering from Crohn's disease. Although her medical advice was that she was in lifesaving need of a blood transfusion, as a devout Jehovah's Witness she had signed an advance directive expressing her wish not to have such transfusions. The Manitoba legislation presumed competence for those sixteen years or older and provided that no medical procedure could be undertaken against these older children's wishes unless this presumption was rebutted. AC was assessed, and all accepted that she was legally competent. She was, in essence, a mature minor. Yet since she was a child under the age of sixteen, the legislation vested the treatment decision in a judge who was to balance a range of factors, ultimately issuing the order that comported with the best interests of the child. AC challenged the legislation on the basis that, as a competent minor who had expressed her wish to follow the dictates of her religion, the legislative scheme violated a number of her rights, including her right to freedom of religion.

A majority of the Court held that the legislation was constitutionally valid but ruled that her religious views ought to be given weight in the analysis of what is "in the best interests of the child" – the governing standard under the legislation. Justice Binnie, dissenting, would have found the legislation unconstitutional on the basis that, as a mature minor, she had the sole authority to make such decisions. Justice Binnie's judgment is a model of perspicuity and humility in the law of religious freedom, a point to which I will return in chapter 4. Justice Binnie observed, "Individuals who do not subscribe to the beliefs of Jehovah's Witnesses find it difficult to understand their objection to the potentially lifesaving effects of a blood transfusion."[111] Nevertheless, he concluded, "The *Charter* is not just about the freedom to make what most members of society would regard as the wise and correct choice. If that were the case, the *Charter* would be superfluous. The *Charter*, A.C. argues, gives her the freedom – in this case religious freedom – to refuse forced medical treatment, even where her life or death hangs in the balance."[112] Yet even with the greater constitutional margin that he affords for AC's religious

---

110  *AC v Manitoba (Director of Child and Family Services)*, 2009 SCC 30, [2009] 2 SCR 181.
     I discuss this case at length in chapter 4.
111  *Ibid* at para 191.
112  *Ibid* at para 163.

views, Justice Binnie's decision discloses something important – indeed, indispensable – about the aesthetics of religious freedom. For both the majority and the dissent, the argument was about autonomy in the present and the impact of past influences on the child. Despite their different conclusions, both decisions work within the temporal frame of the law, including the law of religious freedom.

What is never on the table – what could never be on the table in matters of religious freedom – is the conception of time that framed AC's experiences and her perception of her world. The eternal welfare of her soul was in the balance. This eschatological aesthetic, which informed the exercise of the autonomy that the Court fixed upon, could not be truly comprehended and reckoned with from within the culture of Canadian constitutionalism. Such sharp dissonances between religious and legal conceptions of time demonstrate one way in which reflection about religious freedom takes place within law's aesthetic instincts. However, I want to explore a more subtle way in which the distinctive temporality of legal culture influences the shape of religious freedom and, more generally, law's encounter with religion.

Legal time – the time of the constitutional rule of law – is a compendious reception of all of those moments in the life of the community bound by law that might serve as authority for the present. Kahn identifies the "historicity of law" as "its single most prominent feature":[113] "Law's rule carries forward a past that makes a meaningful claim upon us."[114] The student of the common law will find this feature in the basic principle of *stare decisis* as the building block of the legal rule; the starting point for legal authority is fidelity to the past.[115] As Kahn astutely observes, "Legal arguments do not begin by asking about 'the best outcome, all things considered.' They begin from a commitment to the past."[116] This durable commitment to the past as the starting point

---

113  Kahn, *The Cultural Study of Law, supra* note 4 at 43.

114  *Ibid* at 45.

115  For the centrality of tradition to the rule of law, see also Anthony T Kronman, "Precedent and Tradition" (1990) 99 Yale LJ 1029.

116  Kahn, *supra* note 4 at 43. See also Paul W Kahn, *The Reign of Law: Marbury v Madison and the Construction of America* (New Haven, Conn: Yale University Press, 1997) at 19: "A critical element in our belief in the rule of law is that the future of the political order should be the same as its past. Law's rule is an exercise in the maintenance of political meanings already achieved. It links the future to the past ... To abandon the problem of interpretation of meanings already present in the legal order, and to ask only how we can best order the future, is to abandon the rule of law."

for legal reasoning imprints itself on how law understands and inter-prets the social world. Constitutions express this relationship between time and the rule of law, with the formative documents and events that express both the *is* and the *ought* of a community at one point in history carrying forward to make claims upon us in the present.[117] To the extent that it makes a meaningful claim upon us today, this past both commu-nicates and constitutes political identity.

The most striking feature of law's time is its synchronicity. Like an individual's life story, the historical narrative that frames law's percep-tion and reception of all events is the entirety of its past. "At any given moment, the law appears as the sum total of all that has been done and not yet undone."[118] The past remains present in its claims of legal authority, producing "a curious kind of temporal flatness in the rela-tionship of legal texts and resources to each other."[119] This "temporal flatness" inheres in the possibility that any legal event, any legal deci-sion, may appear as influential in a given contemporary moment. As Martin Krygier observes, "[T]he past of law ... is not simply part of its history; it is an authoritative part of its present."[120] We do not know at any given point whether the best or most relevant authority on the rule of law will be a case decided in 2007[121] or one decided in 1959.[122] Both are available to us as authority. In this sense, law is not on a steady trajectory of progressive discovery, nor is it neatly sequenced, with the past falling away into historical fact, making room for the authority of the present. This is what I mean by law's time as a compendious recep-tion of all of those moments in the life of the community bound by law that might serve as authority for the present.

Seeing law's time in this fashion raises an intriguing issue: can it even be said that law possesses a sense of "history?" Considering the nature of history as a symbolic form in human life, Cassirer observed that, before it could be said that historical consciousness had truly taken up residence in human culture, myth was the prevailing view of time. "In myth," Cassirer wrote, "we find the first attempts to ascertain a chrono-logical order of things and events, to give a cosmology and a genealogy

---

117  See Hanna Fenichel Pitkin, "The Idea of a Constitution" (1987) 37 J Leg Educ 167.
118  Kahn, *The Cultural Study of Law, supra* note 4 at 43.
119  *Ibid* at 51.
120  Martin Krygier, "Law as Tradition" (1986) 5 Law & Phil 237 at 245.
121  *British Columbia (Attorney General) v Christie*, 2007 SCC 21, [2007] 1 SCR 873.
122  *Roncarelli v Duplessis*, [1959] SCR 121.

of gods and men."[123] But he goes on to explain that this cosmology and genealogy is not properly "history," and his explanation reflects provocatively on my description of law's time.

Cassirer distinguishes mythical time from historical time in that, in the former, "[t]he past, present, and future are still tied up together; they form an undifferentiated unity and an indiscriminate whole. ... From the point of view of the mythical consciousness the past has never passed away; it is always here and now."[124] Historical consciousness, by contrast, is diachronic; for the historian, "facts belong to the past and the past is gone forever."[125] In this light, law's synchronic time appears to be a species of mythical time, rather than a brand of historical time. The authoritative immanence of time past is part of a mythical vision in service of constructing a more-or-less coherent national political story through law. Perhaps in this fact we find some explanation for the troubling ineptness evinced by law when forced to deal with redress for historical injustice and, in Canada, claims to Indigenous title. Despite professed attempts to take account of historical truth, the law always meets these compelling cases and claims in thrall to a mythic sense of time – the myth of the community as constituted by law – into which it awkwardly seeks to digest the facts of history. The U.S. Supreme Court's reasoning in an early nineteenth-century Indigenous land rights case is exemplary: "However extravagant the pretension of converting the discovery of an inhabited country into conquest may appear, if the principle has been asserted in the first instance, and afterwards sustained; if a country has been acquired and held under it; if the property of the great mass of the community originates in it, it becomes the law of the land, and cannot be questioned."[126] Whatever we learn about promises made and broken in the political history of

---

123  Cassirer, *supra* note 50 at 173.
124  *Ibid.*
125  *Ibid* at 174.
126  *Johnson & Graham's Lessee v M'Intosh*, 21 US (8 Wheat.) 543, 591, as cited in Eric Dannenmaier, "Beyond Indigenous Property Rights: Exploring the Emergence of a Distinctive Connection Doctrine" (2008) 86 Wash UL Rev 53. Dannenmaier also points to the 1992 Australian High Court decision in *Mabo v Queensland*, in which the tension between the facts of history and what must be assumed for the purposes of legal authority/sovereignty is clear on the face of the judgment. See also Kent McNeil, "The Vulnerability of Indigenous Land Rights in Australia and Canada" (2004) 42 Osgoode Hall LJ 271.

the country, constitutional law is insistent on a story whose moral is its own legitimacy.

The range of secularisms and varieties of religious establishment that one finds in modern Western traditions are constituted in part by the force of these mythic stories, conducted through the authority of law. With this tethering of authority and history, law's time shapes the frame into which issues of religious and cultural difference are received, moulding the sense of what is natural, possible, or unthinkable as a matter of religious freedom. The imprint of this approach to temporality is evident in the religious education cases with which I began this section. Claims of religious freedom had to be disposed of *within* the mythic time of law, in which the purchase of a "solemn pact" made in 1867, and its historical antecedents, was dispositive in a case heard in 1996, and despite the introduction of a *Charter of Rights and Freedoms*. The challenge to the Roman Catholic school funding scheme came to the courts already conditioned by the mythic time defining the Canadian community under its rule of law. The law of religious freedom could not be addressed outside the frame of this temporal aesthetic, this mythic time in which the inter-religious compact reached in the eighteenth and nineteenth centuries had as much authoritative purchase as the claims of religious equality in the modern secular state. When the matter was freed from this temporal frame, when the matter was brought before the UN Committee on Human Rights – operating in its own mythic time – the analysis and result were both manifestly different.

This is, perhaps, one way of understanding the claim that international law does not seem to be "law" in a conventional sense. Law works by appealing to resources within the unfolding story of a particular community wrestling with justice issues over time. Still lacking a strong "us" upon which past authority calls in a meaningful way, without a compendious mythical story of community, international law often seems to lack the authority of this feature of legal reasoning, appearing more aspirational than legal. In *Waldman* the past authorities were not present in the same way, present as part of a temporal identity, and so the committee could state that "the fact that a distinction is enshrined in the Constitution does not render it reasonable and objective."[127] True, but prior to the question of reasonableness and objectivity

---

127 *Waldman, supra* note 105 at para 10.4.

is the question of the aesthetics of religious freedom: the shaping of the boundaries of religious freedom in light of the history of a given community. This is part of the aesthetic intuition that frames the interaction of law and religion in Canada.

## Telling a Different Story about Religion and the Constitutional Rule of Law

The influence of aesthetics on the interaction of religion and the constitutional rule of law will seldom be controlling, but it will never be absent in structuring the experience of the constitutional rule of law in Canada – experience of it both as a world in which we live and an object of encounter. Seeing the shaping influence of such fundamental categories of perception is part of what it would be to tell a story about law and religion in Canada that begins with the experience of constitutional law as a cultural form; to borrow again from Geertz, it is an aspect of understanding Canadian constitutional law in the frame of its own banalities.[128] But these foundational aesthetic categories are only one aspect of the way that law frames experience. That frame also comprises qualitative and normative components. As Charles Taylor argued in his magisterial study, *Sources of the Self: The Making of the Modern Identity*, "[D]oing without frameworks is utterly impossible for us."[129] This book is organized around the idea that, in modern life, the constitutional rule of law is one of the "horizons within which we live our lives and which make sense of them,"[130] and that generating a better account of what is at stake in the interaction of law and religion – sweeping up and making sense of the residue left by our prevailing stories – depends on taking the experience of law as culture as the starting point for analysis.

But enough about starting points. In the next chapter I turn to one of the large questions raised by thinking about the interaction of constitutional law and religion in this way: How is the legal and political experience of religion shaped within the culture of Canadian constitutionalism?

---

128 Geertz, *The Interpretation of Cultures, supra* note 38 at 14.
129 Charles Taylor, *Sources of the Self: The Making of the Modern Identity* (Cambridge, UK: Cambridge University Press, 1989) at 27.
130 *Ibid.*

# Chapter 2

# Law's Religion: Rendering Culture

The more you make religion modern and acceptable, soft and digestible, the less you are faithful to its specific order of difficulty.

Bruno Latour, *Rejoicing:*
*Or the Torments of Religious Speech*[1]

Stories about the contemporary interaction of law and religion in Canada conventionally align the concept of "culture" with only one side of that interaction – the side of religion. Religion, it is thought, is the rich and particular cultural player in this exchange. Law's task in a regime of legal multiculturalism is to understand and manage "the claims of culture," to borrow a phrase from Seyla Benhabib.[2] Yet the location of culture in these encounters turns out to be a much more complicated and subtle question. Does law, indeed, proceed on a "cultural" understanding of religion? Does it apprehend religion in cultural terms? As I explore in this chapter, the answer is interestingly ambivalent, an ambivalence that turns on an appreciation of the way that Canadian constitutionalism frames and gives meaning to phenomena.

When Canadian constitutional law sets its gaze on religion, religion takes on a particular shape, one that accentuates certain aspects of religious life, conscience, and practice while concealing others. In so doing, it shapes the legal and political experience of religion. Law renders religion. Seeking to excavate this peculiar understanding of religion, the chapter

---

1  Bruno Latour, *Rejoicing: Or the Torments of Religious Speech*, translated by Julie Rose (Cambridge, UK: Polity Press, 2002) at 100–1.
2  Seyla Benhabib, *The Claims of Culture: Equality and Diversity in the Global Era* (Princeton, NJ: Princeton University Press, 2002).

asks, If one's only source of information were the constitutional discourse of the courts, what would one conclude about the nature of religion? Otherwise put, what does religion look like when viewed through the lens of modern Canadian constitutional law? By answering this question we can both gain insight into the way that religion is conceived of in contemporary legal analysis and identify the ways in which the phenomenon of religion is tailored to fit within the legal and political imagination.

Religion is never encountered directly; it is apprehended within a broader frame of significance. Freud's core ideas about the psychological reaction to the anxiety borne of the awareness of vulnerability shaped his understanding of religion.[3] We are unsurprised when, reading Durkheim, we find that religion plays a key role in the constitution and sustenance of the group.[4] In an analogous way, when religion is put before the bar of law, law understands and casts its subject in accordance with its own informing commitments. As I identify and describe the various features of law's peculiar understanding of religion, it will become clear that modern Canadian constitutional law casts religion in terms compatible with its own structural assumptions, as well as symbolic and normative commitments, which are themselves informed by the contemporary political culture of liberalism. Although this imagining of religion has a potentially reductionistic and context-stripping effect, it is not simply a defect that calls for remedy; rather, the law has no choice but to conceive of religion in terms cognizable within constitutional liberalism. This selective shaping is an artefact of the cultural nature of the Canadian constitutional rule of law, a consequence of its role in shaping and giving meaning to experience. It must view religion from somewhere, must understand religion in the context of some framing intuitions. This chapter is concerned with exposing those formative

---

3  See Sigmund Freud, "Totem and Taboo: Some Points of Agreement between the Mental Lives of Savages and Neurotics," translated by James Strachey, in Albert Dickson, ed, *The Origins of Religion*, vol 13 (London: Penguin Books, 1990) 43; Sigmund Freud, "The Future of an Illusion," translated by James Strachey, in Albert Dickson, ed, *Civilization, Society and Religion*, vol 12 (London: Penguin Books, 1991) 179, in which Freud explains religion as affording a set of beliefs and practices that give us comfort in the face of our own mortality and help to justify the repression of our urges in the name of social and moral constraint.

4  See Emile Durkheim, *The Elementary Forms of Religious Life*, translated by Karen E Fields (New York: Free Press, 1995) [originally published in 1912], in which Durkheim offers his theory that religion is a symbolic means of binding the individual to the group and committing this individual to the group's welfare.

intuitions and what they mean for how law digests religion. The result of this selective rendering, however, is to trim the phenomenon of religion, both thinning it as a cultural form and taming it for legal and political purposes. That which is left on the cutting room floor – dimensions of religion unaccounted for within constitutional culture – is one aspect of the experiential residue with which this book is concerned.

Before turning to the jurisprudence as a resource from which to draw out Canadian constitutional law's particular understanding of religion, it is worth pausing to acknowledge that by focusing attention on the constitutional discourse of the courts I am narrowing the inquiry to one particular source of information about the state's treatment of religion. The image of religion generated by debates in Parliament or speeches made by members of the executive branch may differ from the image that emerges from the work of the judicial branch. The goal, however, is to deepen our sense of the way in which law understands religion and the respects in which this image diverges from a robust conception of religion as culture. With this appreciation in hand, we are better equipped to understand the nature and challenges of the relationship between religion and the Canadian constitutional rule of law. The courts hold a privileged position in managing this interaction, and it is for this reason that I now turn to the jurisprudence of the Supreme Court of Canada.

## Law's Theory of Religion

Canadian constitutional law has a distinct theory of religion and, influenced by this theory, it shapes religion in its own ideological image and likeness while notionally confining religion to discrete dimensions of human life. In this respect, constitutional analysis engages in a kind of context-stripping whereby the religious is made to fit the range of symbolic and normative commitments essential to Canadian constitutional culture. In this chapter, I analyse claims to religious liberties under the *Charter* as a means of exposing this legal rendering of religion.

This descriptive endeavour is greatly aided by the Supreme Court of Canada's decision in *Syndicat Northcrest v Amselem*,[5] the case about the

---

5  2004 SCC 47, [2004] 2 SCR 551 [*Amselem*]. For analyses of this and other cases discussed in this chapter, see Richard Moon, *Freedom of Conscience and Religion* (Toronto: Irwin Law, 2014) [Moon, *Freedom of Conscience and Religion*]; Mary Anne Waldron, *Free to Believe: Rethinking Freedom of Conscience and Religion in Canada* (Toronto: University of Toronto Press, 2013).

succah on a condominium balcony first introduced in the discussion of law's spatial aesthetics in chapter 1. In *Amselem*, the Court discussed the legal approach to freedom of religion and offered a definition of religion: "Defined broadly, religion typically involves a particular and comprehensive system of faith and worship. Religion also tends to involve the belief in a divine, superhuman or controlling power. In essence, religion is about freely and deeply held personal convictions or beliefs connected to an individual's spiritual faith and integrally linked to one's self-definition and spiritual fulfilment, the practices of which allow individuals to foster a connection with the divine or with the subject or object of that spiritual faith."[6]

Since it offers a relatively clear window onto Canadian constitutionalism's particular understanding of religion, the decision in *Amselem* will serve as a touchstone for exploring and defending this claim. As is always the case, however, the Court's reasoning in *Amselem* is shaped by the specific context in which the issues arose. In particular, *Amselem* was a case about the interaction between public norms and the contractual rights of individuals, and there can be little doubt that this factual matrix coloured the judges' reasons.[7] However, in the context of the Supreme Court's *Charter* jurisprudence on the constitutional status of religion, *Amselem* points to the elements of Canadian constitutionalism's theory of religion. As I unpack *Amselem* and add other strands of jurisprudence to enrich the picture, the particular way in which law frames and shapes religion will become clear.

The argument that will emerge is that Canadian constitutional law's image of religion is best understood as comprising three elements, each

---

6  *Amselem, supra* note 5 at para 39.
7  *Amselem* arose under the Quebec *Charter*, which has certain attributes that significantly distinguish it from the Canadian *Charter*. Perhaps most notably, the inclusion of the protection of peaceful enjoyment of property may have influenced aspects of the reasoning in *Amselem*; indeed, in his dissent, Bastarache J made specific reference to the protection of property in his discussion of how to reconcile rights under section 9.1 of the Quebec *Charter* (paras 164–7ff). However, the majority of the Court explicitly stated, at para 37, that, although enunciated in a Quebec *Charter* case, the principles and analysis set out in *Amselem* are equally applicable to the treatment of religion under the *Canadian Charter of Rights and Freedoms*. Indeed, as I explain later in this chapter, the Court has embraced the *Amselem* approach in its subsequent *Charter* jurisprudence on religious freedom. Many thanks to my friend and colleague Robert Leckey for encouraging me to make this point explicit.

of which leads into and mutually supports the others. The result is a cohesive and particular theory of religion. The elements of this conception are: (1) religion as essentially individual, (2) religion as centrally addressed to autonomy and choice, and (3) religion as private. Though each will be considered separately, this separation is somewhat artificial, given that the three elements are mutually informing. As a result, certain observations could be made in the context of a discussion of more than one of the elements. In the end, the point is that the three elements come together in Canadian constitutionalism's single, integrated rendering of religion, whose informing source – the origin from which these elements are reflected – is the political culture of liberalism.[8]

*Law's Religion as Essentially Individual*

Religion cuts its primary constitutional figure in the protection of religious freedoms. Once religion is embedded within a rights-protecting instrument, as it is in the *Charter*, law's conception of religion quite naturally assumes certain characteristics of the idiom in which it is placed. The modern drive to universal human rights has been dominated by a focus on the rights of the individual. This is eminently true of the *Charter*, which, with the exception of Aboriginal and language rights, attaches its protections to the individual. From the fundamental freedoms found in section 2 to the legal rights of sections 7 to 14 and the equality guarantee in section 15, the *Charter* conceives of legally cognizable interests as ultimately being enjoyed by the individual. Lorraine Weinrib notes that, in the way in which Canadians have come to debate fundamental public policy issues in light of the *Charter*, "[t]he direct and primary relationship of the individual to the state is of paramount importance."[9] This pixilation of human experience has been the subject of academic critique[10] but is characteristic of the structure of rights protection and constitutional adjudication.

---

8  See Paul W Kahn, *Putting Liberalism in Its Place* (Princeton, NJ: Princeton University Press, 2005) at 29 (distinguishing liberalism as "a family of political theories," "a partisan political practice," and "a political culture").

9  Lorraine E Weinrib, "Ontario's Sharia Law Debate: Law and Politics under the Charter" in Richard Moon, ed, *Law and Religious Pluralism in Canada* (Vancouver: UBC Press, 2008) 239 at 261 [Moon, *Law and Religious Pluralism*].

10  See Joel Bakan, *Just Words: Constitutional Rights and Social Wrongs* (Toronto: University of Toronto Press, 1997).

The conceptual individualization of religious experience prepares it for its life in the context of constitutional atomism. The individual is the dominant unit of constitutional rights analysis. It is natural, then, for law to conceive of religion, the protection of which is "one of the hallmarks of an enlightened democracy,"[11] in a way that can be assimilated into the analytic structure of contemporary constitutionalism. In *R v Big M Drug Mart Ltd*,[12] the first significant *Charter* case on freedom of religion, which concerned the constitutionality of Sunday closing legislation entitled *The Lord's Day Act*, Justice Dickson suggested exactly this impact of the *Charter* on legal thinking about religion: "With the *Charter*, it has become the right of every Canadian to work out for himself or herself what his or her religious obligations, if any, should be."[13] But the structure of Canadian constitutionalism is really only the vehicle for the transmission – or perhaps a symptom – of the more foundationally informing political culture of liberalism, which is itself deeply committed to the primacy of the individual. Liberalism understands the individual to be "the elementary unit of explanation"[14] and therefore has difficulty assimilating the religious other than in its individual dimensions.[15] It ought to come as no surprise, then, that the dominant thread in the Court's definition and discussion of religion is its focus on religion as a fundamentally individual phenomenon.

Before drawing out this element of law's religion, it is worthwhile to pause to consider two objections to my argument. First, to be sure, beginning with *Big M*, religious liberties in Canada have been spoken about in a language thick with conceptions of equality. Given the abstract connection between conceptions of equality and group belonging, the equality language that runs through the section 2(a) jurisprudence,

---

11  *Amselem, supra* note 5 at para 1.
12  [1985] 1 SCR 295 [*Big M*].
13  *Ibid* at 351.
14  Kahn, *supra* note 8 at 218.
15  Charles Taylor identifies this liberal individualism as a key feature of modernity leading to what he calls the ideal or ethic of "authenticity" that is peculiar to modern culture. Charles Taylor, *The Malaise of Modernity* (Concord, Ont: House of Anansi Press, 1991) at 2ff [Taylor, *Malaise of Modernity*]. Although he addresses a number of ways in which the ideal of individual authenticity can lead to richer modes of existence, Taylor's concern is that, taken to its full extent, this atomism can lead to the abolition of "all horizons of significance," which "threatens us with a loss of meaning and hence a trivialization of our predicament" (68).

quite independent of the as yet under-used religious equality protection in section 15(1) of the *Charter*, might suggest a more robust role
for the group in law's understanding of religion than I assert. Yet, as a
number of scholars have shown, this prima facie association between
equality and the group has been seriously attenuated in Canadian
equality law, as have been the points in the equality analysis that hold
out the promise of some textured assessment of social context and the
dynamics of group identity.[16] In the end, even equality claims are atom-
ized in the adjudicative realities of Canadian constitutional culture,
always returning to a commitment to the primacy of the individual.
The presence of concepts of equality in discussions of religious liberty
thus offers no rescue from the individualistic orientation of the section
2(a) jurisprudence.

It is also certainly true that there are aspects of Canadian constitutionalism that offer protections to religious groups and that one
can find in the jurisprudence at least some regard for the collective
dimensions of religious experience. Most prominent are the rights and
liberties afforded to the Roman Catholic Church in Canada's early
constitutional documents;[17] furthermore, as John Borrows explains,
section 35(1)[18] appears to offer some possibility for the protection of
Aboriginal religion, though this potential is as yet unrealized and
might merely be "a dim light at the end of the tunnel."[19] But the purpose of what follows is not to argue that Canadian constitutional law
has no regard whatsoever for the collective dimensions of religious
experience. Instead, the claim is that, at base, law's understanding of

---

16  I discuss the relationships between equality, identity, and the Court's understanding
of religion later in this chapter, at 84–9, below.

17  See e.g. *Treaty of Paris* (1763), Britain, Spain and Portugal, 10 February 1763,
reproduced in WPM Kennedy, ed, *Statutes, Treaties and Documents of the Canadian
Constitution, 1713–1929*, 2nd ed (Toronto: Oxford University Press, 1930) 31; *The
Quebec Act*, 1774 (UK), 14 George III, c 83; *Constitution Act, 1867* (UK), 30 & 31
Vict, c 3, s 93, reprinted in RSC 1985, Appendix II, No 5; *Reference re Bill 30*, [1987]
1 SCR 1148.

18  *Constitution Act, 1982*, s 35(1), being Schedule B to the *Canada Act 1982* (UK),
1982, c 11.

19  John Borrows, *Canada's Indigenous Constitution* (Toronto: University of Toronto Press,
2010) at 269. As Borrows argues, and in terms entirely consonant with my argument
in this chapter, "[D]espite the potential of s. 35(1) for recognizing and affirming
Anishinabek spiritual beliefs and practices, it may have difficulty travelling beyond
its own cultural commitments" (269).

religion is powerfully individualistic and that, wherever else its eyes might wander, in the contemporary treatment of religious liberties, Canadian constitutional law invariably returns to a sharp focus on the individual.

Nowhere is this more evident than in the Supreme Court's attempt to define the very subject matter of section 2(a). "In essence," held the majority in *Amselem*, "religion is about freely and deeply held *personal convictions or beliefs*."[20] The majority explained that these personal convictions are religious to the extent that they connect with "an *individual's* spiritual faith."[21] Religion is, at root, a personal rather than a social phenomenon and is located in the individual, not group-based. The ends of religion are also conceived of as individual or personal rather than as goods that redound to a traditional or historical community; religion is ultimately about "an individual's self-definition and fulfilment."[22]

In *Amselem*, this focus on the individual finds expression in the Court's treatment of the doctrinal dispute, internal to Judaism, of whether a personal succah is required or whether a communal one will suffice. The revealing point is not the majority's conclusion that the personal succah is to be permitted, although this conclusion supports my argument. Rather, the treatment of this dispute is telling because the majority of the Court rejected the notion that, for the purposes of the law, religious freedom depends on collective conceptions of religious precept or obligation. Instead, following from its definition of religion, the majority adopted a subjective sincerity test for determining whether religious freedom has been engaged: a claimant need only "demonstrate that he or she sincerely believes in a practice or belief

---

20 *Amselem, supra* note 5 at para 39 [emphasis added]. For an account of *Amselem* that explores the tensions produced by this individualist casting of religious liberty, see Richard Moon, "Religious Commitment and Identity: *Syndicat Northcrest v Amselem*" (2005) 29 SCLR (2d) 201. Moon argues that the priority thus far given by the courts to religious claims in the section 2(a) jurisprudence (rather than other conscientiously based claims) arguably marks a somewhat cultural or identity-based aspect to law's understanding of religion. My claim, which I will explore further below, is that any such identity- or group-based aspect rapidly exhausts itself when religion is actually reasoned about, leaving an overriding priority on individual autonomy.

21 *Amselem, supra* note 5 at para 39 [emphasis added].

22 *Ibid* at para 42.

that has a nexus with religion."[23] There is a tone of discomfort with the collective or the institutional in the majority's holding that religious practices are protected, irrespective of whether they are "required by official religious dogma" or are "in conformity with the position of religious officials."[24]

In this respect, the position articulated in *Amselem* is consistent with the much earlier decision in *Ross v New Brunswick School District No 15*,[25] in which the Supreme Court accepted that Ross's anti-Semitic communications were "of a religious nature"[26] and, thus, protected by section 2(a). Justice La Forest, for a unanimous court, held that it "is not the role of [the] Court to decide what any particular religion believes."[27] This reticence to pronounce on the content of a particular religion's beliefs is understandable and, indeed, the Court reaffirmed this point in *Amselem*.[28] But if this is the case, how does the Court know

---

23 *Amselem, supra* note 5 at para 65. If the interference with this belief or practice is also non-trivial, an infringement of section 2(a) of the *Charter* is made out and the analysis turns to whether the limit on the right can be justified under section 1. This approach was subsequently confirmed in a number of cases, including *Multani v Commission scolaire Marguerite-Bourgeoys*, 2006 SCC 6, [2006] 1 SCR 256; *Alberta v Hutterian Brethren of Wilson Colony*, 2009 SCC 37, [2009] 2 SCR 567 [*Wilson Colony*]; and *SL v Commission scolaire des Chênes*, 2012 SCC 7, [2012] 1 SCR 235 [*SL*]. In *Wilson Colony*, Chief Justice McLachlin summarized the test for an infringement of section 2(a) as follows: "An infringement of s. 2(a) of the *Charter* will be made out where: (1) the claimant sincerely believes in a belief or practice that has a nexus with religion; and (2) the impugned measure interferes with the claimant's ability to act in accordance with his or her religious beliefs in a manner that is more than trivial or insubstantial" (para 32). In *SL*, the Court clarified that although step 1 of that test is subjective, the second stage of that test "requires an objective analysis of the rules, events or acts that interfere with the exercise of the freedom" (para 24).
24 *Amselem, supra* note 5 at para 46.
25 [1996] 1 SCR 825 [*Ross*].
26 *Ibid* at para 67.
27 *Ibid* at para 70.
28 In *Amselem, supra* note 5, the majority justified the subjective sincerity approach partly on the basis that "the State is in no position to be, nor should it become, the arbiter of religious dogma" (para 50) and that "[t]his approach to freedom of religion effectively avoids the invidious interference of the State and its courts with religious belief" (para 55). Seeking to avoid the spectre of adjudicating religious doctrine or arbitrating internal religious disputes, the subjective sincerity approach sets matters on the juridically more familiar and comfortable terrain of credibility. Yet as I explain in this volume, adjudication inescapably involves the courts in matters of religious belief and authority.

which communications are of a religious nature and which are not? In *Ross*, and again anticipating *Amselem*, the Court's ultimate referent is the individual. That Ross might have been reflecting an entirely idiosyncratic view was of no consequence for the Court; the fact that it was his conscientiously held view made it religious. Because "freedom of religion ensures that every individual must be free to hold and to manifest without State interference those beliefs and opinions *dictated by one's conscience*,"[29] a Human Rights Commission's order restricting Ross's capacity to express these views offended his religious freedom.

Nevertheless, aspects of this limitation on Ross's religious freedom were ultimately justified under section 1 of the *Charter*, which allows the government an opportunity to show that the limit imposed on the right is "demonstrably justified in a free and democratic society."[30] In some respects this justification under section 1 of the *Charter* might indicate that Canadian constitutional law's commitment to the individual dimension of religion is not as strong as I have suggested, ultimately giving way to group interests: in the case of *Ross*, the group interests of Jews. To be sure, individual religious liberties sometimes give way to collective goods under section 1 of the *Charter*, and this may well be an aspect of what was going on in *Ross*. This is, however, just part of the picture gleaned from a treetops view. A closer look reveals that, as is so often the case, the justificatory logic has a decidedly individualistic flavour to it. When Justice La Forest explains why Ross's religious freedoms can be justifiably limited under section 1, his reasoning is that the protection of Ross's religious freedoms is weakened because, in his religious expression, Ross has undermined the very purpose of religious freedom: "[A]ny religious belief that denigrates and defames the religious beliefs of others erodes the very basis of the guarantee in s. 2(a) – a basis that guarantees that every individual is free to hold and to manifest the beliefs dictated by one's conscience. The respondent's religious views serve to deny Jews respect for dignity and equality said to be among the fundamental guiding values of a court undertaking a s. 1 analysis."[31]

---

29  *Ibid* at para 72 [emphasis added].
30  The section 1 analysis is, in essence, a rationality and proportionality test that was first set out in *R v Oakes*, [1986] 1 SCR 103, but was importantly elaborated upon in *Wilson Colony*, *supra* note 23, a case discussed later in this chapter. I explore the role and character of section 1 at greater length in chapter 3.
31  *Ross*, *supra* note 25 at para 94.

Ross loses the protection of section 2(a) because his religious views deprive other individuals of their parallel right to believe whatever their consciences dictate, and to do so equally and with dignity. *Amselem* and *Ross* demonstrate that, for the law, what counts as religious is what is meaningful to the individual; institutions and collective traditions are only of derivative importance to the law.[32] Law's approach to religion is characterized by "the centrality of the rights associated with freedom of individual conscience."[33]

This focus on the individual was inscribed into the *Charter* protection of religion in *Edwards Books*,[34] in which Chief Justice Dickson stated, "The purpose of s. 2(a) is to ensure that society does not interfere with profoundly personal beliefs that govern one's perception of oneself, humankind, nature, and, in some cases, a higher or different order of being."[35] The individual's sense of his or her own relationship to the divine or to the object of faith is what lies at the core of law's imagining of religion.[36] As I have explained, this focus on the individual is not unique to religious freedoms; rather, it is a product of the structure and the informing ideology of the *Charter*. One of the hallmarks of the *Charter*'s individualism is its difficulty in taking cognizance of rights claims and social policy measures that seek to empower the groups or institutional contexts that lead to the full enjoyment of the human goods that the Constitution purports to protect.[37] Not only does the

---

32   This is even true of Bastarache J's judgment in *Amselem*, despite being the only judgment to refer to the social dimensions of religion. Although he spoke of the "social significance" of religion, "social significance" refers to formal religious rules and doctrine. This set of rules operates only as an objective limit on the assertions of the individual, who remains always at the centre of his analysis.

33   *Big M, supra* note 12 at 346.

34   *R v Edwards Books and Art Ltd*, [1986] 2 SCR 713 [*Edwards Books*].

35   *Ibid* at 759.

36   More than once, the Court invokes the term *faith* as important to religion. It is unclear, though an interesting question, what the Court understands this term to mean.

37   In its more recent decisions on freedom of association in the labour context, the Court has shown something of a greater appetite to attend to these dimensions of rights protection, recognizing a right to strike in *Saskatchewan Federation of Labour v Saskatchewan*, 2015 SCC 4; and to "meaningful collective bargaining" in *Health Services and Support – Facilities Subsector Bargaining Assn v British Columbia*, 2007 SCC 27, [2007] 2 SCR 391 [*Health Services*]; and *Mounted Police Association of Ontario v Canada (AG)*, 2015 SCC 1 [*Mounted Police Association*].

prevailing equality analysis tend powerfully to extract the individual from her meaningful group context, but breaches of section 15 with clear group dimensions have also been justified as reasonable under section 1, the great limiting clause of the *Charter*.[38] Likewise, in *Chaoulli v Quebec (AG)*,[39] in order to vindicate a wealthy doctor's section 7 right to contract privately for the provision of health care, the Supreme Court struck down legislative restrictions on private health insurance that were designed to protect a public health care system. The *Chaoulli* decision dramatically emphasized the extent to which the dedicated individualism of *Charter* rights makes the law less sensitive to the collective dimensions of social policy. This resistance to addressing the group and institutional contexts in which rights are enjoyed has an economic face that is tied to the positive/negative rights divide, but it also has a deeper informing structure that relates to constitutional law's liberal propensity to see the individual far more clearly than the associational and relational.

Consider also *Adler v Ontario*, discussed in chapter 1,[40] in which a group of parents argued that the state's failure to fund private non-Catholic religious schools was contrary to their section 2(a) freedom of religion rights. Justice Sopinka, writing for the judges who addressed the section 2(a) argument, rejected the claim on the basis that all parents have the choice to send their children to a funded public school. As such, if they choose to send their children to a religious school, Justice Sopinka held that "[they] have no claim cognizable in law since the disadvantage they must bear is one flowing exclusively from their religious tenets ... The fact that no funding is provided for private religious education cannot be considered to infringe the appellants' freedom to educate their children in accordance with their religious beliefs."[41]

This decision emphasizes law's understanding of religion as choice, which I will discuss more fully below, but also manifests law's focus on the individual in the exercise of religious rights. At one level, the reasoning in this case might simply manifest a prudential desire to keep

---

38  See *Newfoundland (Treasury Board) v NAPE*, 2004 SCC 66, [2004] 3 SCR 381.
39  2005 SCC 35, [2005] 1 SCR 79.
40  [1996] 3 SCR 609 [*Adler*]. See the discussion of *Adler* in the section on law's temporal intuitions in chapter 1.
41  *Ibid* at paras 174–5.

the state distant from religious teaching.[42] But at a more fundamental level, *Adler* exposes Canadian constitutional law's awkwardness when claims to religious freedom are made in service of the collective dimension of religious life. The underlying logic of this decision is that religious freedom is fundamentally about the right (in this case) of an individual parent to choose how to educate his or her child. Cast in this light, the state's failure to fund religious schools in the context of universally mandated education does not impose a significant burden on the enjoyment of this parent's rights; parents can individually take steps to teach their children as they see fit.

If Canadian constitutional law's atomism were set aside and the Court had focused upon the centrality of a collective project of education in creating and perpetuating religious community, the issue might have assumed a different complexion. Perhaps an accessible system of publicly funded, community-based education is essential to cultural integrity, including the enjoyment of religion, conceived of as a collective and trans-generational phenomenon. This is not to say that the result in *Adler* is wrong or that the state ought to fund religious schools beyond those guaranteed for historical reasons in the constitutional compact. Rather, the point is an entirely descriptive one: when religion is set before the bar of *Charter* rights, such considerations are not readily cognizable by the law. These dimensions of religious life tend to be filtered out by the structure and commitments of contemporary constitutionalism.

Over the course of Canadian history, the nature and force of law's individualist gaze in matters of religion has been repeatedly revealed by the encounter between Anabaptist religious cultures and the culture of the Canadian rule of law.[43] Alvin Esau has shown that, although the communities have found some success in protecting communal

---

42 For a discussion of the Canadian conception of "state neutrality" in the constitutional protection of freedom of religion, and how it differs from the non-establishment tradition in the United States, see Bruce Ryder, "State Neutrality and Freedom of Conscience and Religion" (2005) 29 SCLR (2d) 169. See also Benjamin L Berger, "Religious Diversity, Education, and the 'Crisis' in State Neutrality" (2013) 29:1 CJLS 103; Richard Moon, "Freedom of Religion under the Charter of Rights: The Limits of State Neutrality" (2012) 45 UBC L Rev 497; David M Brown, "Neutrality or Privilege? A Comment on Religious Freedom" (2005) 29 SCLR (2d) 221 at 229–35.

43 See John McLaren, "The Doukhobor Belief in Individual Faith and Conscience and the Demands of the Secular State" in John McLaren & Harold Coward, eds, *Religious Conscience, the State, and the Law* (Albany, NY: SUNY, 1999) 117.

property rights through the legal system, the Courts have frequently responded to issues raised by and within Hutterite communities with individualist contractual notions and concepts of individual natural justice quite extrinsic to the community's traditions and self-conception.[44] The courts' analytic focus seems to irresistibly return to the individual adherent within a religious group, rather than the group itself.

The case of *Alberta v Hutterian Brethren of Wilson Colony*[45] brought this collision between the communal or group aspect of religion and the law's individualist valuation of religion into a constitutional register. The narrow issue in the case was whether, under a new legislative scheme, a universal requirement for photographs on all driver's licences in Alberta offended this small Hutterite community's freedom of religion and equality. Having one's photograph taken offends this community's interpretation of the biblical second commandment. The community had enjoyed an exemption from the prior scheme, an exemption that permitted them to hold driver's licences such that members of the community could drive for narrow commercial purposes and, thereby, sustain a relatively autonomous, rural, communal lifestyle. The case raises a nest of issues, some of which I will discuss in more detail below. For present purposes, what is of most interest is the way in which the communal dimension of the religious claim was received and handled by the Court. Justice Abella, dissenting in *Wilson Colony*, laid substantial weight on the collective dimensions of the claim. She emphasized the community's concern with self-sufficiency and autonomy, and that these commitments were inextricable from the nature of their claim in this case – they were the heart of the religious freedom and equality claim. She cited Justice Ritchie's explanation in *Hofer v Hofer*[46] of the religious character of the community's lifestyle: "[T]he activities of the community were evidence of the living church."[47] Focusing in this way on the collective dimension of religion for the Hutterites, Justice Abella would have found that the

---

44 See Alvin J Esau, *The Courts and the Colonies: The Litigation of Hutterite Church Disputes* (Vancouver: UBC Press, 2004); Alvin Esau, "Communal Property and Freedom of Religion: *Lakeside Colony of Hutterian Brethren v Hofer*" in McLaren & Coward, *supra* note 43, 97.

45 *Wilson Colony, supra* note 23.

46 [1970] SCR 958.

47 *Ibid* at 969.

impact of this measure of the religious freedom on the community was unjustifiable.

Chief Justice McLachlin, writing for the majority, accepted that religion has a "collective aspect" but made a crucial distinction about the relevance of this "aspect" in the analysis of a *Charter* claim. She held that the "broader impact of the photo requirement on the Wilson Colony community" was relevant in assessing whether a limit on section 2(a) was justified pursuant to section 1 of the *Charter*, when weighing the salutary and deleterious effects of the rights-infringing measure. This community impact did not, however, "transform the essential claim – that of the individual claimants for photo-free licences – into an assertion of a group right."[48] Having thus defined the "essential claim" in this case, by the time the group or community impacts of the government measure factored into the *Charter* analysis, they did so only as incidental "costs" associated with this universal photo requirement, to be weighed against the benefits of this measure to society at large. The Chief Justice conceded that "[o]btaining alternative transport would impose an additional economic cost on the Colony, and would go against their traditional self-sufficiency" but found that "the evidence does not support the conclusion that arranging alternative means of highway transport would end the Colony's rural way of life."[49] "The limit may impose costs on the religious practitioner in terms of money, tradition or inconvenience,"[50] the majority explained, as long as the adherent is left with "a meaningful choice concerning the religious practice at issue."[51] The collective dimensions of religion appear to be assimilated into the language of "tradition"; religious freedom, by contrast, is measured in the heart of the individual.

The jurisprudence shows that, in its deep logic, contemporary Canadian constitutionalism understands religion as a phenomenon that is fundamentally located within the individual and whose goods ultimately redound to the individual, rather than something whose essence

---

48  *Wilson Colony, supra* note 23 at para 31.
49  *Ibid* at para 97.
50  *Ibid* at para 95.
51  *Ibid* at para 95. I offer a fuller discussion of the *Wilson Colony* case in Benjamin L Berger, "Section 1, Constitutional Reasoning and Cultural Difference: Assessing the Impacts of *Alberta v Hutterian Brethren of Wilson Colony*" (2010) 51 SCLR (2d) 25. See also Richard Moon, "Accommodation without Compromise: Comment on *Alberta v Hutterian Brethren of Wilson Colony*" (2010) 51 SCLR (2d) 95.

lies within communities and webs of relationships.[52] In so doing, important dimensions of religious culture may be obscured from the analytic gaze of Canadian constitutionalism. Yet my argument is not that law has "erred" in conceiving of religion in this way, at least not in a way that is the product of a set of doctrinal defects amenable to a quick jurisprudential fix. Rather, law is – quite naturally – viewing religion in terms indigenous and, therefore, sympathetic to this aspect of the ideological structure of modern Canadian constitutional law. Otherwise put, law's commitment to religion as fundamentally individual

---

52 The Supreme Court's decision in *Loyola High School v Quebec (Attorney General)*, 2015 SCC 12, issued while this volume was in final production, offers the Court's strongest statements of regard for the collective dimensions of religious life. Loyola High School, a private Catholic high school founded in the 1840s, objected to the requirement set out in the Quebec government's Ethics and Religious Cultures Program that the curriculum be taught objectively and impartially. Specifically, Loyola claimed that requiring a Catholic school to teach about Catholicism and the ethics of other traditions in a "neutral way" impaired religious freedom. In finding that Loyola could not be compelled to teach about Catholicism "in terms defined by the state rather than by its own understanding of Catholicism" (para 63), Abella J referred to "both the individual *and* collective aspects of religious belief" (para 59) [emphasis in original] and explained that "[r]eligious freedom under the *Charter* must therefore account for the socially embedded nature of religious belief and the deep linkages between this belief and its manifestation through communal institutions and traditions" (para 60). Yet the nature and value of these collective dimensions are indexed to the individual. The collective aspects of religion are understood as "manifestations" of individual religious belief, and the interests involved are framed as those of the members. Justice Abella founds her statements about the collective and social aspects of religion on the recognition "that individuals may sometimes require a legal entity in order to give effect to the constitutionally protected communal aspects of their religious beliefs and practice" (para 33), leading to her conclusion that "[t]o tell a Catholic school how to explain its faith undermines the liberty of the members of its community who have chosen to give effect to the collective dimension of their religious beliefs by participating in a denominational school" (para 62). The minority reasons, written by Chief Justice McLachlin and Justice Moldaver, would have gone further, recognizing that religious organizations themselves could enjoy religious freedom under section 2(a). And yet it is also evident in their decision that regard for the collective is underwritten by solicitousness for the individual. They held that "protecting the religious freedom of individuals requires protecting the religious freedom of religious organizations" (para 91). "The freedom of religion of individuals," they explained, "cannot flourish without freedom of religion for the organizations through which those individuals express their religious practices and through which they transmit their faith" (para 94).

renders religion in a highly digestible state for the purposes of modern constitutionalism.

## Law's Religion as an Expression of Autonomy and Choice

I have pointed to liberalism's commitment to the priority of the individual as the ideological basis for law's individualistic rendering of religion. But liberalism's commitment to the individual is significant to other aspects of law's understanding of religion. The basis for liberalism's focus on the individual is its commitment to the goods of autonomy and individual liberty as the mechanism for human flourishing. Having isolated the individual as the entity of explanatory and experiential priority, liberalism turns to the question of how to empower this entity. In a fusion of Enlightenment individualism and Romantic authenticity,[53] liberalism takes the view that the individual is best able to flourish when left to exercise free choice with respect to the good. On this view of human flourishing, the obligations of the public are twofold: first, not to interfere with individual autonomy and, second, to intervene wherever free choice is constrained. Self-realization is the goal, and autonomous choice is the mechanism.[54] This emphasis on individual autonomy at the core of liberal political culture is the source of the negative conception of liberty.[55] Freedom is secured when the individual can choose freely, and liberty inheres in being left alone. Any social – and, in particular, state – actions that impair this autonomy are, by definition, evils to be guarded against. So, within the liberal imagination, it is impossible to disassociate the priority placed on the individual from the ultimate valuation of autonomy and free choice.

---

53  See Charles Taylor, *Sources of the Self: The Making of the Modern Identity* (Cambridge, UK: Cambridge University Press, 1989).

54  Taylor links this focus on choice to the contemporary liberal culture of authenticity, noting that, with the attenuation of other horizons of meaning, "the ideal of self-determining freedoms comes to exercise a more powerful attraction. It seems that significance can be conferred by *choice*, by making my life an exercise in freedom, even when all other sources fail. Self-determining freedom is in part the default solution of the culture of authenticity." Taylor, *Malaise of Modernity, supra* note 15 at 69 [emphasis in original].

55  See Isaiah Berlin, "Two Concepts of Liberty" in Robert E Goodin & Philip Pettit, eds, *Contemporary Political Philosophy* (Oxford: Blackwell Publishers, 1997) 391.

In Canada, this liberal political culture of autonomy and choice is reflected in the structures of constitutionalism. *Charter* rights are essentially negative in their orientation, guaranteeing a sphere of immunity from state action rather than requiring positive conduct on the part of the state. Although certain notes sounding in the register of positive liberty have issued from the Court, such instances remain either conceived of as exceptional,[56] or confined to dissenting opinions.[57] In law's view, "freedom can primarily be characterized by the absence of coercion or constraint."[58] Indeed, in defining the very concept of liberty for the purposes of the *Charter*, the Court has articulated a thoroughly negative conception that also demonstrates the centrality of autonomy and choice to contemporary Canadian constitutional law: "[L]iberty does not mean mere freedom from physical restraint. In a free and democratic society, the individual must be left room for personal autonomy to live his or her own life and to make decisions that are of fundamental personal importance."[59] The centrality of autonomy, in the form of unencumbered choice, to the Canadian legal imagination is reflected in the fact that the Court has inscribed autonomy as one of those "*Charter* values" – essentially constitutional *grundnorms* – that subtend the

---

56 *Dunmore v Ontario (AG)*, 2001 SCC 94, [2001] 3 SCR 1016. Even the Supreme Court of Canada cases recognizing a right to collective bargaining and a right to strike – breaking from its earlier jurisprudence – cast these decisions in fundamentally negative terms, emphasizing freedom of choice. For example, in *Mounted Police Association, supra* note 37, the majority described freedom of association as protecting "a meaningful process of collective bargaining that provides employees with a degree of choice and independence sufficient to enable them to determine and pursue their collective interests" (para 5), and explained that "[t]he government therefore cannot enact laws or impose a labour relations process that substantially interferes with that right" (para 81).

57 *Gosselin v Quebec (AG)*, 2002 SCC 84, [2002] 4 SCR 429, Arbour J, dissenting.

58 *Big M, supra* note 12 at 336: "If a person is compelled by the state or the will of another to a course of action or inaction which he would not otherwise have chosen, he is not acting of his own volition and he cannot be said to be truly free."

59 *B(R) v Children's Aid Society of Metropolitan Toronto*, [1995] 1 SCR 315 at para 80, La Forest J [*B(R)*]. See also *R v Morgentaler*, [1988] 1 SCR 30 at 166, Wilson J: "Thus, an aspect of the respect for human dignity on which the *Charter* is founded is the right to make fundamental personal decisions without interference from the state. This right is a critical component of the right to liberty. Liberty, as was noted in *Singh*, is a phrase capable of a broad range of meaning. In my view, this right, properly construed, grants the individual a degree of autonomy in making decisions of fundamental personal importance."

whole of the rights-protecting instrument and must be considered in making all legal decisions.[60]

When cast within this constitutional context, religion quite naturally takes on a shape consistent with its mould. Having defined religion in the individualist terms discussed above, the majority in *Amselem* turned to explain the principled basis for the protection of religion. Freedom of religion, the majority asserted, "revolves around the notion of personal choice and individual autonomy and freedom."[61] Religion is to be protected by the law because it is "integrally linked with an individual's self-definition and fulfilment and is a function of personal autonomy and choice."[62] On this view, the value of religion inheres in the fact that it is one of many possible options that an individual might select as an aspect of his or her self-definition and authentic experience. The evil of interfering in religious beliefs and practices is that to do so would constrain freedom and liberty. Religion is cast as one possible component of the autonomous life and, concomitantly, is essentially conceived of as a choice. As the majority states, "The emphasis ... is on personal choice of religious beliefs."[63] Law understands religion as a

---

60  Autonomy is listed in the jurisprudence as being "a fundamental value reflected in our society's Constitution or similar fundamental laws, like bills of rights." *R v Labaye*, 2005 SCC 80 at para 33, [2005] 3 SCR 728. In *Health Services, supra* note 37 at para 81, McLachlin CJ and LeBel J stated that "[h]uman dignity, equality, liberty, respect for the autonomy of the person and the enhancement of democracy are among the values that underly the *Charter*" and explained, at para 80 that "[t]he *Charter* ... should be interpreted in a way that maintains its underlying values." See also *R v Mabior*, 2012 SCC 47, [2012] 2 SCR 584, in which the *Charter* values of "equality, autonomy, liberty, privacy and human dignity" (para 22) are used to interpret the legislation in issue. In *Hill v Church of Scientology*, [1995] 2 SCR 1130 at para 92, the Court stated that "the *Charter* represents a restatement of the fundamental values which guide and shape our democratic society and our legal system." It is thus appropriate to consider these "*Charter* values" as a species of Hans Kelsen's *grundnorm*, understood as "the postulated ultimate rule according to which the norms of [a legal] order are established and annulled, receive and lose their validity." Hans Kelsen, *General Theory of Law and State*, translated by Anders Wedberg (New York: Russell & Russell, 1961) at 113.

61  *Amselem, supra* note 5 at para 40.

62  *Ibid* at para 42.

63  *Ibid* at para 43. See also L'Heureux-Dubé J's dissent in *Adler, supra* note 40, in which she stated at para 72 that "s. 2(a) of the *Charter* is primarily concerned with the necessary limits to be placed on the state in its potentially coercive interference with the original, objectively perceived religious 'choice' that individuals make."

product of choice and, hence, as connected to the liberty and autonomy of the subject.

This aspect of law's rendering of religion also appears in *Amselem* in the dissenting judges' reasoning. Justice Binnie, writing only for himself, focused his attention on the fact that the claimants had voluntarily bound themselves to the terms of the contract and, therefore, could not fairly invoke their religious liberties. In this reasoning, religion is analogous to geography and aesthetics, both subjects of autonomous choice in the selection of a home. If the appellants were unencumbered in their choice of this building then, in compliance with the logic of autonomy and self-determination, the choice cannot be interfered with, even if to do so would be in the name of religious liberties. "It was for the appellants … to determine in advance of their unit purchase what the appellants' particular religious beliefs required. They had a choice of buildings in which to invest."[64] In the end, putting up a succah is a choice to be analysed against other choices, like constructing a garden trellis or opting for satellite television over cable.

This conception of the protection of religious belief as centrally concerned with individual autonomy and choice was inscribed at the foundation of *Charter* jurisprudence on freedom of religion with *Big M*. In finding that the Sunday closing law at issue was unconstitutional, the Court ruled that the legislation did not have a secular purpose but, rather, "binds all to a sectarian Christian ideal."[65] According to Justice Dickson, the essential constitutional infirmity was that the impugned Act "works a form of coercion inimical to the spirit of the *Charter*,"[66] a spirit that is centrally concerned with ensuring equality and freedom. "The essence of the concept of freedom of religion," wrote Justice Dickson, "is the right to entertain such religious beliefs as a person chooses."[67] On this view, protecting autonomy is the core element of religious liberty, and autonomy is secured by ensuring an absence of coercion or restraint. In Justice Dickson's words, "[W]hatever else freedom of conscience and religion may mean, it must at the least mean this: government may not coerce individuals to affirm a specific religious belief or to manifest a specific religious practice for a sectarian

---

64  *Amselem, supra* note 5 at para 185.
65  *Big M, supra* note 12 at 337.
66  *Ibid.*
67  *Ibid* at 336.

purpose."[68] Indeed, this anti-coercion or "protection of autonomy" core of religious freedom was reaffirmed in the *Reference re Same-Sex Marriage*,[69] in which the Court held that, although the proposed same-sex marriage legislation was constitutionally sound, any state compulsion of religious officials to perform such marriages would offend section 2(a) of the *Charter* because it would interfere with "the right to believe and entertain the religious beliefs of one's choice."[70] Since *Big M*, the clear and consistent jurisprudential message has been that religion has constitutional relevance because it is an expression of human autonomy and choice. Indeed, as the jurisprudence has developed, choice and autonomy have evolved from the tacit logical foundation for analysing religion to the overriding barometer for constitutional claims about religion.

*Wilson Colony*[71] shows the maturing of this tendency to focus on choice into a veritable litmus test for the constitutional analysis of religious claims in Canada. It will be recalled that the case concerned a small Hutterite community that sought an exemption from the universal photo requirement on driver's licences. The heart of the claim was that failure to provide such an exemption was an affront to the section 2(a) rights of the community and its members. Given the capacious "subjective sincerity" test established in *Amselem* for what falls within the scope of the section 2(a) right, most of the work was to be done in the section 1 analysis. The Court explained in *Wilson Colony* that the balancing involved in deciding if a limit on section 2(a) was justified under section 1 should generally come down to weighing the benefits of the rights-limiting government action to society against the harms suffered by the section 2(a) claimant. It was in this context that the Supreme Court stated that the ultimate diagnostic for assessing the seriousness of a limit on religious freedom is to ask "whether the limit leaves the adherent with a meaningful choice to follow his or her religious beliefs and practices."[72] This statement reflects the legal coming-of-age of a constitutional conception of religion based on autonomy and choice. After listing the values of equality, of dignity, and of democracy, Chief

---

68   *Ibid* at 347.
69   2004 SCC 79, [2004] 3 SCR 698 [*Reference re Same-Sex Marriage*].
70   *Ibid* at para 57. The Court went on to suggest that such an infringement would likely be unjustifiable under section 1 of the *Charter*.
71   *Wilson Colony, supra* note 23.
72   *Ibid* at para 88.

Justice McLachlin crowned choice as the first among equals, explaining that "[t]he most fundamental of these values, and the one relied on in this case, is liberty – the right of choice on matters of religion."[73] The conception of "meaningful choice" is an essentially formal one, as it is in the section 15 jurisprudence. The Wilson Colony claimed that adhering to their beliefs by ceasing driving would involve serious costs for the community and its religiously inspired way of life. The majority concluded, however, that the deleterious effects of the mandatory driver's licence photograph, "while not trivial, [fell] at the less serious end of the scale"[74] because "it is impossible to conclude that Colony members have been deprived of a meaningful choice to follow or not the edicts of their religion."[75] Chief Justice McLachlin accepted that the legislation may mean that, given their religious commitments, colony members may have to choose not to drive; as such, they will suffer a financial cost, inconvenience, and some disruption to their communal way of life. But these costs "do not negate *the choice that lies at the heart of freedom of religion*."[76] *Wilson Colony* confirms for us that, as far as Canadian constitutionalism is concerned, freedom of religion is ultimately a matter of autonomy and choice.

This centrality of the logic of autonomy is evident in Canadian decisions regarding school prayer. *Zylberberg v Sudbury Board of Education (Director)*[77] involved a claim by three parents – one Jewish, one Muslim, and one non-practising Christian – who challenged an Ontario regulation requiring that schools open or close each day with a reading from the Christian scriptures and a recitation of the Lord's Prayer. The Ontario Court of Appeal agreed and self-consciously reflected on the evolution of constitutional thought about the nature of religion: "In an earlier time, when people believed in the collective responsibility of the community toward some deity, the enforcement of religious conformity may have been a legitimate object of government, but since the *Charter*, it is no longer legitimate. With the *Charter*, it has become the right of every Canadian to work out for himself or herself what his or her religious obligations, if any, should be."[78]

---

73  *Ibid*.
74  *Ibid* at para 102.
75  *Ibid* at para 98.
76  *Ibid* at para 99 [emphasis added].
77  (1988), 65 OR (2d) 641 (CA), 52 DLR (4th) 577 [*Zylberberg* cited to DLR].
78  *Big M, supra* note 12 at 351. Quoted in *ibid* at 589.

No longer a matter of collective or community concern, religious practice has, in the eyes of the law, been decentralized into an expression of individual autonomy. The constitutional defect in this legislation was its coercive nature, interfering as it did with the right of each individual to make choices about religious observance. Indeed, this was so, despite the existence of an "opt-out" clause in the legislation, which allowed a parent to claim an exemption from any religious exercises. The Court reasoned that the appearance of choice here was illusory, and that the true effect of this exclusion clause was a "compulsion to conform to the religious practices of the majority."[79] The Court demonstrated its solicitude about possible constraints on free choice by noting that the exemption is unlikely to be exercised, given "the fact that children are disinclined at this age to step out of line or to flout 'peer-group norms.'"[80] The clear concern of the law is to protect religion as an expression of choice. Any factor – legal or contextual – that might interfere with the autonomy-based core of religious freedom is suspect in the eyes of contemporary constitutionalism. The courts have similarly held that religious education in public schools can be problematic because "teaching students Christian doctrine as if it were the exclusive means through which to develop moral thinking and behaviour amounts to religious coercion in the class-room."[81] The issue is not the separation of church and state per se, but a concern for the autonomy of the child.

*Big M* and *Zylberberg* are particularly interesting cases, as both draw out a seeming tension between the centrality of autonomy and choice, which I have been emphasizing, and the presence of language and reasoning that appears to invoke notions of equality and, with it, identity. There has always been a note of equality language in the Supreme Court's section 2(a) jurisprudence. Themes of equality seem to emerge in places at which the Court speaks of the communicative harm done by favouring one religion over another, even where the interference with the autonomy of the religious claimant is less than clear. Both *Big M* and *Zylberberg* are examples of such cases. In addition to describing a free society as one in which fundamental freedoms are equally

---

79   *Zylberberg, supra* note 77 at 591.
80   *Ibid.*
81   *Canadian Civil Liberties Association v Ontario (Minister of Education)* (1990), 71 OR (2d) 341 at 363 (CA).

enjoyed,[82] Chief Justice Dickson in *Big M* described the harm of the Sunday closing legislation in the following way: "In proclaiming the standards of the Christian faith, the Act creates a climate hostile to, and gives the appearance of discrimination against, non-Christian Canadians."[83] Similarly, in *Zylberberg* the Court spoke of the school prayer, despite its provision to opt out, as "depreciat[ing] the position of religious minorities"[84] and "stigmatizing [students] as non-conformists and setting them apart from their fellow students who are members of the dominant religion."[85] Again, there are notes in this language that seem to sound in the register of equality.

In some respects, this language of equality appears to be in tension with the focus on autonomy and choice described in this section. As Richard Moon argues, in the language of equality there is a seeming invocation of conceptions of cultural identity rather than autonomy: equality logic is about protection from identity-based harms.[86] It might be thought, therefore, that when the Supreme Court invokes the language or logic of equality in its section 2(a) cases, it is appealing to a sense of religion as a cultural or identity-based concept rather than the autonomy-centred phenomenon that I have argued is at the centre of

---

82 *Big M, supra* note 12 at 336–7.

83 *Ibid* at 337. The concern in *Edwards Books, supra* note 34, with competitive disadvantage occasioned by preferential treatment of one religion over another similarly evokes equality-based themes. Mary Ann Waldron is highly critical of this line of reasoning from *Big M*, *Zylberberg*, and other early cases, which she considers having set the section 2(a) jurisprudence "off on the wrong foot." Waldron, *supra* note 5 at 22–53. Waldron suggests that such reasoning is evidence that equality concerns have, in fact, played too significant a role in the courts' analysis of religious freedom claims.

84 *Zylberberg, supra* note 77 at 592.

85 *Ibid.*

86 Richard Moon, "Government Support for Religious Practice" in Moon, *Law and Religious Pluralism, supra* note 9, 217. Analysing a number of SCC cases, including *Big M* and *Zylberberg*, Moon argues that there has been an enlargement of the Court's treatment of the ban on religious compulsion. This enlargement, Moon argues, represents "an ambiguous shift" from thinking about religious freedom in terms of coercion and liberty to conceiving of the right as essentially concerned with exclusion and equality. See also Moon, *Freedom of Conscience and Religion, supra* note 5. For discussion of the "choice approach" and "identity approach" to religious freedom, and an assessment of the risks of an identity approach, see Avigail Eisenberg's important article, "Rights in the Age of Identity Politics" (2013) 50 Osgoode Hall LJ 609 at 615–21. Eisenberg points, in particular, to the risks of essentialism and of the entrenchment of the power of elites associated with identity-based claims.

the Court's treatment of religion. With this language of equality, the Court seems to be reflecting a concern for religion as an aspect of one's identity.

There is no doubt that there is some dimension of religious freedom that has an identity-based component. Most simply, religion is not merely a choice like any other; not all choices are treated with the constitutional protection that religion enjoys. My claim is not that Canadian law's understanding of religion is bereft of a cultural or identity-based dimension. However, the work that "identity" does in Canadian constitutional jurisprudence is actually rather light, and this holds true not only for religion, but also for the constitutional guarantee of equality itself, where one would expect that concept to have its greatest purchase. As others have argued, although the concept of listed and analogous grounds in section 15 of the *Charter* might have been used to emphasize the significance of identity as an indispensable dimension of legal equality, the law has largely denuded those grounds of potential analytic force or substantive meaning in the equality analysis itself.[87]

Under the prevailing interpretation of the constitutional equality guarantee, the essential question is whether a distinction imposed on the basis of an enumerated or analogous personal characteristic creates a disadvantage by perpetuating prejudice or stereotyping.[88] The case law shows that, in this assessment of prejudice and stereotyping, issues of autonomy and choice rise to prominence, frequently controlling courts' judgment of whether discrimination has occurred.[89] Commentators

---

87 Dianne Pothier, "Connecting Grounds of Discrimination to Real People's Real Experiences" (2001) 13:1 CJWL 37. On the way in which the "grounds" analysis has become (particularly after *Corbiere v Canada (Minister of Indian and Northern Affairs)*, [1999] 2 SCR 203) an impediment to, rather than enriching of, the analysis of substantive equality, see Hester Lessard, "Mothers, Fathers, and Naming: Reflections on the *Law* Equality Framework and *Trociuk v British Columbia (Attorney General)*" (2004) 16 CJWL 165 at 190–1. For a reflection on the relationship between freedom of religion and equality jurisprudence in Canada, focusing on what elements of the section 2(a) approach might enhance the analysis of equality claims, see Carissima Mathen, "What Religious Freedom Jurisprudence Reveals about Equality" (2009) 6 JL & Equality 163.

88 *Quebec (AG) v A*, 2013 SCC 5 at para 185, [2013] 1 SCR 61 [*Quebec (AG)*]; *Withler v Canada (AG)*, 2011 SCC 12, [2011] 1 SCR 396.

89 In *Quebec (AG)*, *supra* note 88 at para 256, LeBel J reasoned that the issue of prejudice and stereotyping could be resolved "if the questions of freedom of choice and autonomy of the will of the parties are correctly considered."

have noted that, in many cases, "choice" has served as a stopping or limiting principle in the analysis of equality claims.[90] Such cases suggest a view that the wrong of discrimination inheres in the state treating someone other than as an autonomous chooser.[91] That there has been some legal statement made about the value of your identity may get you in the section 15 door; once there, however, the analytic force of the identity judgment is largely spent, and the law turns instead to questions of choice and autonomy.

The same is true of concepts of equality and identity in religious freedom. Although the jurisprudence sometimes evokes notions of equality, and hence suggests a sense of religion as protected because of some link to identity, one cannot stop there. When one moves to the next question about *why* we want to protect individuals from identity-based mistreatment or harm, the answer collapses the focus back onto conceptions of autonomy and choice. Just as the "identity" aspect of equality is often eclipsed by the concept of choice, the equality/identity aspect of religion is ultimately little more than a marker for a particularly valued manifestation of choice.[92] In both cases – in equality and in religion – law's central concern is to treat the individual fairly as an autonomous choosing agent. Identity itself is valued because it is an expression of who the subject wants to be and to become; identity, on this view, is a function of choice. So when, in its religion cases, the Court invokes language and

---

90  Diana Majury, "Women Are Themselves to Blame: Choice as a Justification for Unequal Treatment" in Fay Faraday, Margaret Denike & M Kate Stephenson, eds, *Making Equality Rights Real: Securing Substantive Equality under the Charter* (Toronto: Irwin Law, 2006) 209; Hester Lessard, "*Charter* Gridlock: Equality Formalism and Marriage Fundamentalism" in Sheila McIntyre & Sandra Rodgers, eds, *Diminishing Returns: Inequality and the Canadian Charter of Rights and Freedoms* (Markham, Ont: LexisNexis, 2006) 291.

91  As the Court stated in an earlier case that guided section 15 analysis for a time, "[T]he equality guarantee in s. 15(1) is concerned with the realization of personal autonomy and self-determination." *Law v Canada (Minister of Employment and Immigration*, [1999] 1 SCR 497 at para 53. This understanding of the gravamen of equality was clearly displayed in *Nova Scotia (AG) v Walsh*, 2002 SCC 83, [2002] 4 SCR 325, in which the Court's finding that there was no breach of section 15(1) turned on the majority's conclusion that the distinction in question was calibrated to the claimant's choices and, as such, "respects the fundamental autonomy and dignity of the individual" (para 62).

92  This point is made clearly in *Adler, supra* note 40 at para 208, when McLachlin J states, "The essence of s. 15 is that the state cannot use choices like the choice of religion as the basis for denying the equal protection and benefit of the law."

approaches that sound in the register of equality, this does not represent a break from the focus on autonomy and choice that I have described; rather, it is the same concern expressed from a different angle. To send the message that someone is less worthy of regard on the basis of his or her religious identity is to fail to respect a choice particularly close to his or her autonomous self-definition. In this way, although there is a note of identity in law's understanding of religion, the major tone turns out always to be the liberal focus on choice and autonomy.

The way in which equality- and identity-based analysis is swallowed up by the insistent return to the logic of choice is illustrated in *Wilson Colony*, the photo-identification case. The small Hutterite community advanced its claim on two grounds. One, which I have already explored, was freedom of religion, which was thoroughly canvassed by the majority and led to the assertion that choice is the "heart" of freedom of religion. But the community also argued that the universality of the photo requirement on driver's licences offended section 15's guarantee of equality. This regulation had a disparate impact on this community, and the special costs borne by the community were suffered as a result of their religious beliefs. This is a seemingly strong foundation for an equality claim, if identity is taken seriously and the government measure is analysed as one that involves adverse effects discrimination flowing from a core dimension of these people's identities. Yet the majority concluded that this claim was "weaker than the s. 2(a) claim and [could] be easily dispensed with."[93] In the terse conclusion to its four paragraphs dedicated to the section 15(1) claim, the majority stated that any claim that might be made under section 15(1) was already folded into the choice-driven section 2(a) analysis: "The substance of the respondents' s. 15(1) claim has already been dealt with under s. 2(a). There is no breach of s. 15(1)."[94] Even the dissenting judgment, penned by Justice Abella, accepts this logic. She would have found the legislation to be unconstitutional, but not because of a breach of some concept of equal religious citizenship or respect for identity; rather, she simply concluded that, on the facts, the legislation did not leave the community with a meaningful choice.[95] She did not

---

93   *Wilson Colony, supra* note 23 at para 105.
94   *Ibid* at para 108.
95   *Ibid* at para 163. Justice Abella explains, "When significant sacrifices have to be made to practise one's religion in the face of a state imposed burden, the choice to practise one's religion is no longer uncoerced" (para 167).

even mention section 15(1). This case dramatizes both the centrality of choice to the way that law imagines religion and also the claim that, in Canada, the constitutional protection of equality is conceptually thinner than we might like to imagine; it is about equal respect, but equal respect for choices made as an autonomous agent.

The strength of law's rendering of religion as being centrally about autonomy and choice is perhaps most clear when one looks to cases in which the quality of the religious subject's autonomy or capacity for choice is somehow in question. Liberalism, and the legal structures that it inspires, has great difficulty with claims to autonomy and personal freedom made by children, the elderly, and the ill or disabled. Law's conception of liberty is centred on free choice and, for these individuals, the law often fears that the choice is not truly free.[96] If choice is not truly free, then the authenticity of autonomy is imperilled, and all bets are off. Thus, given an understanding of religion as choice, if the genuineness of the choice is in question, the force of religion's claim dissipates in the legal imagination. Take, for example, Canadian jurisprudence regarding the right to refuse lifesaving blood transfusions on the basis of religious objection. It is clear that a capable adult is entitled to make such a decision. This is a choice so clearly within the protected realm of personal autonomy that law can make no move to limit the decision, no matter how fundamentally general public attitudes might conflict with this choice. Indeed, to fail to comply with these wishes is viewed by law as an actionable wrong.[97] When the patient is a child, however, the discourse of choice and autonomy shifts and is instead deployed against the claims that religion might make.

Such was the case in *B(R)*,[98] in which the Court accepted the sincerity of the parents' convictions that led to their decision not to permit a blood transfusion for their child, but unanimously held that the *Charter*

---

96  A large and interesting question is under what conditions law is prepared to question the freedom of a given choice. I have identified age and disability as classic bases upon which the law begins to question the quality of a given choice, but perhaps the most contentious current point of debate is the relationship between culture *itself* and choice. For an insightful discussion of this theme arising from the debate on the place of sharia law in Ontario family arbitration, see Natasha Bakht, *Arbitration, Religion and Family Law: Private Justice on the Backs of Women* (Ottawa: National Association of Women and the Law, 2005) at 17–20.

97  See e.g. *Malette v Shulman* (1990), 72 OR (2d) 417 (CA).

98  *B(R), supra* note 59.

did not ultimately protect this manifestation of religious belief.[99] One set of reasons shows the strength of law's conception of religion as choice. Justices Iacobucci and Major reasoned that the child had only been born into the religion and had "never expressed any agreement with the Jehovah's Witness faith."[100] Respect for the child's autonomy meant that she had "the right to live long enough to make [her] own reasoned choice about the religion [she] wishes to follow as well as the right not to hold a religious belief."[101] As compared to the case of the refusing adult, the individual whose autonomy is in question is now not able to exercise choice, and this makes all the difference in the eyes of the law.

This is what made the later case of *AC v Manitoba (Director of Child and Family Services)*[102] so perfectly difficult for the Court. AC was a mature minor (almost fifteen years old) who was refusing a blood transfusion on the basis of her Jehovah's Witness faith. As a mature minor at common law, AC was in a grey zone of autonomy – the quality of her capacity to choose was uncertain. Though still legally a child, she had the maturity and capacity to make informed decisions. Justice Binnie, in dissent, found that legislation that nevertheless subordinated her choice to a judicial determination of her best interests offended her religious freedom.[103] Why? The constitutional fault in the legislation was its failure to respect her autonomous choices. The majority judgment was equally pregnant with discussion of volitional capacity and respect for choice – so much so, in fact, that the religious dimensions of the case recede from view in favour of a debate about choice and capacity. The majority concluded, however, that even mature minors must be placed on a "sliding scale of decision-making autonomy."[104] Accordingly, it was appropriate to have her own wishes factored into the best interests test, but that the ultimate decision was that of the judge. The purpose in looking at these blood transfusion cases is not that the decision should be otherwise. The point is to appreciate that religion has

---

99  The majority reasoned that freedom of religion had been offended, but that it was a justified infringement under section 1 of the *Charter*.

100  *B(R), supra* note 59 at para 231.

101  *Ibid.*

102  2009 SCC 30, [2009] 2 SCR 181 [*AC*].

103  I return to Binnie J's provocative dissent in *AC* in chapter 4.

104  *AC, supra* note 102 at para 115.

force in the eyes of the law to the extent that it is aligned with autonomy and choice.[105]

The clear and consistent jurisprudential message has been that religion has constitutional relevance because it is an expression of human autonomy and choice. Law understands religion as an aspect of personal self-fulfilment. Religion is essentially individual and, correlatively, has its force in law because it is an expression of liberty through choice. Recognizing law's religion as drawing its importance from its nature as personal preference leads us to a final and closely interrelated feature of law's rendering of religion: law assigns religion, albeit unstably, to the private realm.

## Law's Religion as Private

The quintessential domains of the private in liberal thought are the market, the family, and religion.[106] These are domains in which we are governed in our actions and dispositions not by the universalism of reason but by the particularities of love, preference, and belief. The primary role of the public, by contrast, is to create a set of conditions that will guarantee sufficient autonomy and to remain largely agnostic as to the good. The ambition is to banish interest and preference from the realm of public debate, which is instead consecrated to reason. As Paul Kahn writes, what ultimately characterizes the political culture of liberalism is that it "aims to establish a framework of just rules that operate as conditions within which individuals must make their own choices about meaning."[107] Kahn explains that the public/private divide that is so central to liberalism is, in essence, a metaphor for the dividing line between reason and choice or preference: "Arguments among competing conceptions of liberalism are arguments over the location of the border of the public and private, that is, over the point at which there is a crossing

---

105 Another illuminating example comes from *SJB (Litigation Guardian of) v British Columbia (Director of Child, Family and Community Service)*, 2005 BCSC 573, 42 BCLR (4th) 321, in which the court held that an almost-fifteen-year-old girl who did not wish to receive a lifesaving blood transfusion on the basis of her Jehovah's Witness faith was nevertheless required to receive the treatment. For an extended discussion of religious freedom and questions of risk, excess, and harm, a discussion in which the question of Jehovah's Witnesses and blood transfusions features prominently, see Lori G Beaman, *Defining Harm: Religious Freedom and the Limits of the Law* (Vancouver: UBC Press, 2008).

106 See Kahn, *supra* note 8.

107 *Ibid* at 116.

from reason to unreason."[108] That which is public must be governed by reason.[109] When choice and preference enter the picture, we have shifted into the private, and reason is no longer the governing principle.

Canadian constitutional law manifests its commitment to this divide between the private and the public through a number of its doctrines and features. The doctrine of applicability means that the *Charter* binds only government decision-making and leaves the realm of the private to regulation through other mechanisms.[110] Furthermore, a person's enjoyment of his or her *Charter* rights varies depending on whether the particular activity in question is a private or public act; specifically, reason will have a greater limiting claim on public conduct. The constitutional protection of privacy reflects the importance of this distinction. For example, within the framework of constitutional logic, the right to privacy protected in sections 7 and 8 of the *Charter*, which is fundamentally a right to the integrity of one's private domain, is essential because it protects a sphere of autonomy.[111] One's liberty within this sphere of autonomy allows the pursuit of personal interests, the making of personal choices, and the development of one's own sense of the good. The boundary between this sphere and the public is policed by the logic of reasonableness: one's expectation of privacy must be a reasonable one, and one's interests and choices must be acted upon in a reasonable manner, specifically in a manner that gives due regard to the parallel rights of others. In these ways, Canadian constitutionalism expresses liberal political culture's sense of the public and private as the domains of reason and interest, respectively.

---

108  *Ibid* at 123.

109  Kahn describes this as liberalism's own imperial ambition – to claim the whole domain of reason and thereby to occupy the whole field of public values. *Ibid* at 120.

110  For a discussion of the impact of doctrines of applicability on rights constitutionalism, see Gavin W Anderson, "Social Democracy and the Limits of Rights Constitutionalism" (2004) 17 Can JL & Jur 31. Anderson demonstrates that even broader doctrines of rights applicability than that found in the *Charter* end up replicating this private/public distinction so deeply ingrained in the culture of political liberalism.

111  See *R v Spencer*, 2014 SCC 43 at para 15, [2014] 2 SCR 212: "This Court has long emphasized the need for a purposive approach to s. 8 that emphasizes the protection of privacy as a prerequisite to individual security, self-fulfilment and autonomy as well as to the maintenance of a thriving democratic society." See also *R v Tessling*, 2004 SCC 67 at para 15, [2004] 3 SCR 432: "Building upon the foundation laid by the common law, s. 8 of the *Charter* creates for '[e]veryone' certain areas of personal autonomy where 'all the forces of the Crown' cannot enter." Quoting William Pitt (the Elder) in a 1763 speech before Parliament, reproduced in Lord H Brougham, *Historical Sketches of Statesmen Who Flourished in the Time of George III*, vol 1 (London: Richard Griffith and Company, 1855) at 42.

Again, it ought to come as no surprise that, when it turns its analytic gaze to the phenomenon of religion, Canadian constitutional law, itself informed by liberal political culture's commitments, views religion in a manner that comports with the taxonomy of public/private and reason/interest. The primary way in which we see this rendering expressed in the jurisprudence is in the assertion that religion is fundamentally a question of belief. Religion is defined as "freely and deeply held personal convictions and beliefs."[112] The rhetorical focus on belief is not without complexity. In places, the Court speaks of the importance of religious practice,[113] going so far as to note that "the performance of religious rites is a fundamental aspect of religious practice."[114] Although the Court does not entirely blind itself to the practised or lived dimension of religion, close attention to the jurisprudence demonstrates that law manifests a degree of comfort with religion as belief and displays a kind of anxiety and awkwardness with religion as practice. These respective reactions to belief and practice fit comfortably within the liberal framework of constitutional rights. When a belief is accompanied by conduct, its presence as an expression in the world pushes it closer to – or into – the public and, in so doing, threatens the introduction of interest and preference into the realm of reason.

Law's comfort with religion as belief and discomfort with religion as (potentially public) practice appear clearly in *TWU*,[115] which considered Trinity Western University's requirement that all students sign a code of conduct that, among other things, prohibited certain practices "that are biblically condemned," including "homosexual behaviour."[116] Since this code expressed a discriminatory view, the British Columbia College of Teachers (BCCT) refused to certify the university's education program, thus preventing its graduates from serving as public school teachers. The BCCT's refusal was based, at least in part, on its conclusion that students who signed such a code of conduct must have held the belief that homosexual conduct was immoral. Public teachers, the BCCT reasoned, were required to uphold and teach the principles of equality and non-discrimination, and there was no reasonable prospect

---

112 *Amselem, supra* note 5 at para 39. See also *Big M, supra* note 12 at 336–7.
113 See *Big M, supra* note 12; *Reference re Same-Sex Marriage, supra* note 69 at paras 56–9.
114 *Reference re Same-Sex Marriage, supra* note 69 at para 57.
115 *Trinity Western University v British Columbia College of Teachers*, 2001 SCC 31, [2001] 1 SCR 772 [*TWU*].
116 As cited in *ibid* at para 4.

that a student who signed this code of conduct could be relied upon to carry out these public responsibilities.

The Court held that the apparent conflict between equality and religious freedom would be avoided by "properly defining the scope of the rights"[117] involved. In this case, "the proper place to draw the line ... is generally between belief and conduct."[118] Why? The scope of law's protection for conduct is narrower precisely because, once manifest in action, religion takes on a more public aspect. The Court concluded that the BCCT had improperly based its ruling on the "mere" presence of a religious belief, rather than upon evidence that such belief translated into discriminatory conduct in the public realm. Even if the code of conduct was an accurate insight into the beliefs held by the graduates of Trinity Western University, the constitutional ethics of equal treatment and non-discrimination are concerned with public conduct, and the Court was not prepared to predict future conduct based on past evidence of belief. In so ruling, the Court effectively translated the issue into an evidentiary matter, but one that discloses the strong manner in which the constitutional imagination associates religion with the realm of the private. As belief only, religion is a preference that remains solidly and unproblematically within the realm of the personal. As conduct, it might seep into the realm of the public where interest and preference have a troublesome status.

The sense of the rightful presence of the private in the public domain that one finds in the culture of Canadian constitutionalism is, to be sure, complicated. For example, the status of interest and preference as legitimate aspects of public decision-making varies with context. Accordingly, law's understanding of religion as private has a range of implications for the place of religion in the public sphere.[119] At one

---

117  *Ibid* at para 29.

118  *Ibid* at para 36.

119  David Seljak provides an interesting example of the complexity of religion's role in Canadian public decision-making, noting that "[i]n both the 1980 and 1995 referenda, Catholic groups attempted to redefine a public role for the Church in Quebec society." David Seljak, "Resisting the 'No Man's Land' of Private Religion: The Catholic Church and Public Politics in Quebec" in David Lyon & Marguerite Van Die, eds, *Rethinking Church, State, and Modernity: Canada between Europe and America* (Toronto: University of Toronto Press, 2000) 131 at 144. Seljak notes further that these groups' "attempts at the 'deprivatization' of religion take the form of resistance to the dominant political culture, which would relegate both religion and alternative ethical perspectives to the 'private' realm of subjective values and experiences" (145).

end of the spectrum, the justifiability of the influence of religion on the way in which an individual casts his or her ballot is hardly questioned. One might disagree with the religious principles brought to bear, or whether the voter ought to be guided by religion, but the idea that religious commitments can legitimately influence voting is not generally in question. At the other end of the spectrum, from within the contemporary imagination of Canadian constitutionalism, it would seem anathema to have a judge reason from religious principles in a decision about the validity of a contract or the appropriate division of matrimonial assets upon divorce. Somewhere in the middle, and most contested, is the rightful place of religious principle in representative decision-making and other exercises of public authority.[120] The issue of same-sex marriage highlighted this disputed area in Canada. Should a prime minister be informed by his or her religious views when making policy decisions?[121] Can a public marriage commissioner refuse to perform same-sex marriages on the basis of religious objections?[122] Although the current tendency in Canada is to reject such a role for "private" religion, there is a broader spectrum of opinion on this point. So my claim is not that, within the Canadian constitutional rule of law, religion has no place in the public; rather, law's rendering of religion as belief strongly aligns it with the private and, given legal liberalism's commitment to the public/private divide, this association creates identifiable tensions for law's treatment of public expressions of religious commitment.

---

120  For an argument in defence of reliance upon religious beliefs in public decision-making, see Michael J Perry, "Why Political Reliance on Religiously Grounded Morality Is Not Illegitimate in a Liberal Democracy" (2001) 36 Wake Forest L Rev 217.

121  The stances taken by Prime Ministers Jean Chrétien and Paul Martin (both Catholics) on same-sex marriage are cases in point. Both disavowed the legitimacy of basing the decision on legalizing same-sex marriage on Catholic dogma – and this in spite of papal encyclicals calling upon public decision-makers to do just this.

122  See *Re Marriage Commissioners Appointed Under the Marriage Act*, 2011 SKCA 3, in which the Saskatchewan Court of Appeal held that proposed legislation that would either permit exemptions for all religiously objecting marriage commissioners or would "grandfather" existing marriage commissioners who objected to performing same-sex marriages on religious grounds would be an unjustifiable infringement of the section 15(1) protection against discrimination on the basis of sexual orientation. The positions taken by scholars in the area have been varied. See e.g. Bruce MacDougall, "Refusing to Officiate at Same-Sex Civil Marriages" (2006) 69 Sask L Rev 351; Bruce Ryder, "The Canadian Conception of Equal Religious Citizenship" in Moon, *Law and Religious Pluralism, supra* note 9, 87.

An example of this complex role for religion-as-interest in public decision-making is *Chamberlain v Surrey School District No 36*, first raised in chapter 1.[123] It will be recalled that, in this case, the Court quashed the decision of a school board that, influenced by religious objections among parents in the community to same-sex relationships, refused to approve the use of books that depicted same-sex parented families for a kindergarten/grade one curriculum. The board's decision was challenged on the ground that, by deferring to certain religious views in the community, it had acted contrary to section 76 of its enabling legislation, which required that all schools be conducted on "strictly secular and non-sectarian principles."[124] Although the case did not formally raise questions of constitutional rights, by addressing this administrative law question – and, with it, the demands of "secularism" – the Court was involved in the analysis of constitutional themes.[125]

The Court rejected an interpretation of this demand for "secularism" that would prohibit religious concerns from informing the board's decision-making altogether. Instead, the section meant that, if the board gave credence to the religious views in the community, it had to ensure that it did so "in a manner that gives equal recognition and respect to other members of the community."[126] The Court explained that the role of the board as a public decision-maker and the role of parents were manifestly different. Whereas individual parents are entitled to advocate for policies that are consonant with their religious views,[127] as an elected body exercising powers pursuant to public legislation, the board "must not allow itself to be dominated by one religious or moral point of view, but must respect a diversity of views."[128] Critically, the

---

123  2002 SCC 86, [2002] 4 SCR 710 [*Chamberlain*].
124  *School Act*, RSBC 1996, c 412, s 76. The board's decision was also challenged on *Charter* grounds, but the Court disposed of the case on the basis of administrative law principles.
125  Any boundary between constitutional rights analysis and administrative law has been seriously unsettled by Supreme Court of Canada rulings like *Doré v Barreau du Québec*, 2012 SCC 12, [2012] 1 SCR 395, requiring administrative decision-makers to engage in *Charter*-like analyses. This convergence of administrative and *Charter* law might be more faithful to the traditional (and attractive) view of administrative law as simply a species of constitutional law.
126  *Chamberlain, supra* note 123 at para 19.
127  *Ibid* at para 20: "Parents need not abandon their own commitments, or their view that the practices of others are undesirable."
128  *Ibid* at para 28.

board must also be subject to judicial review for the reasonableness of its decisions. In this case, the Court found that the board's decision was unreasonable, in part on the basis that it had deferred to the particular religious views of certain parents rather than considering the multiplicity of views that might be represented in the community, as mandated by the *School Act*'s requirement for secularity.[129] The underlying dynamic at play in this case is one in which, when anchored in the private, law is unconcerned with the existence of religious preference; however, when wielded by public authority, law is less comfortable with religion and requires that it be tested against the dictates of reason. As private religion becomes increasingly associated with the sphere of public decision-making, it leaves the permissive jurisdiction of interest and enters the scrutinizing domain of reason.

*Amselem* further dramatizes the role of the public and private as symbolic markers for the distinction between interest and reason, as well as law's assignation of religion to the realm of the private/interest. This distinction appears in that crucial question raised in *Amselem*: whether the Court needed to decide whether or not the claimants were correct in their belief that Judaism required a personal, rather than a communal, succah. The majority reasoned that it would be inconsistent with law's commitment to individual autonomy (and here we see the interaction among all three elements of law's vision of religion) "to rule on the validity or veracity of a given religious practice or belief."[130] Instead, the courts should confine themselves to determining whether or not the claimant "is sincere in his or her belief."[131] Reflecting this distinction back on the public/private dichotomy, it seems that objective veracity has no place in the realm of interest – all that matters is the sincerity of one's preference. If this test is satisfied, analysis in the private realm is, for law's purposes, exhausted. By contrast, truth is the ultimate test in the realm of reason. If true, a proposition binds all reasonable persons. Validity is for the public, sincerity is for the private, and all that the law requires of religion is sincerity of belief. Within law's imagination, religion takes on a strong sense of "interest," and a concomitant association with the private, such that an inquiry into truth does not fit comfortably.

---

129  *Ibid* at paras 57–9.
130  *Amselem, supra* note 5 at para 51.
131  *Ibid* at para 56.

Even the dissents in *Amselem* betray law's rendering of religion as, in deep ways, a matter of private interest. Justices Bastarache and Binnie both argued that the law must take cognizance, not only of the claimants' religious interests, but also of the other owners' property rights, with Justice Binnie arguing that the claimants had lost their religious rights when they signed the contract. The contractual terms "express a certain style of architectural austerity or collective anonymity which the co-owners wanted to present to the world in a building shorn of any external display of individual personality."[132] To vindicate the religious right without regard to these aesthetic preferences would be to privilege one form of interest (belief) over another (aesthetic taste), and law, which honours the border between private and public, is extremely reticent to do so. This reasoning casts religion as a fungible interest, interchangeable through the market with other preferences. I am not suggesting that law treats religion as *nothing more* than any other interest. The *Charter* explicitly protects religious freedom, whereas it only obliquely protects other interests, such as aesthetic taste. Yet when rendered by the constitutional rule of law, religion takes on a strong sense of private interest, and this colouring affects the way that the jurisprudence treats religion; specifically, religion is drawn away from the realm of culture and into the realm of preference.

There is, of course, a strong connection between law's sense of religion as centrally a matter of individual autonomy and the translation of religious commitment into matters of preference, a link recognized by Justice Dickson in *Big M*.[133] Religion is to be protected because it is the object of individual choice, and this element of choice is the means by which each individual gains the capacity to seek the satisfaction of private interest and preference. Canadian constitutionalism is committed to the view that "[a] truly free society is one which can accommodate a wide variety of beliefs, diversity of tastes and pursuits, customs and codes of conduct."[134] Religion has a claim within the law, then, because it is an autonomous and private expression of one important set of preferred tastes and chosen pursuits. When pushed through the filter of Canadian constitutional law, religion comes out in a shape easily assimilated into a distinction critical to the liberal political imagination: religion is quintessentially private.

---

132  *Amselem, supra* note 5 at para 195.
133  See *Big M, supra* note 12 and accompanying text.
134  *Ibid* at 336.

**Summary: Law's Triptych**

As I have presented it, Canadian constitutional law's image of religion has three aspects. The first is that, within law's imagination, religion is something that essentially and most purely takes place within the individual. Viewed through the lens of constitutional jurisprudence, religion appears as a personal connection between the individual in his or her solitude and whatever it is that forms the object of his or her spiritual attention. When we ask why this commitment to the individual locus of religion is so strong in the law, we see that this conception feeds off the central philosophical commitment about the good that religion represents. Religion is valuable and deserving of legal protection because it is one possible expression of personal autonomy; that is, to protect religion is to protect the right of an individual to make choices about his or her spiritual life. On this view, religious freedom is a necessary outgrowth of a more general dedication to the good of freedom and autonomy. The relationship between this sense of religion as centrally about autonomy and choice, and religion as a fundamentally individual phenomenon, is apparent. We protect autonomy because we privilege the individual; equally, the individual is valued because that individual is the source of choice, which is understood as the expression of freedom and autonomy. From these intimately interrelated aspects of law's rendering of religion, the jurisprudence leads us naturally to the third aspect of law's understanding of religion – that religion is a private matter. Once religion is centred on the individual and his or her personal choices and expressions of autonomy, the constitutional imagination is led to assign religion to the realm of the private. The relationship works equally in the opposite direction. Not an independently legitimate component of public decision-making, religion falls on the private side of law's conceptual divide. Once so designated, religion is bound not by reason, but by preference. It is therefore a matter of choice and, as such, an expression of the autonomous individual.

This is the triptych of religion painted by the brush of modern Canadian constitutionalism. Like the artistic triptych, it can be described structurally as being composed of three discrete panels. But, also like the triptych, these three faces are really aspects of one larger image. They combine to produce a coherent message, each informing the way that we interpret the others. Although elements of the jurisprudence might emphasize one "panel" over the others, law's religion is fully appreciated only when all of these aspects are viewed together. By identifying these features as the aspects of religion relevant to the legal imagination, we see that the resulting image circumscribes religious experience within rather fixed boundaries. The outer frame of the triptych is the limit of law's rendering of religion; the image excludes even as it displays.

But what accounts for what this particular perception of religion omits and what it foregrounds? I have argued that law's understanding of religion is informed by modern Canadian constitutionalism's foundational assumptions and ideological commitments. The focus on the individual as the elementary unit of explanation, the privileging of autonomy and choice, and the fidelity to a private/public taxonomy all make this particular rendering of religion one that resonates with Canadian constitutional law's ideological underpinnings. Law shapes religion in its own ideological image and likeness and conceptually confines it to the individual, choice-centred, and private dimensions of human life. This particular iconography resonates within the meaningful and meaning-giving framework of Canadian constitutional law, deeply informed as it is by the political culture of liberalism. This is how religion is framed for legal and political experience within the culture of Canadian constitutionalism.

It is interesting to note a strong consonance between this rendering of religion and the definition of religion offered by the influential Protestant thinker William James. In *The Varieties of Religious Experience*, James sought to describe the nature of "genuine" religious experience. For James, "true" religion was best conceived of as *"the feelings, acts, and experiences of individual men in their solitude, so far as they apprehend themselves to stand in relation to whatever they may consider the divine."*[135] In his reflections on James's religious theory, Charles Taylor notes that James's conception of religion participates in a trajectory of thought that began in the high Middle Ages and culminated in the Protestant Reformation, one that placed "increasing emphasis on a religion of personal commitment and devotion over forms centred on collective ritual."[136] Notably, Taylor observes that, in its constituent features, "James's take on religion is well adapted to a confrontation between religion and secular

---

135  William James, *The Varieties of Religious Experience: A Study in Human Nature* (London: Routledge, 2002) at 29–30 [originally published in 1902; emphasis in original].
136  Charles Taylor, *Varieties of Religion Today: William James Revisited* (Cambridge, Mass: Harvard University Press, 2002) at 9.

views."[137] James's theory casts religion in a form that is congenial to a life in the modern secular state: "[I]t operates within common assumptions about the importance of personal commitment, and within these it presents religion in the most favorable light by defining it in terms of intense experience that can galvanize conduct."[138]

Given that law's theory of religion closely mirrors James's understanding of genuine religious experience, Taylor's observation is highly salient for thinking about the interaction of Canadian constitutional law and religion. To the extent that a particular religious culture accords with the law's assumptions about the value and nature of religion – a rendering of religion that has deep sympathies with certain Protestant understandings – the religious conduct at issue will appear less challenging or problematic. We see the truth of this claim in Canadian legal history, with the vast bulk of jurisprudence on this topic generated out of encounters between law and religious traditions that did not participate in, or have since resisted, the trajectory of thought identified by Taylor. The evocative suggestion is that the constitutional rule of law in a modern secular state is not indifferent as to the form of religion that appears within it;[139] rather, the extent and character of legal tolerance for religion may turn on a religion's conformity with the law's conceptual commitments about religion. It seems that as the conceptual gap between law's religion and the culture of a particular religious tradition expands, the instances and extent of conflict between law and religion will increase. This is the cultural force of law's religion, the dynamic to which I will turn in the next chapter.

---

137  *Ibid* at 14.
138  *Ibid* at 15.
139  See Winnifred Fallers Sullivan, *The Impossibility of Religious Freedom* (Princeton, NJ: Princeton University Press, 2005) at 7–8. Sullivan identifies two broad conceptions of religion at play in the U.S. tradition of religious freedom: the first is a highly Protestant-influenced conception of religion akin to that offered by James; the second – which Sullivan notes, "was, and perhaps still is, the religion of most of the world" – is the public, enacted, and communal form of religion represented historically by the Catholic Church and, today, by Islam. "Crudely speaking," she argues, "it is the first kind – the modern protestant kind – that is 'free.' The other kind is closely regulated by law." Though analytically illuminating, there is a risk that over-relying on such ideas of "protestant religion" (or my own tracing of Canadian legal renderings of religion to particular brands of Protestant thought) can mislead, obscuring the ways in which the public assertiveness of certain forms of Protestantism – in the United States, Canada, and elsewhere – are posing some of the most fraught issues in the modern interaction of law and religion.

I can now return to and explain the ambivalent answer to the question raised at the outset of this chapter: does law apprehend religion in cultural terms? In one important sense the answer to the question must be "yes." My analysis of law's rendering of religion shows the cultural dimensions of law. Law seeks to understand religion in terms that make sense within the horizon of significance endogenous to law. Canadian constitutional law's understanding of religion is "cultural" in the sense that it is demonstrative of the culture of Canadian constitutional law, understood as the frameworks in which law makes sense of experience. In this respect, law's understanding of religion is cultural. But the corollary is that law therefore processes religion in terms exogenous to religious cultures; in so doing, it may fail to take seriously the meanings and structures of significance involved in religion. In this sense law's understanding is not a cultural understanding of religion. It does not seek to understand religion as an interpretive horizon, composed of sets of symbols, practices, and categories of thought, out of which meaning can be given to identity, history, and experience. Law's understanding of religion is a Procrustean product of law's own symbolic commitments and frameworks of understanding.

One might object that I am asking too much of law by questioning whether its approach to religion is cultural. Perhaps law is not excluding the cultural dimension at all but, rather, remaining agnostic on this question. Otherwise put, is law actually defining religion – making a claim about what religion *is* – or is law simply dealing with religion in the terms necessary for adjudication and withdrawing from any essential claim about the nature of religion? My analysis may seem to make the greater claim that law is actually asserting something about the true nature of what it is protecting: that it is making a sociological determination about what religion *is*. But perhaps law merely takes a slice of religion – only that which is necessary to answer the question before it – and leaves open a whole set of issues about the nature of religion for others to answer. That is, it does not speak to the social, identity-based, or public facets of religion because those aspects are not at issue in a court of law and, therefore, law leaves these other aspects to be worked out and spoken to by other disciplines and other social institutions. Just as the law might not deny (or confirm) that language has a socially constructive dimension when deciding a language rights case, why would I assume that law's rendering of religion is a comprehensive claim about the very nature of religion?

There is some truth in this critique. Canadian constitutional law might not understand itself as making the larger claim about the very nature of religion at large. Law begins from the premise that it is making only the first claim – that it is merely concerned with that slice of religion necessary to decide the case before it and is quite happy to allow other understandings of religion to flourish. But law's modesty is always false. Because law defines rights and uses power to implement its vision, its claim rapidly assumes the greater form – the comprehensive claim about religion. Because it both commands the coercive power of the state and always implicitly assumes the ultimacy of its authority, law's rendering of religion assumes the force and significance of a total claim about what matters about religion, what religion relevantly *is*. This is the essence of Cover's insight that law is *jurispathic*: that, whether it intends to or not, the very nature of law is that it kills other normative arrangements and interpretations.[140] This is the reason that law's rendering of religion matters so much when discussing the nature of the relationship between law and religion: even when it begins with a modest claim, the nature of law and its violence is such that its claims quickly expand into a more comprehensive form. Cover calls this law's jurispathic character; I would perhaps call it epistemologically colonial – it may be that law is saying only that it is making a limited claim about religion for its own purposes, but when the courts are called on to adjudicate the relationships among rights and interests, law's understanding of religion quickly becomes the only game in town. Law says, "For *my purposes* religion is the following." However, in this modest claim is the seed of the larger: "And if you appear before me, this is the only definition that will attract the recognition of the state." This is why appreciating the way in which Canadian constitutional law frames and understands religion – how it renders religion – is so essential to generating a more satisfying account of the interaction of law and religion.

## Conclusion

My claim in this chapter is neither that law merely "has it wrong," nor that its conception of religion must change. The framing intuitions, symbolic commitments, and interpretive practices that inform

---

140  Robert M Cover, "The Supreme Court 1982 Term – Foreword: *Nomos* and Narrative" (1983) 97 Harv L Rev 4.

Canadian constitutional law's understanding of religion are no more or less mutable than those that comprise a religious culture. In this way, it is not the case that law has *misunderstood* religion. Law has *understood* religion; it has simply done so in keeping with the culture of Canadian constitutionalism. As such, this understanding is just one possible rendering of religion and not one that necessarily reflects the nature of religious life and its relationship with the law. In particular, it does not afford religion the same significance, reach, and impact that law, however tacitly, assumes for itself.

What this discussion does point to is the experiential residue left by conventional accounts of the interaction of law and religion. Religious life can be more complex, more interpretively ambitious, and therefore less manageable than law would have it. Religion is not only what law imagines it to be. Law's religion is but a corner of lived religion, lived religion being simply too unruly to subsist within the imagination of the constitutional rule of law. That being so, even if successful at accommodating or tolerating what it understands to be religion, aspects of religion remain entirely unattended to and, therefore, unresolved in their tension with the constitutional rule of law. And with this insight we come to one important part of the explanation for why the story we conventionally tell about law and religion in Canada has proven so unsatisfactory: it fails to fully appreciate the cultural nature of – and dynamics involved in – the encounter between religion and the Canadian constitutional rule of law.

# Chapter 3

# The Cultural Limits of Legal Tolerance

A regime which is nominally liberal can be oppressive in reality. A regime which acknowledges its violence *might* have in it more genuine humanity.

Maurice Merleau-Ponty, *Humanism and Terror*[1]

In Canada the judicious use of principles of tolerance and accommodation of difference, inspired by constitutional rights, has produced certain positive legal outcomes in matters concerning sexual orientation, disability, political dissent, and, in some instances, religion. It is, no doubt, these practical legal achievements of tolerance and accommodation – aspects of the triumph of law – that have so cemented in our imagination the role of a tolerantly implemented set of constitutionalized rights and freedoms as the framework within which to address such issues. Indeed, tolerance has become central to the organizing grammar for talking about the interaction of law and religion in Canada. Conventional wisdom holds that the problem of religious diversity is to be responded to with the legal tool of toleration: these have become the natural terms for describing the encounter of law and religion. But, as this chapter explores, this language has proven to be not just natural but *naturalizing*, obscuring the currents of power, history, and politics that are at work underneath this pacific idea of toleration.

That capacity to conceal itself flows from the underlying assumption of law's autonomy from culture – a claim of autonomy that Wendy

---

1 Maurice Merleau-Ponty, *Humanism and Terror: An Essay on the Communist Problem*, translated by John O'Neill (Boston: Beacon Press, 1969) at xv.

Brown characterizes as a central "conceit" of modern legal orders.[2] Combined with its commitment to the autonomy of the subject from culture, Brown argues that these "twin conceits ... enable liberal legalism's unique positioning as fostering tolerance and liberal polities' unique position as capable of brokering the tolerable."[3] Putting law "above" culture in this way means that the tools used by the law in this managerial endeavour – including the device of "toleration" – are themselves seen as distinct from any particular cultural system and, hence, not exerting cultural force. As Winnifred Fallers Sullivan argues, theorists "tend to work with a definition of law as problematic as that of religion. There is a tendency to accept modern law's representation of itself as autonomous, universal, and transparent. Such a representation makes religion, not law, the problem."[4]

But chapter 2 exposed the way in which law frames its experience of religion, providing a context for both interpreting and evaluating the claims of religion and, in so doing, serving a cultural function. Religion is experienced – it is met and analysed – through the culture of Canadian constitutionalism. When religious groups find themselves before the bar of the law, the terms of the debate are, in important ways, always already settled. This bounded openness whereby the core assumptions of the law are bracketed even as space is left open to assess the just is an intrinsic feature of law's rule. This means that law not only shapes experience and interpretation, but that, in the particularity of these framings (what they capture and what they leave out) and the exercise of power to realize and defend them, law can itself be experienced as a cultural force. So although a pliant, accommodative "toleration," drawing strength from an informing conceit of law's autonomy from culture, frequently serves as the self-described mode of law's management of religious difference, that concept is in truth a marker for a much more

---

2 Wendy Brown, *Regulating Aversion: Tolerance in the Age of Identity and Empire* (Princeton, NJ: Princeton University Press, 2006).
3 *Ibid* at 171. And if the capacity to engage in toleration is also a mark of civilization, Brown argues, liberalism thus becomes definitional of civilization and the tolerated becomes definitionally uncivilized or "barbaric." Martha Minow similarly notes that tolerance "perpetuates assumptions that some – who put up with others – are actually superior to those others ... [T]he very injunction to put up with others may be experienced as putting down some ways of life." Martha Minow, "Putting Up and Putting Down: Tolerance Reconsidered" (1990) 28 Osgoode Hall LJ 409 at 410.
4 Winnifred Fallers Sullivan, *The Impossibility of Religious Freedom* (Princeton, NJ: Princeton University Press, 2005) at 153.

complicated intercultural encounter, one in which the law assiduously conserves its symbolic, structural, and normative commitments.

A phenomenological turn in understanding the interaction of law and religion must try to push past the descriptive language of toleration and inquire into the experience of being worked upon by a legal regime that operates from a posture of toleration. That experience is the subject of this chapter. How does legal toleration of religion actually operate within the contemporary culture of constitutionalism? If one accepts that the interaction between law and religion is profitably thought about as a cross-cultural interaction, what is the particular character – including the limits and possibilities – of that engagement?

### Looking through the Lens of Cross-Cultural Encounter

In 1763, the *Treaty of Paris*[5] brought an end to the imperial wars in Canada. Building upon similar provisions in the *Articles of Capitulation, 1759*,[6] Article IV of the *Treaty of Paris* included the following guarantee: "His Britannick Majesty, on his side, agrees to grant the liberty of the Catholick religion to the inhabitants of Canada: he will, in consequence, give the most precise and most effectual orders, that his new Roman Catholic subjects may profess the worship of their religion according to the rites of the Romish church, as far as the laws of Great Britain permit." From its early inception, then, Canada held itself out to be a place of religious accommodation through the legal toleration of religion. By modern comparison, of course, this was a modest form of multiculturalism. Yet, as part of an attempt to settle the peace and establish government in a volatile incipient nation, this provision of religious tolerance was a recognition that the legitimacy of a state met with the fact of internal cultural diversity depends, at least to some degree, on the extent to which it provides some room for cultural difference.[7]

---

5 *Treaty of Paris* (1763), Britain, Spain and Portugal, 10 February 1763, reproduced in WPM Kennedy, ed, *Statutes, Treaties and Documents of the Canadian Constitution, 1713–1929*, 2nd ed (Toronto: Oxford University Press, 1930) 31.
6 *Articles of Capitulation of Quebec, 1759*, 18 September 1759, reproduced in Kennedy, *ibid* at 23–4.
7 For a related claim generated from the historical U.S. setting, see Evan Haefeli, *New Netherland and the Dutch Origins of American Religious Liberty* (Philadelphia: University of Pennsylvania Press, 2012).

"Multiculturalism" is, in the first instance, a description of a state of affairs, referring to the fact of a number of cultures existing in relationship to one another. In Canada, the language of multiculturalism – rooted in these early experiences of religious and cultural difference – is also something more; it is the name of a policy adopted by the federal government in 1971, a policy that took a normative position on this descriptive state of affairs – that multiculturalism was a good to be cultivated.[8] In neither the descriptive nor the aspirational use, however, does this language tell us much of practical interest. It says nothing in itself about the quality or nature of the interaction between and among the multiple cultures that it contemplates. It says nothing about the details of how this state is to be achieved or worked out. It says nothing, furthermore, about the experience of this interaction for those living within it, or about the possibilities and room for commensurability of strong cultural difference within this interaction. To begin to assess, in detail and with sensitivity, the meeting of constitutional law and religion, one must move beyond the merely descriptive or aspirational language of multiculturalism and set in place lenses appropriate to assessing the internal dynamics – an idiom for analysing the essential character – of this cross-cultural interaction.

This chapter will work with one such idiom, offered by Fred Dallmayr in his book *Beyond Orientalism*.[9] Although his focus is on the particular cross-cultural encounter that began in the Americas in 1492, Dallmayr provides a non-exhaustive taxonomy of "modes of cross-cultural encounter." Dallmayr's language of "encounter" carries with it the risk of effacing the complexity, overlap, and messiness inherent in the legal relationship to cultural pluralism, as well as the shifting, porous, and internally contested nature of the cultures themselves. Moreover, the historical result of these interactions is always much messier than such language suggests.[10]

---

8  For the history of the development of the policy of official multiculturalism in Canada, see Joseph Eliot Magnet, "Multiculturalism and Collective Rights" (2005) 27 SCLR (2d) 431; Jack Jedwab, "To Preserve and Enhance: Canadian Multiculturalism before and after the *Charter*" (2003) 19 SCLR (2d) 309. See also Will Kymlicka, "Canadian Multiculturalism in Historical and Comparative Perspective: Is Canada Unique" (2003) 13:1 Const Forum Const 1.

9  Fred Dallmayr, *Beyond Orientalism: Essays on Cross-Cultural Encounter* (Albany, NY: SUNY, 1996).

10  For a sense of the overlap and hybridity involved in such interactions, see Homi K Bhabha, *The Location of Culture* (London: Routledge, 1994), especially at 112–16; James Tully, *Strange Multiplicity: Constitutionalism in an Age of Diversity* (Cambridge, UK: Cambridge University Press, 1995).

Nevertheless, Dallmayr's model is useful insofar as it describes various postures of engagement between cultures, with their associated attitudes to difference and understandings of the relation between the self and other. Focusing on these postures and attitudes helps get us closer to a more phenomenological account of legal toleration.

Dallmayr's taxonomy contains three broad categories. The first comprises modes of encounter that, in one way or another, ultimately deny difference. Here we find three closely related and frequently, though "not always or necessarily," linked modes: *conquest, conversion,* and *assimilation/acculturation*.[11] Colonialism is the quintessential modern form of conquest, involving the subjugation, complete assimilation, or even extermination of the encountered culture. As has been all too apparent in the context of European "engagement" with various Indigenous populations, encounter through conquest is predicated on a particular way of conceiving of other cultures. Specifically, conquest demands a confidence in one's own cultural assumptions and a conviction that the dissemination of this way of being is not only permitted, but justified. Typically, "conquest entails the physical subjugation of alien populations and sometimes also their forced cultural assimilation."[12]

When the dominant feature of a cross-cultural meeting informed by this mindset is the forced cultural assimilation of the alien population, the mode is best described as *conversion*, Dallmayr's second mode of encounter. Whereas conquest operationalizes a denial of difference in a "radical-hierarchical way" that inscribes a schism between the two cultures, in the case of conversion, "difference is denied through the insistence on a common or identical human nature" that marks the encountered population as a target for proselytization.[13] Any instance of cultural encounter in which one culture, operating on the basis of an assumed identity of human nature, seeks to transform the other to its own way of being can be described properly as a practice of conversion.[14] Closely related is the idea of *assimilation/acculturation*, which is best thought of as a form of conversion that involves "the spreading

---

11  Dallmayr, *supra* note 9 at 9.
12  *Ibid.*
13  *Ibid* at 9–10.
14  Dallmayr is vague on the role of force in this and his other modes of encounter. Presumably, conversion can take the form of violent imposition, rhetorical persuasion, or something between the two.

of diffuse cultural patterns of ways of life (of religious and/or secular vintage),"[15] usually targeted at marginalized ethnic, linguistic, and national groups within a given country. Otherwise put, this third mode of cross-cultural encounter involves the conversion of internal minority cultures to the dominant way of life.

These first three modes of cross-cultural encounter are cut from the same cloth. They share a universalist ethic that translates into a dedication to the preservation of a single cultural form at the expense of others. Whether by violence and force of arms (conquest) or by ideological means either abroad (conversion) or at home (assimilation), each shares a core characteristic: a commitment to asserting the dominance of one's own culture, including its basic ways of knowing, its symbolic and normative commitments, and its ways of life.

A second category in this way of thinking about the varieties of cross-cultural encounter reacts against the universalism and ideological violence of the first set of modes and, instead, counsels *minimal engagement*. This is the familiar response of *modus vivendi* liberalism in which the hope is to stave off conflict by adopting a posture of indifference to cultural diversity and using procedural and formal mechanisms to buffer interactions between cultures. In pursuit of "a tolerant juxtaposition of cultures and life-forms predicated on relative mutual disinterest and aloofness,"[16] liberalism seeks a stable division between public procedures and institutions that we share, and private, culturally specific aspects of life that are owed hands-off tolerance. The cultural violence found in the conquest/conversion/assimilation modes is thought to be forestalled by minimizing substantive engagement, which is seen as inherently risky.

But perhaps engagement need not take this universalistic and potentially violent form. Dallmayr outlines a final category of modes of encounter that, like liberal minimal engagement, rejects the first category of modes as unjust, but finds its solution in a different attitude or ethic informing cross-cultural engagement, one in which "the respective cultures must face each other on a more nearly equal or roughly comparable basis."[17] Once the rigid hierarchy assumed in the first three forms is softened and the cultures in question begin to borrow

---

15 Dallmayr, *supra* note 9 at 14.
16 *Ibid* at 24.
17 *Ibid* at 18.

from one another, anything from cultural incorporation to genuine cultural self-transformation can take place. *Cultural borrowing* is a form of engagement that "involves a prolonged, sometimes arduous process of engagement in alien life-forms, a process yielding at least a partial transformation of native habits due to a sustained learning experience."[18] More ambitious yet is the mode of encounter that Dallmayr views as the "normatively most commendable"[19] – *dialogical engagement*. This form of encounter also relies upon a non-hierarchical view of cultures but goes further, demanding a kind of "caring respect" and "agonistic mutuality" in which both cultures are willing "to undergo a mutual learning process while simultaneously preserving the distinctiveness of difference of their traditions."[20] In stark contrast to the monism at the core of conquest, conversion, and assimilation, a dialogic mode of cross-cultural encounter actively encourages pluralism and diversity, and does so expecting to have one's own way of being changed through the influence of the other.[21]

All of these models proceed from the proposition that a culture sits on both sides of every encounter. Each mode is descriptive of a different posture informed by a very different set of assumptions and attitudes regarding the nature and possibilities of self-other relations in the context of cross-cultural encounters. Viewed through the lens of this taxonomy, how can we best characterize and understand the interaction between the culture of the Canadian constitutional rule of law and religious cultures, guided as it is by the terms of legal tolerance?

---

18  *Ibid* at 24. Dallmayr notes, however, that the results of cultural borrowing can be various, ranging from "complete absorption of foreign ingredients in the prevailing cultural matrix" to "reciprocal give-and-take" or even "genuine self-transformation" (18). In any case, such borrowing requires "a willingness to recognize the distinctiveness of the other culture, coupled with a desire to maintain at least some indigenous preferences" (18).

19  *Ibid* at 31.

20  *Ibid* at 36. See also Tzvetan Todorov, *The Conquest of America: The Question of the Other*, translated by Richard Howard (New York: Harper & Row, 1984). An interesting question is whether true openness to dialogue and its effects is commensurable with an a priori commitment to preservation of one's own cultural distinctiveness.

21  As I will discuss in detail below, Dallmayr is not alone in holding this commitment to dialogic modes of cross-cultural engagement. See e.g. Tully, *supra* note 10; William Connolly, *Identity/Difference: Democratic Negotiations of Political Paradox*, expanded ed (Minneapolis: University of Minnesota Press, 2002), advancing an approach that he calls a "discursive ethic of cultivation" or an "ethic of agonistic care."

The answer will depend on the details, which are sometimes buried beneath the surface. I began this section with a description of the legal status given to Roman Catholicism in early Canadian constitutional documents. The British Crown confirmed that Catholics in Canada would be entitled to "profess the worship of their religion according to the rites of the Romish church, as far as the laws of Great Britain permit." The stance appears to be one of liberal minimal engagement and tolerance. But the very day that the *Royal Proclamation of 1763* was issued, and in the same year as the signing of the *Treaty of Paris*, Governor Murray was issued a set of secret instructions in which he was directed to actively limit the influence of the See of Rome and to establish the Church of England in Quebec so that the inhabitants "may by degrees be induced to embrace the Protestant religion, and their Children be brought up in the Principles of it."[22] Beneath the veneer of emerging liberal tolerance was the deep grain of a conversionary impulse.

### Law's Approach

One can discern the particular "mode of encounter" that law assumes in its interaction with religion by looking to the *Charter* jurisprudence governing the management of strong claims of religious freedom.[23] The starting point is the fountainhead case on religious liberties in Canada,

---

22 *Instructions to Governor Murray, 7 December, 1763*, reproduced in Kennedy, *supra* note 5 at 47–8.

23 One could legitimately look to other institutional sites to examine law's interaction with religion, but judicial decisions are a particularly rich and helpful source: for, as George Grant put it, "Theories of justice are inescapably defined in the necessities of legal decision." George Grant, *English-Speaking Justice* (Toronto: House of Anansi Press, 1998) at 69 [originally published in 1974]. Furthermore, since the introduction of the *Charter*, the courts have been both viewed and treated as the authoritative speakers about the shape and claims of the rule of law. Even when the legislatures and Parliament have chosen to cast an issue in a constitutional and rights-based register, their terms of reference have been overwhelmingly those taken from the law as spoken by the courts. As lamentable as this state of affairs may be to many commentators (see e.g. Lawrence G Sager, "Justice in Plain Clothes: Reflections on the Thinness of Constitutional Law" (1993) 88 Nw UL Rev 410; Robert C Post & Reva B Siegel, "Legislative Constitutionalism and Section Five Power: Polycentric Interpretation of the Family and Medical Leave Act" (2003) 112 Yale LJ 1943), in a work aimed at generating a more satisfying account of the relationship between religion and the constitutional rule of law in Canada, it makes sense to focus on the jurisprudence.

*R v Big M Drug Mart Ltd.*[24] In holding the *Lord's Day Act* unconstitutional, Chief Justice Dickson linked the notion of religious freedom to the very nature of a free society, stating that such a society "is one which can accommodate a wide variety of beliefs, diversity of tastes and pursuits, customs and codes of conduct."[25] The concept of freedom of religion, then, is centrally concerned with permitting the free and unconstrained expression of religious belief and conduct. Freedom of religion is, in the jurisprudence, an ideal that revolves around the notion of tolerance. In *Syndicat Northcrest v Amselem*, the Supreme Court of Canada explained that "respect for and tolerance of the rights and practices of religious minorities is one of the hallmarks of an enlightened democracy,"[26] going so far as to declare that "mutual tolerance is one of the cornerstones of all democratic societies."[27] The Court has characterized Canada as "a diverse and multicultural society, bound together by the values of accommodation, tolerance and respect for diversity."[28] The story that law tells about its encounter with religion is shot through with the language of tolerance.

In *Amselem*, the Court described this commitment to tolerance as directly linked to the fact of living in a "multiethnic and multicultural country such as ours, which accentuates and advertises its modern record of respecting cultural diversity and human rights and of promoting tolerance of religious and ethnic minorities."[29] Our policy of multiculturalism produces the commitment to religious tolerance, and the constitutional manifestation of this commitment is the protection of religious freedom in section 2(a) of the *Charter*. This is the first plank in law's approach to religion: given the multicultural character of the state, tolerance is the guiding feature of law's engagement with

---

24  [1985] 1 SCR 295 [*Big M*].

25  *Ibid* at 336.

26  2004 SCC 47 at para 1, [2004] 2 SCR 551 [*Amselem*].

27  *Ibid* at para 87.

28  *Chamberlain v Surrey School District No 36*, 2002 SCC 86 at para 21, [2002] 4 SCR 710 [*Chamberlain*].

29  *Amselem, supra* note 26 at para 87. In *Regulating Aversion, supra* note 2 at 1, Brown emphasizes and critiques the centrality of the concept of tolerance in modern multicultural democracies, asking how and why tolerance has become "a beacon of multicultural justice and civic peace at the turn of the twenty-first century" when "[a] mere generation ago, tolerance was widely recognized in the United States as a code word for mannered racialism."

religion, affording a healthy margin of freedom for a broad diversity of beliefs, tastes, and pursuits.

The picture is, of course, rather more complex. In *Big M*, Chief Justice Dickson explained that the corollary of freedom of religion is freedom *from* religion. If the basis for religious freedom is, in the first place, respect for the autonomy and freedom of each person, then it is equally antithetical to our commitments to allow the religious beliefs of one individual or group to be imposed upon the unwilling or the non-believing. This holding gestures towards the potential – frequently actualized in contemporary issues of religious freedom – of the conflict of rights. The Supreme Court of Canada has explained that "respect for religious minorities is not a stand-alone absolute right; like other rights, freedom of religion exists in a matrix of other correspondingly important rights that attach to individuals."[30] The issue is not solely one of the parallel individual rights of others. The tolerance of religious difference takes place within a society with its own concerns, needs, and imperatives. As such, "[r]espect for minority rights must also coexist alongside societal values that are central to the make-up and functioning of a free and democratic society."[31]

In recognition of this embeddedness within a context of other rights and other pressing societal interests and needs, the Canadian legal story adds to its aspiration of tolerance a second feature: limits on freedom of religion may be justified in order to protect broad social interests or preserve the rights of others. Since *Big M*, there has been some ambiguity and debate within the jurisprudence as to whether the right to religious freedom found in section 2(a) may be internally – or "definitionally" – limited by certain powerful public interests, such as public safety and order, or by the rights and freedoms of others.[32] Latterly, the Court has expressed a strong preference for managing such conflicts

---

30  *Amselem, supra* note 26 at para 1.

31  *Ibid.*

32  On the one hand, in *Big M, supra* note 24 at 337, the Court stated that religious freedom was "subject to such limitations as are necessary to protect public safety, order, health, or morals or the fundamental rights and freedoms of others." On the other hand, in *B(R) v Children's Aid Society of Metropolitan Toronto*, [1995] 1 SCR 315 at para 109 [*B(R)*], La Forest J, writing for the majority of the Court, stated that the Court had "consistently refrained from formulating internal limits on the scope of freedom of religion in cases where the constitutionality of a legislative scheme was raised; it rather opted to balance the competing rights under s. 1 of the *Charter.*"

not by declaring that the religious practice falls outside the protection of section 2(a), but by recognizing a breach of religious freedoms and then moving on to assess whether a limit on that right is reasonable. In *Multani*,[33] discussed below, as well as the *Reference re Same-Sex Marriage*,[34] the Court explained that the most appropriate means of dealing with tensions between religious freedom and other rights or other social interests is to balance them under the rubric of section 1 of the *Charter*, which states that a right can be limited when such limitation is "demonstrably justified in a free and democratic society."[35] In *Wilson Colony*, a case in which a majority of the Court found the requirement for a photograph on a driver's licence to be a justified limit on a Hutterite community's religious freedoms, the Court emphasized this central role for section 1 in the analysis of claims for legal toleration or accommodation, while at the same time making the test even more solicitous of state concerns and objectives.[36] The analysis under section 1 is, in essence, a form of means-ends proportionality review exemplary of contemporary liberal constitutional logic.[37] In the result, the

---

33 *Multani v Commission scolaire Marguerite-Bourgeoys*, 2006 SCC 6, [2006] 1 SCR 256 [*Multani*]. The Court confirmed, at para 26, that it had "clearly recognized that freedom of religion can be limited when a person's freedom to act in accordance with his or her beliefs may cause harm to or interfere with the rights of others" but emphasized that it had "on numerous occasions stressed the advantages of reconciling competing rights by means of a s. 1 analysis."

34 2004 SCC 79, [2004] 3 SCR 698.

35 This section 1 test is governed by the "Oakes test," established in the case of *R v Oakes*, [1986] 1 SCR 103 [*Oakes*]. For discussion of the section 1 test as an expression of the duty to accommodate, see José Woehrling, "L'obligation d'accommodement raisonnable et l'adaptation de la société à la diversité religieuse" (1998) 43 McGill LJ 325.

36 *Alberta v Hutterian Brethren of Wilson Colony*, 2009 SCC 37 at para 88, [2009] 2 SCR 567 [*Wilson Colony*]. I offer a more extensive assessment of the impact of the *Wilson Colony* decision on the approach to section 1 in Benjamin L Berger, "Section 1, Constitutional Reasoning, and Cultural Difference: Assessing the Impacts of *Alberta v Hutterian Brethren of Wilson Colony*" (2010) 51 SCLR (2d) 25. I argue that the irony of the decision is that the Court's analytical approach deepens the very difficulties involved in adjudicating religion that the majority laments at the outset of the decision. See also Richard Moon, "Accommodation Without Compromise: Comment on *Alberta v Hutterian Brethren of Wilson Colony*" (2010) 51 SCLR (2d) 95; Richard Moon, *Freedom of Conscience and Religion* (Toronto: Irwin Law, 2014) at 94–9 [Moon, *Freedom of Conscience and Religion*].

37 See Aharon Barak, *Proportionality: Constitutional Rights and Their Limitations*, translated by Doron Kalir (Cambridge, UK: Cambridge University Press, 2012); David M Beatty, *The Ultimate Rule of Law* (Oxford: Oxford University Press, 2004).

toleration of religious difference suggested by the guarantee of freedom of religion is circumscribed by a constitutional limiting apparatus that looks to law's view of the socially reasonable in order to decide upon the justifiable boundaries of legal toleration. This doctrinal framework serves as the rules of engagement for law's cross-cultural interaction with religion, shaping the posture that the Canadian constitutional rule of law assumes in its relationship with religion.

In light of the modes of cross-cultural encounter described in the previous section of this chapter, how is law's approach, conditioned as it is by these rules, best understood? On the surface, law begins firmly in the posture of liberal minimal engagement. The law claims that our society is strongly dedicated to multiculturalism and this commitment demands tolerance of the ways that people choose to live their lives, including the free expression and manifestation of cultural beliefs and cultural practices. However, there is no assumption that religious cultures might offer something valuable from which the legal culture might borrow. Law and religion are certainly not engaging in a conversation as relative equals, one that may result in the transformation of either. Law's formal encounter with religion is an instance neither of cultural borrowing nor of dialogic engagement. Neither, though, is there an attempt – at this point – to subordinate difference by means of the kind of ideological force that characterizes conversion or assimilation. Instead, the law affirms diversity, but at arm's length. Religious cultures are entitled to the benefit of a liberal *modus vivendi* tolerance.[38]

The difficulty with tolerance, as Bernard Williams has argued, "is that it seems to be at once necessary and impossible."[39] Tolerance becomes a robust virtue at points at which the tolerating group "thinks that the other is blasphemously, disastrously, obscenely wrong."[40] A virtuous toleration that will "accommodate a wide variety of beliefs, diversity of

---

38  See John Gray, *Two Faces of Liberalism* (New York: New Press, 2000).

39  Bernard Williams, "Tolerating the Intolerable" in Susan Mendus, ed, *The Politics of Toleration in Modern Life* (Durham, NC: Duke University Press, 2000) 65 at 65. For an important work on the politics of toleration, one that also draws on phenomenological sources and argues for "active tolerance," see Lars Tønder, *Tolerance: A Sensorial Orientation to Politics* (New York: Oxford University Press, 2013).

40  Williams, *supra* note 39 at 65. See also Rainer Forst, "The Limits of Toleration" (2004) 11 Constellations 312. In providing his definition of the concept of toleration, Forst articulates the "objection component," which holds that "it is essential for the concept of toleration that the tolerated beliefs or practices are considered to be objectionable and in an important sense wrong or bad" (314).

tastes and pursuits, customs and codes of conduct"[41] must be one that finds it difficult to accept these practices and beliefs within its own system of meaning and commitments. As Williams explains, "We need to tolerate other people and their ways of life only in situations that make it really difficult to do so. Toleration, we may say, is required only for the intolerable. That is its basic problem."[42] Otherwise put, "When tolerance is contextually possible, it is untenable; tolerance, I want to suggest, is paradoxical."[43] The doctrinal structure of Canadian constitutional law as I have described it reflects this "basic problem" or "paradox" and, in so doing, points to important characteristics of law's treatment of religion.

The easy language of "toleration" exhausts itself juridically at the capacious section 2(a) stage of the analysis. That which has come before the law is "religion," and religious difference should be tolerated. Yet if the religious conduct or beliefs in question are arguably "intolerable," the law moves to the section 1 means-ends proportionality analysis that asks whether the limit on legal tolerance is justified. With this move, the law quickly collapses into a conversionary mode of engagement. A particular instance of religious pluralism has been deemed problematic and the law now asks whether the limit imposed on the tolerance of this religious culture is justified. When asking if a limit on religious freedom is justified, the question is assessed within the values, assumptions, and symbolic commitments of the culture of Canadian constitutionalism itself.[44]

---

41  *Big M, supra* note 24 at 336.

42  Williams, *supra* note 39 at 65.

43  Joshua Halberstam, "The Paradox of Tolerance" (1982–83) 14:2 Philosophical Forum 190 at 190. Halberstam also sees a paradox in the idea of tolerance, but constructs it somewhat differently: "[G]enuine tolerance is in fact impossible for anyone. An examination of just why the true believer cannot be tolerant uncovers the less obvious conclusion that any conviction potentially precludes tolerance toward dissidence from that conviction. Yet at the same time it is only those with convictions who can be tolerant, for it is only when one has a strong belief that a different point of view can be considered an opposing view toward which tolerance is possible."

44  See *Oakes, supra* note 35 at 136: "The underlying values and principles of a free and democratic society are the genesis of the rights and freedoms guaranteed by the *Charter* and the ultimate standard against which a limit on a right or freedom must be shown, despite its effect, to be reasonable and demonstrably justified." See also *Gosselin v Quebec (AG)*, 2002 SCC 84 at para 353, [2002] 4 SCR 429, Arbour J: "[I]t would not be far from the truth to state that the types of limits that are justified under s. 1 are those, and *only* those, that not only respect the content of *Charter* rights but also *further* those rights in some sense – or to use the language of s. 1 itself, 'guarantee' them – by further advancing the values at which they are directed" [emphasis in original].

Chief Justice McLachlin made this eminently clear in *Wilson Colony*, when she explained that the overall balancing of the benefits and harms of any limit on freedom of religion – the stage of the analysis that the Court gave pride of place in this decision – involved assessing the deleterious impact of the limit "in terms of *Charter* values, such as liberty, human dignity, equality, autonomy, and the enhancement of democracy."[45] As described in chapter 2, the Court reasoned from the *Charter* value of autonomy to declare that being unable to drive would be merely a source of cost and inconvenience and, as such, this limit on freedom of religion was justified because it "[did] not negate the choice that lies at the heart of freedom of religion."[46]

As this reasoning in *Wilson Colony* makes clear, law's conception of religion expresses itself strongly in the assessment of the justifiability of limits on religious freedom. As explored in chapter 2, law never really meets religion; rather, it engages with its own projected image of religion's nature and value, one that may make it more accepting of certain forms of religion than others. In this respect, law is operating as any culture might, for it is always the case that "our understandings of other cultures' practices are refracted and distorted through our own cultural or ideological preoccupations."[47] The law assesses whether the religious expression in question has deviated – and if so, how much – from "acceptable religion." Here, the relevant questions include whether the controverted practice is closely linked to individual flourishing, whether it was merely private or encroached on the public, and whether it limited the autonomy or equality of another. These are the criteria that determine if this instance of cultural difference will be tolerated or not. Crucially, these criteria are drawn from inside the culture of Canadian constitutionalism itself. The more that a given religious culture or practice accords with law's understanding

---

45  *Wilson Colony, supra* note 36 at para 88. In Moon, *Freedom of Conscience and Religion, supra* note 36, Richard Moon argues that courts do not – and cannot – "engage in anything that could properly be described as the 'balancing' of competing public and religious interests" (132) because "[t]he court has no way to attach specific value or weight to a religious practice" (131). Instead, he states that "they have sometimes sought to create space for religious practices at the margins of law" (132).

46  *Wilson Colony, supra* note 36 at para 99.

47  Jeremy Webber, "Multiculturalism and the Limits to Toleration" in André Lapierre, Patricia Smart & Pierre Savard, eds, *Language, Culture and Values in Canada at the Dawn of the 21st Century* (Ottawa: International Council for Canadian Studies & Carleton University Press, 1996) 269 at 271.

of religion, the less abrasive and challenging to law's commitments it will be and, hence, the more likely it is that it will fall within the limits of legal tolerance. When, however, a claim to religious freedom begins to grate or put pressure on the law, it appears legally intolerable. As Sullivan puts it, "The right kind of religion, the approved religion, is always that which is protected, while the wrong kind, whether popular or unpopular, is always restricted or even prohibited."[48] The deeming of a particular manifestation of religion as "intolerable" – and, hence, the limitation of religious freedom as justified – can always be read as the product of a misfit between the claimant's religion or religious practice and what law understands as tolerable religion.

Note the analytic upshot of this juridical posture: if the limit on tolerance is justified, it is justified by virtue of its fidelity to the commitments, values, and overarching objectives of the rule of law. Importantly, however, if the limit on tolerance is not justified, the reason is the same. It is not justified because we erred in thinking that the practice actually offended the basic commitments of Canadian constitutionalism. The limitation was unduly onerous or we did not appreciate that, in fact, the religious practice or belief in question could be viewed as or rendered consonant with these commitments – commitments such as autonomy, the protection of individuals, and the maintenance of a private sphere characterized by personal values and a public sphere cleansed of the influences of choice and taste. Within this analytic structure, law always vindicates its own cultural understandings.

With this, law's encounter with religion takes on salient features of the conversionary/assimilationist mode of cross-cultural encounter.[49] Characteristic of conversionary and assimilationist modes of cross-cultural encounter, there is an underlying denial of difference, a repudiation of the diversity recognized, from a distance, in the minimal engagement posture. Law tolerates that which is different only so long as it is not *so different* that it challenges the organizing norms, commitments, practices, and symbols of the Canadian constitutional rule of law.

---

48 See Sullivan, *supra* note 4 at 154.
49 This experience of an encounter with law as an experience of cultural imperialism or as conversion/assimilation is, of course, something all too familiar for the Aboriginal peoples of Canada. For a reflection on the assimilationist policies concerning Aboriginal communities in Canada as part of the story of Canadian constitutional engagement with cultural diversity, see Colleen Sheppard, "Constitutional Recognition of Diversity in Canada" (2006) 30 Vt L Rev 463 at 466–7.

The conversionary move has both a universalist and a culturally specific dimension: the assertion that there is a single and indissoluble package of criteria that is appropriate to judging the result of such conflicts of rights and the fact that these criteria are all drawn from within the culture of the rule of law itself. Once this move has taken place, there exist only two possibilities: the courts will either deem the conduct intolerable and require the religious group or individual to conform to the norms and commitments of Canadian constitutionalism, or the courts will conclude that the state was wrong in limiting this instance of religious diversity because this expression of cultural pluralism is itself consistent with those values and commitments. In this way there is the simultaneous marking of the group that is the candidate for tolerance as factually different and an assertion of the dominance of the meanings and perspectives of the culture of Canadian constitutionalism that renders marginal the perspectives or meanings of the group in question.[50] Ultimately, one is either required to conform one's way of life to the symbols, values, and meanings of the constitutional culture, or permitted to carry on without interference because the law recasts the meaning of one's practices and beliefs as already consistent with those cultural commitments. In either case, the law spreads a cultural pattern or way of life that has, at its base, "the insistence on a common or identical human nature."[51] In either case, the individual is sent the message that, despite the values at stake for him or her at this analytic moment, what really matters is the set of values and commitments held by the rule of law and, whether by proscribing certain behaviour or by recasting the meaning of that behaviour, one will be made to conform to the culture of law's rule. This is one juridical manifestation of what Tully calls an "imperial culture embodied in most liberal constitutions."[52]

---

50 Iris Marion Young identifies just this "paradox of experiencing oneself as invisible at the same time that one is marked out and noticed as different" as the central experience of cultural imperialism. Iris Marion Young, "Five Faces of Oppression" (1988) 19:4 Philosophical Forum 270 at 286.

51 Dallmayr, *supra* note 9 at 9–10. This dynamic that I am arguing is at the core of Canadian constitutionalism's engagement with difference is described by Tully, *supra* note 10 at 164: "The words and deeds of one side are redescribed and adjudicated in the monological framework of the other, thereby providing further evidence for the correctness of their comprehensive and exclusive view from the safety of the sidelines" (164).

52 Tully, *supra* note 10 at 7.

Consider two examples drawn from the jurisprudence, one in which religion "wins" and one in which religion "loses." What is the message about the nature of legal tolerance expressed in each of these cases? *Multani v Commission scolaire Margeurite-Bourgeoys* is an interesting example of apparent legal tolerance, in part because it also contains a passionate plea by the Court for the importance of religious tolerance in Canadian society and the need to teach this value to Canadian youth.[53] *Multani* involved an Orthodox Sikh boy who felt that his faith required him to wear a kirpan, a small ceremonial dagger, at all times. His school's governing board held that he was prohibited from wearing the kirpan at school on the basis of its policy that prohibited students from carrying any "weapons and dangerous objects." Given that it was the product of a sincerely held religious belief, the Court had no difficulty finding that the policy offended Multani's section 2(a) right. The bulk of the analysis turned on section 1. Although the school authority argued that the prohibition was justified as a safety measure and that the kirpan's presence could have an adverse impact on the school environment, the Court concluded that this absolute prohibition was not a proportional limit on Multani's religious right. Dismissing the safety concern as ill-founded, the Court noted that there was no history of kirpan-related violence and that Multani had already agreed to wear the kirpan under his clothes and in a wooden sheath, itself wrapped and sewn in a cloth envelope. Contrary to the submission that the presence of a kirpan would damage the school environment, the Court explained that it was, in fact, the absolute prohibition that would have this effect, by sending "the message that some religious practices do not merit the same protection as others."[54] By contrast, the Court reasoned, "accommodating Gurbaj Singh and allowing him to wear his kirpan under certain conditions demonstrates the importance that our society attaches to protecting freedom of religion and showing respect for its minorities."[55]

So this religious practice is entitled to legal tolerance. But note that before arriving at this conclusion, the Court has cast the meaning of Multani's religious expression in a form consistent with law's understanding of religion, whether that comports with his understanding or not.

---

53  *Multani, supra* note 33.
54  *Ibid* at para 79.
55  *Ibid*.

The logic of the section 2(a) analysis says that Multani's religious expression is constitutionally cognizable because it is an aspect of an "individual's self-definition and fulfilment and is a function of personal autonomy and choice."[56] Although it takes place at school, this religious practice is an expression of individual difference, does not touch the domain of public reason, and does not threaten the autonomy, choice, or equality of any others. Sheathed, sealed, and tucked away inside the folds of young Multani's clothing, religion does not threaten any of the values or structural commitments of the rule of law. *Multani* holds that this religious difference will be "tolerated," but the underlying message is that it will be tolerated because it conforms to law's understanding of religion and does not meaningfully grate upon any of the central cultural commitments of Canadian constitutionalism. In this way, even as it tolerates, law asserts its cultural superiority and performs the dominance of public norms.[57] The message sent is that Multani's religion should be tolerated because it ought not to be of genuine public concern.

What, on the other hand, is the message sent when the law curbs religious freedom? In *B(R)*[58] discussed in chapter 2, the religious freedom issue was whether the government of Ontario had interfered with the religious liberties of Jehovah's Witness parents by overriding their decision not to permit a blood transfusion for their infant child. The majority of the Court accepted that this decision was an expression of the parents' religious freedom as protected by section 2(a). When, however, the judges turned to the section 1 analysis, they reasoned that the state's actions were justified limitations on this religious freedom. The judges explained that the child had "never expressed any agreement with the Jehovah's Witness faith" and that respect for the child's

---

56 *Amselem, supra* note 26 at para 42.
57 Brown notes that the object of tolerance is always marked "as naturally and essentially different from the tolerating subject." Brown, *supra* note 2 at 15. She explores the way in which this core dynamic within tolerance has the effect of legitimating the state and its role in reproducing the dominance of certain groups, while having profound identity effects for the "tolerated." Although his explanation of the mechanism is different, Robert Paul Wolff similarly complains of the maintenance of social dominance as one of "the covert ideological consequences" of pluralism and tolerance as ideals of social policy. Robert Paul Wolff, "Beyond Tolerance" in Robert Paul Wolff, Barrington Moore Jr & Herbert Marcuse, eds, *A Critique of Pure Tolerance* (Boston: Beacon, 1965) 3 at 39ff.
58 *B(R), supra* note 32.

autonomy demanded that she be allowed to "live long enough to make [her] own reasoned choice about the religion [she] wishes to follow,"[59] if any. The parents had found the limit of legal tolerance at the border of individual autonomy and choice. There was simply no way that the Canadian constitutional rule of law would cede the necessary territory to make room for the parents' sincerely held ethical and epistemological commitments. The message sent in *B(R)* is that, in the presence of a religious difference that actually challenges the fundamental commitments of the Canadian constitutional rule of law, tolerance is at an end.

This overall point comes through powerfully in *R v NS*, the 2012 Supreme Court of Canada's decision addressing whether a sexual assault complainant and witness should be permitted to wear a face covering – her niqab – while testifying in court.[60] Given that the issue arose in the context of a criminal trial, one in which the accused's fair trial right and right to full answer and defence were engaged alongside the complainant's freedom of religion claim, the Supreme Court held that a somewhat different doctrinal approach to analysing the competing interests was appropriate.[61] The majority's reasoning nevertheless preserves the economy of legal toleration that I am describing, this time showing religious difference being reasoned about within the frame of the structural and aesthetic commitments of the rule of law. Having applied the expansive *Amselem* sincerity test[62] to find that NS's freedom of religion was engaged by the prospect of a judge ordering her to remove her niqab, the balance of the decision centred on whether and when, assessed within the baseline commitments of the criminal trial, having a witness's face covered would be, in effect, tolerable. The majority of the Court explained that it was unwilling to set aside

---

59  *Ibid* at para 231.

60  2012 SCC 72, [2012] 3 SCR 726 [*NS*].

61  Chief Justice McLachlin explained, *ibid* at para 7, that given that "[t]wo sets of *Charter* rights are potentially engaged – the witness's freedom of religion (protected under s. 2(a)) and the accused's fair trial rights, including the right to make full answer and defence (protected under ss. 7 and 11(d))," it would be appropriate to apply the framework used in publication ban cases (the "*Dagenais/Mentuck*" framework) used "for identifying and resolving rights conflicts that arise at common law." Like the section 1 analysis, if there is a genuine conflict between the two claimed rights, this framework ultimately asks a judge to arrive at the constitutionally appropriate result by weighing the salutary and deleterious effects at issue in the case.

62  The *Amselem* subjective sincerity test for whether a claimant's right under section 2(a) of the *Charter* is engaged is described in chapter 2.

"the long-standing assumptions of the common law"[63] regarding the importance of seeing a witness's face to the proper conduct of cross-examination and to the assessment of credibility, meaning that any time a niqab-wearing witness's evidence was contested, the accused's fair trial rights would be in play. Chief Justice McLachlin explained that, if there is no way of dissolving or avoiding this clash of rights, such cases would turn on a proportionality analysis. In *NS*, the deleterious effects of being asked to remove her niqab were as high as one could imagine: the practice was important to the complainant, the state's interference was substantial, and the overall context of the case was a prosecution of sexual crime. Yet weighing on the other side of the scales, the majority explained, is the fact that "[t]he right to a fair trial is a fundamental pillar without which the edifice of the rule of law would crumble."[64] As such, if the evidence is important in the case and if credibility is at issue, the niqab will likely have to be removed.[65] In the result, according to the majority judgment,[66] when might a witness be permitted to wear a niqab when giving evidence in a Canadian court? Only when that evidence is uncontested or peripheral; otherwise put, only when the religious practice does not really matter to the law.

A similar dynamic emerges from two cases that touch upon the role of religion in the provision of public education. In both cases, the Court chose to decide the issue in administrative law terms, but in both cases, extensive resort was made to the constitutional status of religious freedom and the rights contained in and values reflected by the *Charter*. In *Trinity Western University*,[67] examined in chapter 2 in the discussion of law's religion as "private," the Court was called upon to review the BC College of Teachers' refusal to certify the university's education program, thus preventing its graduates from serving as public school teachers. Recall that the basis for the College of Teachers' decision was the fact that Trinity Western required all students to sign a code of conduct

---

63  *NS, supra* note 60 at para 22.

64  *Ibid* at para 38.

65  *Ibid* at para 44.

66  Justice LeBel (Rothstein J concurring) would have given even more weight to the traditions of the common law, foreclosing any possibility that a witness could give testimony wearing a niqab. Justice Abella, dissenting, would have allowed greater room for the accommodation of the niqab.

67  *Trinity Western University v British Columbia College of Teachers*, 2001 SCC 31, [2001] 1 SCR 772 [*TWU*].

in which they agreed to refrain from practices "that are biblically condemned," including "homosexual behaviour."[68] The College of Teachers held that it would be contrary to the public interest to approve the program of an institution whose students had to sign a document that reflected beliefs so inconsistent with the non-discrimination and equality principles of the *Charter* and human rights legislation. In quashing this decision, the Court explained that even if it was fair to impute this religiously based belief to those who signed the code of conduct, until there was evidence that teachers acted upon these beliefs in the public schools, the College of Teachers' decision was an unfair limitation of the students' religious freedom. Trinity Western and its students were entitled to religious tolerance. But what were the conditions of this legal tolerance? The Court explained that, in such matters, "the proper place to draw the line … is generally between belief and conduct."[69] So long as the issue was belief held within a private religious school rather than practice manifested in a public institution, the discriminatory religious views would be tolerated. *TWU* was interpreted as a "win" for the religious group in question. Yet the underlying logic of the decision is that tolerance was in order inasmuch as the religious beliefs comported with law's understanding of religion as dominantly a private issue and could be contained within law's architectural commitment to the public/private divide.

Although it concerned interestingly similar issues to *TWU*, in *Chamberlain* the claims of religion "lost" when tested against a legislative demand that public education be conducted on the basis of "strictly secular and non-sectarian principles."[70] As I explained earlier in this volume, in *Chamberlain* the Supreme Court quashed the decision of the school board to ban the use of books that depicted same-sex parented families in the kindergarten/grade one curriculum, a decision based on the religious sentiments of a group of parents in the school district.[71] In arriving at this decision, the Court made clear that the role of the board as a public decision-maker and the role of individual parents were fundamentally different. Although the demand for "secularism" did not entirely prohibit religious concerns within the community from

---

68  *Ibid* at para 4.
69  *Ibid* at para 36.
70  *Chamberlain*, *supra* note 28 at para 18.
71  See the discussion of *Chamberlain* in the discussion of space in chapter 1 and of law's sense of religion as private in chapter 2.

informing the board's decision-making, the Court emphasized that the board's public role demanded that it "must not allow itself to be dominated by one religious or moral point of view, but must respect a diversity of views."[72] Furthermore, its decision would have to be guided by the public values reflected in the *Charter*, including the strong constitutional value of equality, a value to which the board had inadequately attended. This case imparts the message that, although religion is a legitimate, perhaps even laudable, component of private life, it must not be the dominating consideration in public decision-making. The presence of religious influence in the formation of public education policy must be circumscribed by the powerful public law value of equality. In short, the deep logic of this decision is that this expression of religion is impermissible because it fundamentally offends law's conception of the public/private divide; once in the public realm, religion had to comply with the value of equality that has been so deeply internalized in Canadian constitutional culture.

A pattern appears in *Multani*, *B(R)*, *NS*, *TWU*, and *Chamberlain*: to the extent that religion can be contained within the structural and aesthetic commitments of the constitutional rule of law, interpreted as comporting with its values and read as consistent with its understanding of religion, tolerance is the mode of cross-cultural engagement. The grant of tolerance is based on the implicit judgment that the cultural differences found in the "tolerated" really ought not to bother the law. The point at which religion transgresses these commitments and defies these conceptions is the point at which tolerance gives way to the forceful imposition of the culture of Canadian constitutionalism.

This is certainly not law's self-understanding in matters of constitutional law's treatment of religious diversity. Judges, for example, understand their analyses and debates with one another as being about the genuine potential for the law to "make room" for religion. It is in this vein that Justice Abella speaks of an "evolutionary tolerance for diversity and pluralism" characteristic of Canadian legal multiculturalism.[73] But I have proceeded from the assumption that law's internal account is already afflicted by a double blindness to its own cultural nature and to the cultural way in which it renders religion. Canadian constitutional law is deeply committed to a self-presentation as

---

72 *Chamberlain, supra* note 28 at para 28.
73 *Bruker v Marcovitz*, 2007 SCC 54 at para 1, [2007] 3 SCR 607 [*Bruker*].

neutral and, concomitantly, free from particular cultural commitments. Acceptance of this self-presentation is precisely the means by which law is set "above culture," the configuration that I have argued is at the root of the failure of the conventional story about the interaction of religion and constitutionalism. Accordingly, my interest is in generating an account that can illuminate the way in which the dynamic between law and religion can be experienced by those living within religious cultures.[74]

In his essay "Tolerating the Intolerable," Bernard Williams refers to an apparent form of tolerance in the history of the relationship among various churches and denominations within the Christian world. One means of managing this pluralism was to assert that, despite seeming differences, all of these brands of Christianity were, in essence, the same. Since all were ultimately concerned with the same goals, one need not care much about the details of what the other believed. Although Williams acknowledges that this solution produces certain practical political goods, he cautions against an excessively sanguine evaluation of this state of affairs, stating that "as an attitude, it is less than toleration. If you do not care all that much what anyone believes, you do not need the attitude of toleration, any more than you do with regard to other people's tastes in food."[75] Instead, the attitude being relied upon beneath the language of toleration is, in truth, indifference.

As I have described it, Canadian constitutionalism treats religion with just such a tolerance as indifference. Insofar as religious culture either produces no apparent conflicts with what centrally matters to the law or the basic ways in which law understands the world, toleration is the mode of engagement. Yet this kind of tolerance ends at the point at which the religious culture genuinely begins to grate on the values, practices, and ways of knowing of Canadian constitutional culture. When religious practice actually starts to *matter* to the law by

---

74 Minow, *supra* note 3 at 421, notes that "[s]ecular humanism, from the vantage point of certain religious subcommunities, is not a solvent of tolerance for all points of view but a conflicting belief system that threatens the integrity and viability of their own culture." Accordingly, she argues that the idea of tolerance must be re-thought in such a way as to "include the vantage point of members of traditional subgroups that do not share the dominant liberal commitments to individual choice, experimentation, and value relativism" (440).

75 Williams, *supra* note 39 at 67. Halberstam, *supra* note 43 at 192, puts it somewhat differently, but in a way that echoes with my analysis: "Tolerance is paradigmatically exemplified when one allows a *meaningful* challenge to a deeply-felt conviction" [emphasis in original].

challenging something central to the culture of law's rule, we begin to see the depth and force of law's commitments. Legal tolerance of religion re-enacts the public/private divide that is so central to law's culture. The law is able to tolerate those religious beliefs and practices that exert little pressure on the public norms and commitments of Canadian constitutionalism. There is an irony in this point. The rhetoric of multiculturalism is usually levied against a vision of religious and cultural difference as a purely private matter. I am suggesting that, while in certain ways resisting the easy relegation of difference to the private sphere, the invocation of legal tolerance has the simultaneous effect of, in other ways, shoring up that border between the public and private. As Wendy Brown writes, "Tolerance of diverse beliefs in a community becomes possible to the extent that those beliefs are phrased ... as being constitutive of a private individual whose private beliefs and commitments have minimal bearing on the structure and pursuits of political, social, or economic life."[76] When the law can no longer be indifferent – when the religious belief or practice begins to trouble the law – we encounter the cultural limits of legal toleration.

This designation of a religious belief or practice as something that "troubles the law" triggers an interesting symbolic economy. Sometimes these issues crystallize around practices about which the symbolic stakes are, ex ante, symmetrically high for both law and religion. Law's tolerance may run out precisely at the point that it matters most to the religious culture. *B(R)*, the Jehovah's witness blood transfusion case, is an example. Yet even if the religious expression is less central to the culture in question, the symbolic stakes are not, in the result, so different. Once marked as a matter of cultural significance to the law, the religious practice assumes deep importance to the religious culture because the practice has become a site for negotiating the relationship between cultures.[77] For this reason, we sometimes see practices not at

---

76 Brown, *supra* note 2 at 32. See also Talal Asad, *Formations of the Secular: Christianity, Islam, Modernity* (Stanford, Cal: Stanford University Press, 2003) at 199. Writing of the force of the state conception of the private and public within modern secularism, Asad observes, "From the point of view of secularism, religion has the option either of confining itself to private belief and worship or of engaging in public talk that makes no demands on life. In either case such religion is seen by secularism to take the form that it properly should have. Each is equally the condition of its legitimacy."

77 The debate about the hijab in France is a sharp example of this symbolic economy, showing how a particular practice can become a kind of synecdoche for the cultural negotiation between religion and constitutionalism.

the self-understood core of a religious tradition suddenly embraced as uniquely definitional of a given religious culture. This describes the dynamic in *TWU*[78] well, in which the demand to sign a heterosexist code of conduct in order to gain entrance to a teacher training program became a rallying point for certain arguments about the status of Christianity in modern Canadian public life. In such a case, the practice in question has become the emblem of something larger than itself: the power and politics of engagement with the culture of the Canadian constitutional rule of law. At such points there is felt to be genuine difference; yet it is at such points that toleration as indifference runs out and the structural and cultural reticence of law to give anything up of significance takes shape.

Law's tolerance as indifference is neither simple nor without virtue.[79] Recall the constitutional logic employed when analysing whether an aspect of religious culture that might appear to chafe on the commitments of the liberal rule of law ought to be tolerated: before limiting the right, the courts should carefully consider whether the religious expression that is producing the apparent conflict can actually be satisfyingly digested within the values and commitments of the rule of law. This reflective process demands a continual refinement and perhaps even expansion of the realm of indifference. Law asks itself to reconsider and reconfigure the geography of indifference using its own categories, like the private/public, and its own values, like autonomy and choice. Perhaps what we thought, on first glance, was objectionable is actually something that we can convince ourselves we should not really mind after all. At first blush, the code of conduct at issue in *TWU* appears beyond the pale when seen through the values dear to the culture of Canadian constitutionalism. On reflection, though as always within the boundaries of law's structural and normative commitments, its aesthetic frame, and its conception of religion, the Court concluded that the

---

78 *TWU, supra* note 67.

79 Being either myopically critical or overly aspirational can lead us to take for granted more modest but nevertheless very real political goods. In this vein, in Bernard Williams, "Realism and Moralism in Political Theory" in Geoffrey Hawthorn, ed, *In the Beginning Was the Deed: Realism and Moralism in Political Argument* (Princeton, NJ: Princeton University Press, 2005) 1 at 2, n 2, Williams chastises Rawls for his repeated use of the phrase "mere *modus vivendi*": "The very phrase 'a mere *modus vivendi*' suggests a certain distance from the political; experience (including at the present time) suggests that those who enjoy such a thing are already lucky."

belief was sufficiently private so as not to trouble the law. On the face of the situation that arose in *Amselem* – a condo owner's religiously motivated desire to erect a sukkah on his balcony despite condo regulations to the contrary – Mr Amselem was simply breaching the aesthetic rules to which he had agreed when he purchased his unit. Nevertheless, irrespective of whether Mr Amselem viewed his religion in this manner, the Court ultimately concluded that, because it was both essentially a matter of private expression of preference and "integrally linked with an individual's self-definition and fulfilment and is a function of personal autonomy and choice,"[80] the law ought not to object to this practice.

Seen in this way, modern legal tolerance takes place within the margins set by culturally conditioned points of incommensurability between law and religion at which law will move to a posture of enforcement or "conversion." Although very much consistent with the roots of liberal thinking about the nature of political tolerance of religion,[81] this is a more modest practice than suggested in the conventional story about legal tolerance and multiculturalism. But by imposing the reflective demand to learn about the nature and contours of the religious practice or commitment appearing before it and asking whether it should really matter that much to the law, there is the abiding prospect that the law will stay its violent hand in more cases than it otherwise might, absent this demand for the refinement of indifference. Alexander Bickel famously described the political importance of a court's declaration that legislation is "not

---

80  *Amselem, supra* note 26 at para 42.
81  Locke's *Letter Concerning Toleration* is still often invoked as the basis for modern political practices of religious toleration. It is interesting to recall that Locke himself was counselling only a relatively modest form of toleration that fundamentally inhered in leaving alone that which ought not to concern civil society. The kind of accommodation imagined in the prevailing story of legal multiculturalism is entirely foreign to his concept of toleration. Of the three limits to tolerance that he outlined, the first was the border of public law and the general interests of society. He held that no magistrate should tolerate conduct that contravenes laws of general application enacted for a valid public purpose, stating, "No Opinions contrary to human Society, or to those moral Rules which are necessary to the preservation of Civil Society, are to be tolerated by the Magistrate." John Locke, *A Letter Concerning Toleration*, ed by James H Tully (Indianapolis: Hackett, 1983) at 49. What were the other two limits? First, a magistrate need not tolerate religion that counsels loyalty to a foreign political power, and second and most emphatically, "Those are not at all to be tolerated who deny the Being of a God" (51).

unconstitutional."[82] The tacit or express declaration that a particular religious expression is "not intolerable" is, similarly, a kind of political intervention with virtues and significance that it would be a mistake to ignore. There are goods to be found – a space of liberty and cultural diversity – in this margin created by an expanded and continually refined indifference. As I will explore in chapter 4, an assiduously cultivated liberal "tolerance as indifference" is a meaningful virtue.

Nevertheless, when toleration of a given religious commitment would require the law to actually cede normative or symbolic territory, law trumps it in the name of procedural fairness, choice, autonomy, or the integrity of the public sphere; with this, tolerance gives way to conversion. Dallmayr describes conversion as a form of universalism of ideals, and perhaps this description provides some insight into why religion and law have been locked for so long in this form of cross-cultural encounter. Like religion, the rule of law is concerned with shaping meaning and it is not modest in its claims. As I have argued in this book, living within the Canadian constitutional rule of law is living within a culture that makes claims about the relevance of space and time, about the source and nature of authority, and about what is of value about the human subject. So, too, does religion. Law and religion are, in this sense, homologous; through norms, rituals, institutions, and symbols both constitute meaningful worlds. This homology means that religious claims and practices can come into direct competition with those of the law.[83] And within a liberal democratic rule of law, the

---

82  Building his argument for the more robust judicial exercise of the "passive virtues," Bickel observed that although finding a statute "not unconstitutional" is not a compliment, "neither is it an inconsequential appreciation. To declare that a statute is not intolerable in the sense that it is not inconsistent with the principles whose integrity the Court is charged with maintaining – that is something, and it amounts to a significant intervention in the political process." Alexander M Bickel, *The Least Dangerous Branch: The Supreme Court at the Bar of Politics*, 2nd ed (New Haven, Conn: Yale University Press, 1986) at 129. Though more modest than the robust ethic of tolerance that is invoked in the story of legal multiculturalism, a tolerance based in indifference, in Bickel's terms, *is something*.

83  As I have suggested in chapter 2, depending upon the shape of their symbolic, normative, and practical commitments, religious cultures will be more or less comprehensively challenging to the law. As Réaume puts it, "One minority community may adhere to a way of life that is comprehensively incompatible with the lifestyle of others; another may differ in relatively contained spheres." Denise G Réaume, "Legal Multiculturalism from the Bottom Up" in Ronald Beiner & Wayne Norman, eds, *Canadian Political Philosophy: Contemporary Reflections* (Oxford: Oxford University Press, 2001) 194 at 195.

tacit but powerful assumption is that law's understandings and commitments must prevail. Perhaps this instinct is natural enough – every culture assumes that its way of seeing is basically correct; however, in the modern liberal state, law is uniquely privileged and equipped to enforce its sense of centrality. As a result, at such points of strong cultural difference law asserts its dominance, and law's asserted dominance is experienced as a conversionary effort for those committed to the religious culture's way of being in the world. These are the unacknowledged cultural stakes of law's interaction with religion.

"Once we see that the rule of law is a way of being in the world that must compete with other forms of social and political perception, a range of questions about the actual forms and character of this competition open up. We need to study the places at which conflict emerges and the ways in which law has succeeded or failed in these conflicts."[84] Studying the points of conflict between the culture of law's rule and religious forms of being in the world has revealed an unacknowledged complexity. Law's self-understanding speaks of multiculturalism, toleration, and accommodation as the key principles. Yet, as I have shown, this brand of toleration depends upon a kind of indifference (no matter how cultivated) and at precisely the points at which the law can no longer be indifferent – tellingly, often at the points at which the stakes for the religious culture concerned have themselves become the highest – its conversionary aspirations appear. The conventional story that we tell about the nature of tolerance and accommodation in a multicultural society is far more comforting but far less satisfying.

### The Limits of Theory

Modern theories of multiculturalism have tended to offer approaches that suffer from the same limitations as the conventional legal account.[85] These theories also suffer from the explanatory failure that I have

---

84 Paul W Kahn, *The Cultural Study of Law: Reconstructing Legal Scholarship* (Chicago: University of Chicago Press, 1999) at 84–5.

85 Réaume, *supra* note 83, stands out as a strong counter-example. In her compelling plea for a "bottom-up" approach to legal multiculturalism, Réaume states that "[t]he challenge of multiculturalism is that of negotiating the relationship between two or more normative systems within a political unit" and emphasizes that "[t]he legal system is also a normative system – a complex set of rules guiding behaviour and facilitating human activity" (194).

described, giving neither a strong account for the realities and difficulties of the conflict of law and religion nor a meaningful sense of the stakes of this encounter for these cultures. Although there is no dearth of theoretical ink spilled on the question of the just means of approaching the interaction of law and religious culture, this explanatory shortfall and its conceptual root can be seen by turning to consider two accounts that have been influential in the Canadian scholarly debate.

In *Multicultural Citizenship*, Will Kymlicka takes up the project of developing a liberally defensible theory of minority rights.[86] Kymlicka's theory is based largely on the distinction between internal and external restrictions: minority cultures should be afforded external protections that enhance the equality of these groups within broader society; they should not, however, be afforded support for internal restrictions that limit the autonomy and freedom of members.[87] Based as it is in liberalism, Kymlicka's idea of tolerance is bounded by the goods of equality, autonomy, and freedom and guided by the categories of the inside/outside, private/public. He offers a theory of legal multiculturalism that is different in its details from the conventional legal approach, but one that similarly affords tolerance only to the extent that the given culture comports with the values, symbols, and practices of the law, which is itself set apart from the multicultural fray. As with the legal approach, the boundaries of toleration are always already set, and set in a fashion that structurally insulates the norms and assumptions of legal culture from meaningful engagement and contestation. Thus, "[l]iberals can only endorse minority rights insofar as they are consistent with respect for the freedom or autonomy of individuals."[88] Beyond this point of

---

86 Will Kymlicka, *Multicultural Citizenship: A Liberal Theory of Minority Rights* (Oxford: Clarendon Press, 1995).

87 Martha Minow suggests an approach very similar to Kymlicka's inside/outside model. She offers the concept of "oppression" as the figurative canary in the mineshaft, arguing that, although measures taken to protect the subgroup from the dominant culture are acceptable forms of tolerance, "[w]hen a religious subgroup implements practices that systematically subordinate some of its members, such as women and children, deference to the self-government and autonomy of the groups, from the vantage point of a liberal society, is not well-placed." Minow, *supra* note 3 at 433. She argues that a theory and approach centred on oppression could serve as a "winning solution" to the seemingly intractable difference between the perspectives of the dominant social groups and subgroups because the demands for tolerance made by the subgroup and the demand for conformity to certain liberal norms made by dominant society are joined in their concern with anti-oppression (436).

88 Kymlicka, *supra* note 86 at 75.

tolerance as indifference, in the face of illiberal cultures, the general rule is that the ultimate goal of liberals should be "to seek to liberalize them."[89] Kymlicka offers a full working out of a liberal theory of multiculturalism, demonstrating how far liberalism can go while working within its own categories. In so doing, he reflects in the realm of liberal theory the same limits of toleration that I have identified in liberal legal discourse. He demonstrates the degree to which the discourse of tolerance "is an exercise of hegemony that requires extensive political transformation of the cultures and subjects it would govern."[90]

As is the case with legal multiculturalism, Kymlicka's brand of tolerance as indifference flows from his initial conception of culture. Kymlicka states that, for his purposes, a culture is understood as "an intergenerational community, more or less institutionally complete, occupying a given territory or homeland, sharing a distinct language and history."[91] A state is multicultural if it is composed of members who belong to or have emigrated from different nations, "and if this fact is an important aspect of personal identity and political life."[92] Two features of this conception of culture are of particular salience. First, it is "thin" in the sense that there is no ideological, symbolic, or belief-based component. In this respect, religious minorities might well find themselves fitting awkwardly within this understanding of culture, just as I have argued they might struggle to fit themselves within law's understanding of religion. Second, law does not figure in as a culture. The law oversees and moderates, but does not itself engage as a cultural

---

89  *Ibid* at 94. See also Joseph Heath, "Immigration, Multiculturalism, and the Social Contract" (1997) 10 Can JL & Jur 343 at 359, in which Heath argues that "it would be highly misleading to regard this as a form of assimilation. The correct term would be *liberalization*, which we can use to denote an endogenous transformation that renders cultural value systems institutionally compatible with a plurality of other cultural forms" (359). Like Kymlicka's, Heath's argument is compelling from within the horizon of liberal thought, which is – it must be emphasized – the horizon that both overtly seek to occupy. But whether ultimately liberally defensible or not, as experienced by a religious culture, "liberalization" as the "endogenous transformation that renders value systems institutionally compatible with a plurality of other cultural forms" may have a decidedly euphemistic ring to it.

90  Brown, *supra* note 2 at 202. Brown critiques Kymlicka's approach for "deploying Kantian liberalism in a distinctly non-Kantian way: that is, treating tolerance as a means for transforming others rather than as an end in itself, and treating individual autonomy as a bargaining chip rather than as an intrinsic value" (202).

91  Kymlicka, *supra* note 86 at 18.

92  *Ibid*.

actor in, the multicultural terrain that he imagines. By locating culture on only one side of the issue, Kymlicka obscures the dominance and power at play in the cross-cultural encounter between law and religion, even as his theory performs it.

Another Canadian theorist of multiculturalism whose ideas have been influential in debates about the management of religious difference, Ayelet Shachar takes a critical stance towards Kymlicka's liberal theory of multiculturalism, arguing that his external/internal binary is inadequate inasmuch as it "fails to provide a workable solution in practice for certain real-life situations involving accommodated groups."[93] She rightly notes that his approach could exacerbate the invidious position of historically disadvantaged or vulnerable members "where the external protections that promote justice between groups uphold the very cultural traditions that sanction the routine in-group maltreatment."[94] Yet in attending to these concerns, Shachar's theory of "transformative accommodation" ultimately replicates the mode of cross-cultural engagement between law and religious pluralism found in Kylmicka's work and Canadian jurisprudence alike.

Shachar's laudable goal is to find an approach to multiculturalism that shows a concern for cultural integrity but that is also sensitive to the distributional social costs borne primarily by women when such cultures are afforded too much autonomy from the influence of public norms. She wants to add the individual to the normally dyadic debate about multiculturalism that focuses on the interaction of the state and the group. Shachar is critical of the "unavoidable costs" approach to multiculturalism, which holds that if you want to take multiculturalism seriously you must simply bear the costs of possible in-group

---

93 Ayelet Shachar, *Multicultural Jurisdictions: Cultural Differences and Women's Rights* (Cambridge, UK: Cambridge University Press, 2001) at 18. Shachar also notes, at 26, the curious fact that Kymlicka "pays relatively little attention to religiously defined minority communities," a point of limitation in Kymlicka's theory and on which Shachar is much stronger. For her detailed critique of Kymlicka, see 29–32. Equally critical of Kymlicka on this point, Modood's "institutional integration approach" to multiculturalism that centres on "a moderate and evolutionary secularism based on institutional adjustments" is quite close to Shachar's theory in certain other key ways. In particular, Modood similarly adopts an essentially functional/institutional conception of law and assumes the values of public law as the framing limits of his approach. Tariq Modood, *Multiculturalism: A Civic Idea* (Cambridge, UK: Polity Press, 2007) at 79.

94 Shachar, *supra* note 93 at 18.

rights violations. Yet she is equally critical of the "reuniversalized citizen option," which says that the only way to resolve this tension is to pick the primacy of individual rights over group cultural integrity. Shachar's preferred approach leans heavily on the concept of "jurisdiction" to achieve a form of balance that she calls "transformative accommodation." In this vision of multiculturalism, there are overlapping, non-exclusive jurisdictions shared between the state and the group, leading both to compete for the loyalties of citizens and, thus, creating incentives for both to speak to the needs of individuals within minority groups. Yet as she unfolds her theory of transformative accommodation through "joint governance," we see that the transformation envisioned is really one whereby religion is forced to change to take better account of the normative commitments of Canadian constitutional culture. On the one hand she claims that "[t]he object of harnessing this individual-group-state dynamic is not to strip communities of their distinctive *nomos*."[95] This claim is important to her because she wants to respect group and individual commitment to traditional cultures. Yet on the other hand, she argues that the very goal of this model of transformative accommodation – a goal reflected in her chosen label itself – is to make in-group practices that are inconsistent with the equality and autonomy norms of the constitutional rule of law very costly and, thus, to "create incentives for the group to transform the more oppressive elements of its tradition."[96] The goal is to "lead to the internal transformation of the group's *nomos*."[97] Ultimately, Shachar's is a conversionary model of encounter.

Shachar offers an imaginative and legally crafty alternative model of multiculturalism that admirably seeks to ameliorate the in-group social costs too often borne by women. But it is also a good example of a theory that concerns itself with *nomoi* that are "over there" while failing to account for the extent to which the manipulation of concepts of jurisdiction and authority is a project that is itself firmly embedded in a *nomos*, this time law's *nomos*. Throughout, Shachar presents law in an overwhelmingly functional light – as a tool for managing culture – and in so doing elides the presence and influence of law's culture in

---

95  *Ibid* at 126.

96  *Ibid*.

97  *Ibid* at 124. In this respect, Shachar's approach is a kind of anti-pole to Tully's, who seeks to reorient legal practices towards recognition and understanding of the other group's *nomos*. Tully's approach is discussed more fully below.

her analysis. Indeed, as I discussed in chapter 1, Shachar's controlling concept – jurisdiction – is itself a history- and meaning-laden way of understanding the intersection of authority and space that is specifically tied to the culture of law's rule.[98] In effect, she imposes law's symbolic categories in service of enforcing values that are, themselves, internal to the culture of Canadian constitutionalism. Shachar's theory is fairly described, in Dallmayr's terms of cross-cultural encounter, as a model of gradual or "soft" conversion. She assumes certain boundaries regarding the tolerable beyond which cultural transformation is the goal. Her means of protecting these boundaries is simply more nuanced and gradual than a direct imposition or outright demand for change. Yet whether the product of "toleration," "internal vs. external restrictions," or the hyper-cultural legal concept/symbol of jurisdiction, the process of being forced to change to comply with a given cultural system can be experienced as a power dynamic characteristic of conquest, conversion, or assimilation. This experience demands attention as a meaningful aspect of the politics of legal multiculturalism. As was the case for Kymlicka's avowedly liberal theory, Shachar's underlying understanding of law hides the intercultural dimensions of the encounter between law and religion.

Despite their differences, these two models are both exemplary of conventional theorizing about legal tolerance as it relates to religious difference. Both amount to theoretical reconfigurations of the geography of legal tolerance, preserving the cultural dynamics that I have described. The efforts of those like Kymlicka and Shachar to soften law's force and to expand and refine the margins of indifference are important. Nevertheless, these accounts essentially replicate the pattern of engagement found beneath law's story about religious pluralism. Each views law as something quite apart from the cultures that it is overseeing. Accordingly, each assumes limits to tolerance and means of managing difference that do not force law to critically examine its own

---

98 One is reminded of Cover's observation, "We construct meaning in our normative world by using the irony of jurisdiction, the comedy of manners that is *malum prohibitum*, the surreal epistemology of due process." Robert M Cover, "The Supreme Court 1982 Term – Foreword: *Nomos* and Narrative" (1983) 97 Harv L Rev 4 at 8–9. See also Richard T Ford, "Law's Territory (A History of Jurisdiction)" (1999) 97 Mich L Rev 843 at 855: "[J]urisdiction is … a way of speaking and understanding the social world"; Kal Raustiala, "The Geography of Justice" (2005) 73 Fordham L Rev 2501.

symbolic and normative assumptions or seek cross-cultural understanding; as a result, toleration tends to expire at precisely the point
at which these assumptions are threatened. This produces a strong
tendency to collapse into assimilationist modes of engagement with
religious and cultural groups. Herein lies the source of the durable and
protracted tensions between religious communities and the constitutional rule of law, tensions that we have seen build in recent years. If,
under the banner of multicultural tolerance, religious diversity is being
subject to conversionary force at precisely those points of meaningful
cultural difference, the experience of those minority cultures is not one
of respect for pluralism and accommodation of diversity but, rather, of
coercion at the hands of the law.

What other forms of legal tolerance of religious difference can be
imagined? An apparently promising candidate would be an approach
to constitutionalism based on theories of dialogical engagement. This
is the approach that Dallmayr urges. Drawing strongly from Todorov
and Gadamer, Dallmayr imagines a form of cross-cultural tolerance
that is "understood not as outgrowth of neutral indifference but as the
appreciation of otherness from the vantage of one's own life world (and
its prejudgments)."[99] A constitutional order dedicated to the ethics of
dialogic cross-cultural engagement would be more than an attempt
at normative agreement. Rather, it would manifest "a willingness to
enter the border zone or interstices between self and other, thus placing
oneself before the open 'court' of dialogue and mutual questioning."[100]
"Wedged between surrender and triumph, dialogical exchange has an
'agonal' or tensional quality which cannot be fully stabilized."[101] For
theorists such as Dallmayr, Todorov, Gadamer, Connolly, and others, it
is this kind of cross-cultural encounter that could navigate the "precari-
ous course between (or beyond) assimilation and atomism."[102]

Taken from the heights of political and hermeneutic theory, this
approach to the encounter between cultures seems both to offer a more
satisfying recognition of the stakes for law and religion and to chart
a possible new path. So can we find the answer to the cultural limits

---

99  Dallmayr, *supra* note 9 at 55–6.
100  *Ibid* at 47.
101  *Ibid* at xviii.
102  *Ibid* at 33. See e.g. William E Connolly, *Pluralism* (Durham, NC: Duke University
       Press, 2005) at 125 [Connolly, *Pluralism*]: "In a relation of agonistic respect, some-
       thing in the faith, identity, or philosophy of the engaged parties is placed at risk."

of legal toleration in these contemporary dialogic theories of cross-cultural interaction? I argue that we cannot. The distinctive character of the culture of contemporary constitutionalism limits the possible modes of cross-cultural encounter and precludes the kind of dialogical engagement imagined in these theories.

One of the common features of dialogic theories of cross-cultural encounter is the demand that each culture face a degree of risk in the encounter with the other. Dallmayr, for example, describes dialogic encounter as requiring that both cultures open themselves to mutual questioning and a "willingness to 'risk oneself.'"[103] Connolly requires that "something in the faith, identity, or philosophy of the engaged parties is placed at risk."[104] Otherwise put, a precondition to this form of cross-cultural understanding is the "risk of self-critique and self-decentering, which entails that 'one has to believe that one could be wrong.'"[105]

One of the distinctive features of law's rule is that it is, in a very particular and practical respect, never wrong. This is not, of course, to say that law never admits error and makes changes accordingly; it surely does this. The point, rather, is that the ultimate authority and correctness of the law is never in question for itself. Even when it accepts that the application of its principles was misguided in a given case or that certain rules should adjust to account for changes in society, there is a permanent conservation of law's authority and, contrary to the dialogic demand to be open to the risk of "self-decentering," a structurally perduring affirmation of its place at the centre of the management of all public dispute. As Kahn explains, "Law does not win localized victories over action; it cannot tolerate defeats as long as they are balanced by victories. ... Law never explicitly concedes defeat; it never admits powerlessness."[106] Thus, although it might, in a given case, concede that the line between the private and public was incorrectly drawn in the past, we cannot imagine Canadian constitutional rule of law disavowing the organizing significance of this conceptual trope. Similarly, although the legal configurations necessary to protect individual autonomy and choice might be hotly debated in the law, the normative primacy of

---

103 Dallmayr, *supra* note 9 at xviii.
104 Connolly, *Pluralism, supra* note 102 at 125.
105 Dallmayr, *supra* note 9 at 48–9.
106 Paul W Kahn, *The Reign of Law: Marbury v Madison and the Construction of America* (New Haven, Conn: Yale University Press, 1997) at 167.

these values is never itself at stake. If this is true, it leaves little room for dialogic engagement.

When religious cultures claim the protection of rights that are a part of modern legal multiculturalism, there is no openness to the possibility that the law might not be the ultimate arbiter of the terms and conditions that will settle this dispute.[107] Another way of seeing this very particular feature of the culture of contemporary Canadian constitutionalism is in linguistic terms. In his plea for a form of dialogic constitutionalism that can better serve the needs of deep diversity, Tully concludes that "if there is to be a post-imperial dialogue on the just constitution of culturally diverse societies, the dialogue must be one in which the participants are recognised and speak in their own language and customary ways. They do not wish either to be silenced or to be recognised and constrained to speak within the institutions and traditions of interpretation of the imperial constitutions that have been imposed over them."[108] My argument is that once cast as a claim about legal tolerance or accommodation within contemporary Canadian constitutional culture, the possibility of the use of a language other than law's own is foreclosed. The language becomes the language of rights constitutionalism, privileging the terms *autonomy, equality,* and *choice.* The salient concepts are those of the public and the private, jurisdiction, and standing. The ways become the way of legal process, and the matter is firmly set within the institutions and traditions of interpretation of the culture of law's rule. It is little wonder that for many cultural groups, including Indigenous North Americans, dialogue with the law under the rubric of legal multiculturalism can be

---

107  This is where Forst's argument for a "respect conception" of toleration founders when applied to the interaction of religious culture and the culture of Canadian constitutionalism. See Forst, *supra* note 40. Forst's reflections are provocative and helpful for many contexts in which toleration is salient (he calls for attention to the "*context of toleration*" himself at 314) but, in his analysis, law is always a background consideration or mechanism, never a tolerating agent itself. As a result, some of his predicate demands for toleration based on respect seem structurally inconsistent with the constitutional rule of law as it is currently constituted.

108  Tully, *supra* note 10 at 24. See also Charles Taylor, "Understanding and Ethnocentricity" in *Philosophy and the Human Sciences: Philosophical Papers 2* (Cambridge: Cambridge University Press, 1985) 116. Tully is not alone in seeking a new form of constitutionalism that centres on dialogic forms for engagement. See Sheppard, *supra* note 49 at 486: "For a growing number of scholars ... dialogue across group-based differences is the essence of constitutionalism."

so deeply unappealing. As Tully himself concludes, "[A] just dialogue is precluded by the conventions of modern constitutionalism," including the assumption that understanding the other inheres in translating cultural claims "within an inclusive language or conceptual framework in which it can then be adjudicated."[109] Indeed, it is this conclusion that impels Tully's search for a means of entirely reconceiving and reconstructing modern constitutionalism.

The meaningful form that law gives to experience is not the only form imaginable; indeed, law's meanings are always and essentially in competition with other ways of imagining and interpreting the world – other cultures.[110] This is what makes the dialogic form of cross-cultural encounter so attractive. But, in a liberal constitutional democracy, the law is privileged among such possible interpretations, and it is this feature of legal culture that seems to put this more promising form of cross-cultural encounter out of reach.[111] Once cultural conflict is

---

109  Tully, *supra* note 10 at 56. Whereas I have discussed the impact of this modern constitutional dynamic as one of "assimilation," Tully describes it as the imposition of uniformity. Tully expresses this point with characteristic clarity and force when he concludes that "the language of modern constitutionalism which has come to be authoritative was designed to exclude or assimilate cultural diversity and justify uniformity" (58).

110  As Van Praagh writes in her penetrating discussion of the role of the Court in matters of diversity and pluralism, "Despite a tendency for students and practitioners of law to presume its paramount importance, the law is but one set of influences that direct our behaviour and relationships." Shauna Van Praagh, "Identity's Importance: Reflections of – and on – Diversity" (2001) 80 Can Bar Rev 605 at 608.

111  Van Praagh, *ibid* at 617, notes that although law is "never solely determinative of our relations and interactions … its presence is significant in our collective existence and our shared experience of living our pluralist lives. When it offers a judgment, it not only adjudicates the particular dispute before it, but traces the contours of our liberal, diverse society." There is a strand of scholarship that goes further, seeing law's meaning-shaping capacity as so powerful as to destroy or threaten to destroy other forms of the social. See e.g. Stanley Diamond, "The Rule of Law Versus the Order of Custom" (1971) 38 Social Research 42 at 44: "No contemporary institution functions with the kind of autonomy that permits us to postulate a significant dialectic between law and custom. We live in a law-ridden society; law has cannibalized the institutions which it presumably reinforces or with which it interacts"; Jürgen Habermas, *The Theory of Communicative Action*, translated by Thomas McCarthy, vol 2 (Boston: Beacon Press, 1984) at 356–73, arguing that "juridification" constitutes a colonization of the lifeworld. Habermas understands juridification "from the viewpoint of the uncoupling of system and lifeworld and the conflict of the lifeworld with the inner dynamics of autonomous subsystems" (358).

embedded within the language of rights and legal accommodation, by its very nature the constitutional rule of law exerts a kind of structural dominance immiscible with dialogic forms of cross-cultural encounter. So, in the end, whereas disregard for the shape and character of the culture of contemporary Canadian constitutionalism consigns legal multiculturalism to a form of cultural assimilation, seeing the precise nature of this contemporary legal culture forecloses the possibility of the promising dialogic form of cross-cultural engagement.

## Conclusion: The Challenges of Seeing Culture

The challenging cultural dynamics of legal tolerance that I have explored in this chapter can be found wherever legal multiculturalism is invoked as a tool for the management of religious pluralism. Consider the framing adopted in *Bruker v Marcovitz*,[112] a case that confronted the Supreme Court of Canada with the very difficult question of how the law should relate to religious beliefs and practices relative to marriage and divorce. Specifically, the Court was called upon to compensate a claimant for the harms that she suffered arising from her ex-husband's failure to deliver on his agreement to provide her with a *ghet*, the divorce document required by Jewish law. Justice Abella set the tone and context for the majority decision: "Canada rightly prides itself on its evolutionary tolerance for diversity and pluralism. This journey has included a growing appreciation for multiculturalism, including the recognition that ethnic, religious or cultural differences will be acknowledged and respected. Endorsed in legal instruments ranging from the statutory protections found in human rights codes to their constitutional enshrinement in the *Canadian Charter of Rights and Freedoms*, the right to integrate into Canada's mainstream based on and notwithstanding these differences has become a defining part of our national character."[113] One sees here the extent to which contemporary legal debate about the interaction of law and religion remains very much in thrall to the conventional account of legal multiculturalism. Justice Abella paints a picture that reflects the familiar and comforting story about the

---

112 *Bruker, supra* note 73. Discussed more extensively in chapter 4, this case was fundamentally a *Quebec Civil Code* case concerning the law of obligations, but it squarely raised the question of the relationship between religious traditions and contemporary Canadian law.

113 *Ibid* at para 1.

management of religious pluralism by means of legal tolerance. Yet her words also betray the way in which this story fails to adequately reflect the deeper and more complex reality of the interaction between law and religion. With the suggestion that the constitutional protections for religious, cultural, and ethnic differences exist to facilitate integration into a Canadian mainstream "based on and *notwithstanding*" these elements of pluralism, Justice Abella gestures, perhaps unwittingly, towards the true character of legal tolerance. The dominance and indifference that I have argued characterizes the cross-cultural engagement of law and religion shows itself in the midst of the official rhetoric of legal tolerance.

The conceptual core of this chapter is the suggestion that the conventional story about the relationship between the rule of law and religious cultures depends upon the conceit of law's autonomy from culture, a conceit that hides the fact that law is not merely an overseer or instrumental force in the politics of multiculturalism. When analysed as a cultural force in its own right, the boundaries of legal doctrines of tolerance and the nature of the cross-cultural interaction between religion and law become more transparent. What is thereby revealed is that legal tolerance is a more modest posture towards religious pluralism than the rhetoric of multiculturalism would suggest. In the end, law's tolerance is a form of cultivated and continually refined indifference towards religious cultures, and when the boundaries of this indifference are found – when religious belief and practice begin to push on the law in a way that would force contemporary constitutionalism to cede, reconsider, or revise its core cultural commitments – this posture of tolerance collapses into one that is assimilationist or conversionary. Understood in terms of cross-cultural encounter, the stakes of this interaction are high, and it becomes clear that the culture of law's rule is structurally positioned and very much prepared to assert its dominance.

Understanding the meeting of law and religion as a cross-cultural encounter breaks down our complacencies about what it means for law to accommodate strong forms of religious pluralism and exposes the cultural limits of legal toleration. It is a more honest account of what is occurring between law and religion under the rubric of legal multiculturalism. Yet with the limits exposed by this more satisfying account of the cross-cultural nature of law's interaction with religion in clear view, the horizon is somewhat bleak when we turn to look for other, more satisfying modes of engagement. It may be that Tully is correct that the only way of properly attending to deep cultural diversity is by reconstructing another form of constitutionalism. Such a form would have to differ fundamentally in its basic assumptions and self-understanding from the one that we currently possess.[114] Or, as I will explore in the next chapter, perhaps we can do no better than to work to expand the borders of our indifference. If so, we are faced with the continuing challenge of explaining why, at points of genuine friction, the culture of law's rule is entitled to dominance over other forms of culture. Irrespectively, if viewing – with detail and precision – the interaction of law and religion as a cross-cultural encounter causes us to see this experience of encounter as decidedly fraught and durable, then it is an account that has served us well because it has helped us to see better.

---

114 See Tully, *supra* note 10. Tully's reconstructed/reimagined form of constitutionalism is built upon the three conventions of mutual recognition, consent, and continuity. He argues that, in order to adequately recognize cultural diversity, rather than the prevailing approach to constitutionalism, a "constitution should be seen as a form of activity, an intercultural dialogue in which the culturally diverse sovereign citizens of contemporary societies negotiate agreements on their forms of association over time in accordance with the three conventions of mutual recognition, consent and cultural continuity" (30).

# Chapter 4

# The Stories We Live By: Religious Difference and the Ethics of Adjudication

… theories are at work in the decisions of the world, and we had better understand them.

George Grant, *English-Speaking Justice*[1]

For even though theory may be serving us, the social scientists, simply as an instrument of explanation, the agents whose behaviour we are trying to explain will be using (the same or another) theory, or proto-theory, to define themselves. So that whether we are trying to validate a theory as self-definition, or establish it as an explanation, we have to be alive to the way that understanding shapes practice, disrupts or facilitates it.

Charles Taylor, "Understanding and Ethnocentricity"[2]

"Life," wrote nineteenth-century German philosopher Wilhelm Dilthey, "is the basic fact that must form the starting point of philosophy."[3] For Dilthey, lived experience is the bedrock of human understanding. It is that "behind which we cannot go."[4] A central figure in the development of philosophical hermeneutics, one of Dilthey's singular contributions

---

1 George Grant, *English-Speaking Justice* (Toronto: House of Anansi Press, 1998) at 47 [originally published in 1974].
2 Charles Taylor, "Understanding and Ethnocentricity" in *Philosophy and the Human Sciences: Philosophical Papers 2* (Cambridge: Cambridge University Press, 1985) 116 at 116 [Taylor, "Understanding and Ethnocentricity"].
3 Wilhelm Dilthey, *Selected Works: The Formation of the Historical World in the Human Sciences,* Rudolf A Makkreel & Frithjof Rodi, eds, translated by Rudolf A Makkreel & William H Oman, vol 3 (Princeton, NJ: Princeton University Press, 2002) at 280.
4 *Ibid*.

was to build from this essentially phenomenological insight to argue for the centrality of narrative to the way in which we understand our worlds. This is true, for Dilthey, whether one is concerned with the way in which an individual interprets and understands his or her own life or whether, engaged in the *Geisteswissenschaften* ("human sciences"), one is attempting to understand social institutions and collective life. For those concerned with interpreting the expressions of humans' understandings of their worlds – in ritual, institutional, sociological, or legal form – Dilthey held that the process of generating meaning from experience is essentially the same as the way in which individuals, awash in a present of infinite complexity, make sense of their experiences.

Understanding – for Dilthey, the process of generating meaning from this complex lived experience – is a process of continual narration and re-narration. The individual meets the world equipped with a story that enables him or her to make sense of the present in relation to a remembered past and imagined future. Life experiences gather significance from their narrated relationship to our pasts and futures. Structurally, these experiences derive meaning from the larger story of our worlds, but there is also a reciprocal demand made by experience upon the pre-existing narrative. It may be that the whole must be retold in a way that makes sense in light of present experience. Equipped with this retelling, we then turn back to encounter life again. This circulating dynamic of meaning between part and whole, story and event – the hermeneutic circle[5] – is, for Dilthey, the basic mechanism of human understanding, the means by which we understand our lives.

Dilthey argued that this concern with *understanding* was, similarly, the core of the human sciences. "The method pervading the human sciences," Dilthey wrote, "is that of understanding and interpretation. All the functions and truths of the human sciences are gathered in understanding."[6] The project of understanding our collective lives involves the creation of narratives that help to make sense of our social and political experiences. Yet these stories that we tell about our social, political, and legal lives are not merely questions of understanding. They have implications for the way in which society is shaped. Equipped with

---

5  Dilthey drew this notion of the hermeneutic circle from Ast and Schleiermacher, before him. "Meaning," wrote Dilthey, "is the special relation that the parts have to the whole within life. We recognize this meaning, as we do that of the words in a sentence, by virtue of memories and future possibilities." *Ibid* at 253.

6  *Ibid* at 226.

these narratives that lend a particular significance or meaning to the phenomena of social life, we are led to act in particular ways, judge in particular fashions, and thus to create particular political realities. When these social and political realities – the experiences of collective life – prove undesirable or unsatisfying, we must return to expose, critique, and demand re-narration of our larger stories.

Without recognizing the affinity to Dilthey's thought, many contemporary scholars have engaged in precisely this kind of critique of prevailing narratives about social phenomena. Troubled by the unsatisfying political configurations that they yield, scholars have questioned the conventional narrative of marriage and family, the story about the aetiology of crime and techniques of crime control, and the link between the free market and economic prosperity, to name just a few examples. Among the most forceful of these critiques have been radical reassessments of stories that we tell about the place of religion in modern life. Tomoko Masuzawa has retold the story of "world religions" as a story about European colonialism rather than the pluralization of religious consciousness in the West.[7] Talal Asad's retelling of the genealogy of the concept of the "secular" and the idea of "secularism" is another powerful case in point.[8] This book is an effort to re-narrate the story that we use to make sense of the interaction between religion and Canadian constitutionalism. As Dilthey anticipates, the need for this re-narration arises from lived experiences that suggest certain inadequacies of the story we tell about the interaction of law and religious difference in contemporary Canada.

To understand better is rarely, however, to be more comforted. My account disrupts constitutional law's self-presentation as a field that can serve as a neutral meeting ground for diverse forms of culture. It does so principally by denying law the conceit that it is autonomous from – that it stands apart from and above – culture. There is no doubt that it is unsettling to see law's Procrustean instinct, conceptually forcing religion into conformity with law's own assumptions, values, and meanings. To see this is to understand that law never really meets religion in its cultural richness and variety; rather, the interaction is always

---

7  Tomoko Masuzawa, *The Invention of World Religions: Or, How European Universalism was Preserved in the Language of Pluralism* (Chicago: University of Chicago Press, 2005).
8  Talal Asad, *Formations of the Secular: Christianity, Islam, Modernity* (Stanford, Cal: Stanford University Press, 2003).

mediated by law's projected image of religion's nature and value. By placing law as a participant in the cultural fray, one can then examine the particular mode and character of cross-cultural encounter between constitutional law and religion. Again, it is unsettling to see that law's posture towards religion is far more forceful and normatively ambitious than is conveyed by prevailing accounts of law's role in the management of religious difference.

Met with these uncomfortable lessons, one might be tempted to inaugurate a project of legal reform. Such a response might be based, in part, on a sense that the results in some of the cases that I have described in this book are wrong. And so a reader might expect to find a final chapter that offers an alternative doctrinal scheme for law's analysis of religious freedom and equality claims, or perhaps one that argues for a structural reconfiguration of the guiding commitments involved in the culture of Canadian constitutionalism. Yet as I explained in chapter 1, those kinds of responses involve a perspective and methodological posture altogether different from the one I assume in this volume. This book is concerned with appreciating what the contemporary interaction of law and religion reveals about the experience of living within and encountering the culture of law's rule. This approach is about understanding Canadian constitutional law as a way of framing and shaping experience; it is not an enterprise of imagining how it might otherwise be.[9]

To abstain from this kind of project of reform is not, however, to eschew all critical reflection arising from the account that I have offered. Two important normative questions still offer themselves, both asking what this different framing might mean for our legal and political practices around the meeting of law and religion. First, is my account actually one that we ought to embrace in the way that we approach and discuss issues of religious diversity and law in Canada? That an account helps one to understand better does not necessarily mean that its insights should inform our public understandings. I have argued that Canadian constitutionalism is best understood as a cultural form,

---

9  "[A] cultural form is never a failed form of something other than itself. The rule of law exists first of all as an experience of meaning, a way of being in the world for the individual and the community. It is not the product of someone's or some community's effort to be something, which has been only partially achieved." Paul W Kahn, *The Cultural Study of Law: Reconstructing Legal Scholarship* (Chicago: University of Chicago Press, 1999) at 92 [Kahn, *The Cultural Study of Law*].

that it proceeds under its own cultural conception of religion, and that there are cultural limits to the practices of legal tolerance. Should these understandings actually inform the way we talk publicly about religious pluralism? Or might we be better off carrying on with the old story about law's relationship to religion?

Second, what might an appreciation of the cross-cultural dynamics at play in the encounter between religion and Canadian constitutionalism mean for the role and responsibilities of legal actors? In particular, constitutional adjudication of religious claims has been at the centre of my analysis. Equipped with a new account of the nature and dynamics of the interaction of law and religion, different ways of conceiving of the function of the judge may emerge and new adjudicative virtues may come into focus. If we adopt this new story, what is the nature of the virtuous conduct of judges tasked with adjudicating claims arising from the cross-cultural encounter between law and religion?

I take up these two questions in this final chapter. My argument is that the conventional narrative has certain insidious effects that can be exposed and palliated by understanding the relationship between law and religion in the way that I have suggested. Accordingly, there is value in seizing this new story rather than continuing on in the grip of the old. Furthermore, this new account offers a fresh perspective on how judges might approach religious diversity from within the culture of law's rule and how they should go about doing so. And so, based on the account that this work has generated, this chapter does make an argument for a certain kind of reform. It is not, however, reform of the culture of Canadian constitutionalism or the doctrinal rules governing the analysis of religious freedom and equality. It is, instead, a change in the stories we tell about the nature of legal multiculturalism, and an associated shift in our understanding of the practices and virtues of adjudication.

## Why the Conventional Account Is Not a Noble Lie

In the opening paragraph of *English-Speaking Justice*, George Grant's fierce critique of the sufficiency of contractarian liberalism to sustain an adequate sense of justice, Grant pauses to reflect upon the meaning and novelty of the word *technology*. Grant's particular interest is in scientific technology and its capacity to expose facts about the world that pose ontological questions that liberalism does not have the resources to answer, resulting in a "terrifying darkness which has fallen upon modern justice."[10] But in the first steps that he takes towards this distressing conclusion, Grant observes that in the word *technology* one finds the novel idea of a link between making and knowing – of *techne* and *logos*. Technologies are tools by which a particular way of knowing is married with a creative instinct, a project of making.

Our public stories are social technologies. They marry ways of understanding the social world with the project of social creation. The conventional public story that we tell about the relationship between law and religious diversity is one such social technology. This story purports to know certain things both about religion and about the constitutional rule of law. On the strength of this knowledge we engage in a project of social creation. "Religious multiculturalism" is not a state of affairs; rather, it is a craft. It contains within it that admixture of knowing and making that characterizes technology. But if this conventional story is a social technology, what kind of social technology is it? By what process does it work and what are its effects? My claim is that the conventional public story about the interaction of law and religion is a technology of *depoliticization* that has a certain set of undesirable effects on the larger body politic. It is a dangerous technology that has negative impacts upon the very issue it seeks to resolve: the challenge of religious pluralism within liberal constitutionalism.

As Wendy Brown describes it, to depoliticize "involves removing a political phenomenon from comprehension of its *historical* emergence and from a recognition of the *powers* that produce and contour it."[11] This kind of divestment of social phenomena from their constituting context of history and power relations means that "there is no acknowledgment of the norms, the subject construction, the subject positioning, or the civilizational identity" at stake in the phenomenon in question.[12] The technologies of depoliticization are multiple. Liberalism effects this kind of depoliticization by means of privatization and an emphasis on individualism, thereby pushing explanations for social phenomena away from power and history, towards questions of self-making. Merleau-Ponty argued that one could recognize what he called "aggressive liberalism" precisely "by its love of the empyrean of principles, its failure to ever mention the geographical and historical circumstances to which it owes

---

10  Grant, *supra* note 1 at 86.
11  Wendy Brown, *Regulating Aversion: Tolerance in the Age of Identity and Empire* (Princeton, NJ: Princeton University Press, 2006) at 15 [emphasis in original].
12  *Ibid* at 19.

its birth, and its abstract judgments of political systems without regard for the specific conditions under which they develop."[13] Market rationality is also a discourse of depoliticization, for "[w]hen every aspect of human relations, human endeavor, and human need is framed in terms of the rational entrepreneur or consumer, then the powers constitutive of these relations, endeavors, and needs vanish from view."[14]

The conventional account of law's role in the management of religious difference depoliticizes by treating the encounter between law and religion as a relationship of management rather than a cross-cultural interaction in which the dynamics of power are always at issue.[15] Understanding the constitutional rule of law as separate from culture withdraws it from its historical construction and embeddedness, thereby removing the burden of knowledge of its own contingency and specificity. Law is essentialized and naturalized as something fundamentally different and separate from culture, while religion is essentialized and naturalized in the shape understood by law. To depoliticize religious pluralism within legal multiculturalism means reading the experience of religious difference in public life as the product of private struggles with neutral law rather than an instance of social and cultural conflict that calls for political analysis and responses. One sees this effect of the conventional story in Canada when the political and cultural contours of the interaction of law and religion have seeped out from under the edges of this controlling account, as they did in the 2003–6 debate about sharia-based arbitration in Ontario and in the controversy surrounding the proposed "Charter of Quebec Values" in 2013–14.[16] In both instances, the role of history, culture, and power in the use of law

---

13  Maurice Merleau-Ponty, *Humanism and Terror: An Essay on the Communist Problem*, translated by John O'Neill (Boston: Beacon Press, 1969) at xxiv.

14  Brown, *supra* note 11 at 18.

15  As Kahn explains, seeing that the rule of law is a form of understanding in competition with other cultural forms means that the dynamics of power are central to a cultural study, but "power" understood in a particular way: "Because of this competitive diversity in the forms of understanding, every cultural form must be analyzed from a perspective of power. Power here is not a function of violence, coercion, and exclusion – although all are elements of a legal regime. Rather, power is the capacity to exclude or dominate competing ways of understanding the event." Kahn, *The Cultural Study of Law*, *supra* note 9 at 66.

16  Anna C Korteweg and Jennifer A Selby's volume *Debating Sharia: Islam, Gender Politics, and Family Law Arbitration* (Toronto: University of Toronto Press, 2012) is an excellent critical guide to the "sharia debate" in Ontario.

to address religious difference became obvious and undeniable. As a result, these events were interpreted as exceptional crises in the relationship between law and religion, rather than seen for what they were: focused expressions of the ordinary, everyday character of the interaction of law and religion.

Speaking of the way in which processes of depoliticization efface this everyday influence of power and history, Brown explains that "[w]hen these two constitutive sources of social relations and political conflict are elided, an ontological naturalness or essentialism almost inevitably takes up residence in our understandings and explanations."[17] As I have shown, this is precisely what has become of our explanation of law's interaction with religion. An ontological naturalness has been taken up in respect of both law and religion. Law and religion simply *are* as they are presented in legal analysis and this breeds complacency about our current account of the relationship between constitutionalism and religious difference, despite its descriptive insufficiency.

But perhaps depoliticization is a good thing. The political involves certain dangers and passions that it is tempting to suppress. There are winners and losers and the stakes are high. To make manifest the power, history, and culture at stake in the relationship between law and religion is to put these features of the political into open circulation. And so perhaps there is virtue in concealing the power and culture at play in the relationship between law and religion. Even if the conventional public story is not descriptively accurate, maybe we live better together if we continue to proceed under that account. Perhaps, in short, the conventional story is a kind of noble lie.

In what follows, I want to take that possibility seriously, arguing, to the contrary, that there are real harms for a diverse constitutional democracy to carry on in the thrall of a public story whose effect is to depoliticize by obscuring the cultural core of the interaction of law and religion. As a matter of sustaining a healthy democracy and valuing political respect, I suggest we do not live better under the conventional account. Rather, as Brown argues, the attempt "to remove from the political table as much of our putatively 'natural' enmity ... undercuts the cultivation both of shared citizen power and of a substantive public sphere devoted to the fashioning of democratic political culture and community."[18]

---

17  Brown, *supra* note 11 at 15.
18  *Ibid* at 89.

I want to expose, in particular, four concrete effects of this depoliticiza-tion of the relationship between law and religion in Canada: it leads to over-reliance on adjudication, it deeply alienates religious communities, it exposes public life to particular vulnerabilities, and – perhaps most significantly – it breeds disingenuous forms of political engagement.

## Tethering Religious Difference to the Limits of Adjudication

The conventional account of law's relationship to religious difference turns on an optimistic image of the managerial capacities of the law and the accommodative potential of rights-based multiculturalism in mat-ters of religious difference. When faced with matters of political and social difficulty, the promise of a malleable, accommodative, a-cultural law is a seductive one, offering escape from our ethical anxieties. In this way, the depoliticizing effect of the conventional account is linked to the juridification of issues of religious difference. This is yet another instance of the legalization of politics found not only in modern Cana-dian constitutionalism,[19] but also as a characteristic feature of modern governance. As Comaroff and Comaroff explain, the contemporary appeal to legal instruments and procedures to address matters once remitted to democratic politics is a neoliberal response to the challenges of deep ethical difference. Consistent with my argument in this chapter, they argue that the apparent neutrality of legal language seems to offer an appealing respite from the political and social challenges produced in conditions of cultural diversity: "[T]he language of legality offers an ostensibly – note, *ostensibly* – neutral register for communication across lines of social and cultural cleavage. ... The pragmatic promise of jural instruments is that they have the capacity to create equivalence amidst contrast, providing a currency that appears to allow for the transac-tion of incommensurable interests across otherwise intransitive bor-ders. Thus it is that law offers a common denominator, and a means of imposing coherence, in socially and ethically incoherent circumstances. Therein, in part, lies its hegemony – although in itself, it is anything but

---

19 See e.g. Andrew Petter, "Legalise This: The *Chartering* of Canadian Politics" in James B Kelly & Christopher P Manfredi, eds, *Contested Constitutionalism: Reflections on the Canadian Charter of Rights and Freedoms* (Vancouver: UBC Press, 2009) 33; Joel Bakan, *Just Words: Constitutional Rights and Social Wrongs* (Toronto: University of Toronto Press, 1997); Michael Mandel, *The Charter of Rights and the Legalization of Politics in Canada*, revised ed (Toronto: Thompson Educational, 1994).

a guarantor of equality."[20] It is natural (and common) enough, then, to focus upon rights discourse and constitutional law as a uniquely promising means of resolving issues of religious difference and public policy. The conventional story thus has a funnelling effect on public debate, offering an attractive legal casting of questions about religious difference and thereby channelling them before the courts.

Doing so, however, tethers the issue to the imaginative and practical limits of adjudication within the culture of law's rule. Some of those limits are those explored at length in chapters 2 and 3 – the cultural limits of legal tolerance itself. As cases like *Wilson Colony*[21] and *AC*[22] made clear, once submitted to the processes of adjudication, religion will be rendered in a form congenial to the law and we will be bound to the humble practices of legal toleration.

But there are also structural and remedial limits at play, with legal processes offering only a select range of outcomes to highly complex social disputes, as well as epistemological limits at work, with the rules of evidence (and the tyranny of relevance) stripping away salient dimensions of the experience of religious difference and diversity. When such questions are funnelled before the courts, other means of addressing the question of deep religious difference are either foreclosed or substantially displaced. In this way, tethering the question of religious difference to the courts has steep opportunity costs. Taking these issues up in a more overtly political context offers at least the promise of a more searching, inclusive, and diverse debate unconstrained by the adversarial structure and evidentiary rules of adjudication. Moreover, the range of solutions possible from a creative political process is vastly broader than that available within the institutional constraints of adjudication, a point that has become clear in matters ranging from health care to Indigenous rights. In short, the conventional story about the interaction of law and religion breeds over-reliance on the problem-solving capacity of law and adjudication, directing issues of religious difference before the courts and marginalizing other possible forms of multicultural justice.

---

20  Jean Comaroff & John L Comaroff, *Theory from the South: Or, How Euro-America Is Evolving toward Africa* (Boulder, CO: Paradigm, 2012) at 145 [emphasis in original].
21  *Alberta v Hutterian Brethren of Wilson Colony*, 2009 SCC 37, [2009] 2 SCR 567 [*Wilson Colony*].
22  *AC v Manitoba (Director of Child and Family Services)*, 2009 SCC 30, [2009] 2 SCR 181 [*AC*].

The processes and structures of rights adjudication did not serve the Hutterites of Wilson Colony terribly well, a community that had, until 2003, enjoyed the benefits of a political answer to the demands of religious diversity. The political decisions that engendered and shaped this case were effaced as religion was turned into a matter of individual autonomous choice, and creative solutions to the problem were sloughed off as the adversarial and binary (valid-invalid) nature of constitutional adjudication determined the range of remedial options. The majority's decision in *Bruker v Marcovitz*,[23] discussed again later in this chapter, vindicated the claims of a woman whose husband had denied her a religious divorce. The result of her twenty-six-year ordeal was a legal precedent and an award of damages in the amount of $47,500 (before legal fees). Yet the Supreme Court decision has nothing substantial to say about the informal, low-level exercises of coercion and power at work in issues of marriage and divorce within religiously orthodox communities – the much more difficult and pressing social and political issue raised by the fact of religious law operating within Canadian society. This is not to fault the Court's judgment; rather, it is a natural artefact of dealing with such issues through adjudication. Or consider the *Trinity Western University*[24] case, concerning the accreditation of TWU's teacher training program by the BC College of Teachers in light of the school's exclusionary code of conduct. The deeper political structure of this issue involved questions about the relationship of private Christian post-secondary education to public life, the conditions precedent for the discharge of a public role in a diverse society committed to equal treatment, the history and purpose of human rights exemptions for religious institutions, and a whole set of local questions about the way that post-secondary institutions in the interior of British Columbia had collaborated in the preparation of schoolteachers. Once the issue was set within the terms of a section 2(a) claim about religious freedoms, the Court resolved the case on the basis of a distinction between religious belief and discriminatory conduct, holding that the BC College of Teachers had acted without the right kind of evidence. *TWU* is often interpreted as a "win" for that religious community; yet, having sidestepped the deeper structural issues at work in the case by funnelling

---

23  2007 SCC 54, [2007] 3 SCR 607 [*Bruker*].
24  *Trinity Western University v British Columbia College of Teachers*, 2001 SCC 31, [2001] 1 SCR 772 [*TWU*].

the question before the courts, the essential issue reappeared a decade later in debates about whether the code of conduct precluded TWU from having an accredited law school. Addressing the immediate issue through the adjudicative process meant that, in the intervening years, no meaningful attention was given to the deeper questions regarding the relationships between private religious education, discrimination on the basis of sexual orientation, and the discharge of public duties.

My concern here is exposing the harms of carrying on with the conventional account of law's role, location, and capacities in the management of religious difference. This close binding of the political and social challenge of religious diversity to the limits of adjudication is just the first such harm. Once the issue is firmly set within the courts and thereby tied to the logic and structures of rights-based adjudication, the stage is set for the conventional story about the interaction between law and religion to produce three further and, in some respects, more deeply pernicious effects, to which I now turn.

## The Alienation of Religious Claimants from the Political Community

In its fealty to the conceit of law's autonomy from culture, the conventional story imposes strong discursive constraints on adjudication. These constraints parallel one of the core aspirations of liberal political theory: the desire to keep public reason thoroughly non-partisan. The fear that motivates the commonly asserted need for a public sphere divested of "comprehensive doctrines"[25] is that one who approaches the institutions of justice and finds a pre-existing conception of the good may suffer a form of alienation from the public sphere. Within this story, the institutions of law are mechanisms for social cohesion; whatever the various cultural disputes that might emerge in society, the hope is that if the conception of law and justice is sufficiently arid, it might just be a climate that is hospitable to all.

The advocate of the "noble lie" approach to the conventional story about law and religion worries that, even if it is true that Canadian constitutional law engages in the exercise of cross-cultural power when dealing with religion, the risks of making this overt are simply too great. If the law were to speak in ways that made its own cultural stance manifest, a religious individual or group would lose the necessary sense

---

25 John Rawls, *A Theory of Justice*, revised ed (Cambridge, Mass: Belknap Press of Harvard University Press, 1999).

that the law is capable of non-partisan justice. There is great risk, on this view, in a judge saying, "I have heard your claim but, from within the law's framework of meaning and significance, the law's commitments to the structure of experience and what is of value in the human, I cannot accede to your view." The litigant will walk away feeling that the law is not for her, that she cannot really be understood within the culture of constitutionalism. The good of loyalty to the conventional account is that it hides the partisan nature of the law. When stripped of its cultural nature, law becomes a kind of haven from the politics – the power, the history – surrounding it. To suggest that law present itself otherwise is to jeopardize an important point of social cohesion. Better to maintain the conceit that law stands apart from the cultural fray than to risk this kind of alienation.

In truth, it is the conceit that is deeply alienating.

Consider first the claimant who, under the conventional account, engages the adjudicative process and loses. Under this telling of the relationship of law to religious and cultural difference, the rule of law offers itself as a common meeting ground for – and despite the differences among – various cultural forms. Such a culturally non-partisan conception of the rule of law is always based on some sense of what reasonable people would view as fair and just, whether the device for arriving at these rules is imagining a state of nature, positing the original position, or leaning on the claims of proportionality. When the law is presented as non-partisan, non-historical, *non-cultural*, it is trading in the currency of reasonableness. When I come before this non-cultural law and lose, it is as if I have been invited behind the veil of ignorance and shown that – if only I could see things reasonably – I would concur with the result. As a reasonable member of the political community, I should see that the fair and just stand against me. On this account, the law's aridity is really an appropriation of my voice as a reasonable, dispassionate member of the political community. There is a certain alienation in this, but note that it is one suffered by any claimant who loses in court – it is not specific to the experience of the adjudication of religion.

The special alienation suffered by the religious claimant lies in the fact that, by hiding the cultural nature of the rule of law, the conventional account denies a salient reason for that loss. As a religious claimant, I lost not because the law has cultural commitments that are at odds with mine – a result that might lead me to politically engage and contest the partisan legal culture. Instead, neither my culture nor that of the law was a factor in the legal result. Worse than disputed or rejected, my culture is deemed immaterial. It is, of course, material to me; I am conscious of its ineluctable influence on the structure of my experience of the world and my sense of the good and true. Yet the conventional story precludes a legal debate about those stakes, about culture. This severs me from the law as a forum for public debate about what most concerns me and, hence, from an important source of political community and social cohesion.

The *Wilson Colony* case again serves as a useful illustration of this kind of effect. The bulk of the analysis in *Wilson Colony* focused on the proper approach to addressing questions of proportionality under section 1 of the *Charter*. Given the broad sincerity test for section 2(a) established in *Amselem*,[26] little analysis of the beliefs of the members of the Wilson Colony was necessary and, having passed through that generous portal, everything turned on the all-in assessment of whether the limit was reasonable/proportional. The constitutional din of whether the limit is reasonable, all things considered, muffles the particularities of the community, its beliefs, lifestyle, and practices. In the end, the Wilson Colony was unsuccessful not because the particular texture of its beliefs, lifestyle, and practices were carefully assessed but deemed incommensurable with the demands of public life, but rather because the Court held that the reasonable conclusion was that they retained a choice regarding their religious practices. To make the point squarely, would members of the Wilson Colony see themselves and their realities engaged with in the Court's reasoning?

The nature of this estrangement comes into even sharper focus when one recognizes that it does not depend on the result in a given case – interestingly, it occurs even if one wins. Even if I am successful in my religiously motivated claim, culture was irrelevant to the legal conclusion. If my position is legally acceptable, it is so *despite* my cultural commitments and only to the extent that I was capable of stripping my claim of the terms that make it meaningful to me in the first place.[27]

---

26 *Syndicat Northcrest v Amselem*, 2004 SCC 47, [2004] 2 SCR 551 [*Amselem*]. See the description of *Amselem* and this test in chapter 2.

27 James Tully, *Strange Multiplicity: Constitutionalism in an Age of Diversity* (Cambridge, UK: Cambridge University Press, 1995) at 39, makes an analogous point using an example from the realm of Indigenous engagements with constitutional law: "When, for example, Aboriginal peoples strive for recognition, they are constrained to present their demands in the normative vocabulary available to them. That is, they seek recognition as 'peoples' and 'nations,' with 'sovereignty' or a 'right of self-determination,' even though these terms may distort or misdescribe the claim they would wish to make if it were expressed in their own languages."

The "win" is not a product of cross-cultural understanding; rather, it turns on the successful suppression of the dimension of culture. In this sense, the alienation begins before I enter the courtroom. It happens at the very moment that I am forced to reframe my claim as one about reason and right, not about culture. As Tully puts it, "[T]he injustice of cultural imperialism occurs at the beginning, in the authoritative language used to discuss the claims in question."[28] The conventional story's commitment to an a-cultural conception of law, abetted by the juridification of questions of religious difference, estranges the religious claimant from law, a crucial instrument of political community.

The case of AC,[29] discussed earlier in this book, offers an evocative example of this effect. AC was the almost-fifteen-year-old girl who required a blood transfusion. As a Jehovah's Witness she would not consent to this treatment. The director of Child and Family Services apprehended her as a child in need of protection and sought authorization from the courts to order the transfusion on the basis that this was in her best interests as a child. AC challenged the legislation, which she claimed offended her religious freedom because it denied her the ability to make a decision consistent with her religious beliefs, irrespective of her maturity. The decision is fascinating in a number of dimensions, facets of which I will return to later in this chapter. For present purposes, most interesting is the way that the majority cast what was really at stake in the case. AC "won" inasmuch as the majority of the Court found that her views should be taken into account within the legislative scheme (thereby interpreting it in a way that rendered it constitutionally compliant). But her claim was recast in the language of adolescents having "an interest in exercising their capacity for autonomous choice to the extent that their maturity allows,"[30] and the legal solution was to ensure that the best interest of the child took into account this "decisional autonomy commensurate with [the young person's] maturity."[31] There is nothing especially religiously attuned about this analysis; the nature and quality of AC's beliefs do not figure at all in the majority's

---

28  *Ibid* at 34. In a manner sympathetic to my argument here, Tully goes on to note, at 35, that "[t]he language employed in assessing claims to recognition continues to stifle cultural differences and impose a dominant culture, while masquerading as culturally neutral, comprehensive or unavoidably ethnocentric."

29  *AC, supra* note 22.

30  *Ibid* at para 105.

31  *Ibid* at para 114.

reasons. AC "wins," but so too would have any adequately mature child arguing for the legal recognition of her exercise of autonomy. In the end, the case is not really about religion at all; in the hands of the law it becomes a question of perfecting a rationally generalizable claim about the exercise of autonomous choice. AC's particular beliefs – the specific and deeply religious motivations animating her claim – are legally irrelevant.

This is the insistently alienating effect of maintaining the conventional public story about law's engagement with religion. In an attempt to make justice arid enough to feel hospitable, the conventional a-cultural story opens up the potential for law to be a device for alienating the religious individual from the political community. To be sure, there are risks to calling upon the law to be more overt about its cultural nature. To do so repoliticizes the law and, hence, makes it yet another object for social contestation. Met with a story about law that is transparently cultural, one may invite increased political engagement over the commitments found in law. Whatever the risks involved in such a display, it keeps the religious individual engaged in and part of the common social practice of political debate and contestation. To use Chantal Mouffe's terms, it is better to have the religious actor as an "adversary" rather than an alienated "enemy," cast outside the common social practices.[32] Crucially, as adversaries, "while in conflict, they see themselves as belonging to the same political association."[33] Such a sense of common engagement despite cultural difference seems necessary to avoid the violence of cultural alienation and is, hence, important to a healthy and functioning democratic polity in the context of deep pluralism.

This pernicious effect of maintaining the conventional public story about law's engagement with religion is an effect borne directly by religious individuals or communities. Of course this kind of alienation also ramifies more broadly because it fractures a sense of political community and produces estrangement from legal institutions. But there is another more specific and fundamental sense in which maintaining

---

32 See Chantal Mouffe, *The Democratic Paradox* (London: Verso, 2000). Mouffe's thought is helpful in demonstrating the way that this kind of display of strong difference is essential to healthy democracy insofar as it turns enemies into adversaries.

33 Chantal Mouffe, *On the Political* (New York: Routledge, 2005) at 20. Mouffe writes that, understood in this way, "'the adversary' is a crucial category for democratic politics."

the story of an a-cultural law harms not just religious individuals and communities, but the constitutional rule of law itself.

## The Vulnerability of Law

The conventional account of law's role and nature in the management of religious difference makes law acutely vulnerable to partisan attack on the grounds of hypocrisy and disingenuousness. A religious individual or community met with the sets of cultural commitments and ways of understanding intrinsic to the law, and forced into the analytic mould in which religion is asked to fit, sees law's culture very sharply, indeed. The predictable result is the charge that although it purports to be above the cultural fray, the law is, in fact, partisan. This charge takes a number of forms: the "backlash" of the Christian religious right, which claims that law and its actors are liberally sectarian; non-Christian commentators who observe the thorough imbrication of Protestant sensibilities and conceptions of religiosity in the law; a liberal critique that the law has illegitimately enforced a vision of the good life. The essence of these charges is that the law claims to be one thing but is, in fact, something quite different; it claims to operate in one fashion but, in truth, works quite differently. And, of course, this allegation is quite right.

Recall Justice Ritchie's reasons in the *Brassard v Langevin* case with which this book opened. Faced with deciding whether the community advocacy of the Catholic Church during an election to the House of Commons constituted undue influence, Justice Ritchie concluded that this was not "at all a religious question";[34] rather, electoral law was a statutory civil right "pure and simple" and was, therefore, "simply a constitutional legal question."[35] To those involved in *Brassard*, the intervention of the courts was deeply cultural, intervening in and pronouncing upon fundamental questions of ontology and authority. Even if one views the result in that case as entirely legitimate, it is disingenuous to claim that the law was operating above the cultural fray, dealing simply in a common currency of constitutionalism.

The same is true of the many contemporary examples of cases involving claims about religious freedom and religious equality. To

---

34  (1877), 1 SCR 145 at 215 [*Brassard*].
35  *Ibid.*

the religious communities involved in such cases – indeed, to all those involved – these matters are emphatically about contending cultural visions, and when the law weighs in at the end of the day, it does so as a player in the realm of culture, complete with claims about ontology, authority, what is of value in the individual, and the nature of a good society. The only place that such decisions appear as non-partisan exercises of something like common constitutional reason is on the face of these judgments – in the public presentation of such matters consistent with the conventional narrative of legal multiculturalism. All those involved sense the wizard behind the curtain.

Ironically, then, the more the story about law is divested of cultural content the more open it becomes to cultural critique.[36] But this is only half of the picture. Thick substantive judgments are being made about the content of the law's positions. What resources does legal culture have to meet these objections? It has great difficulty formulating substantive ethical responses, because any such responses ultimately involve a cultural view from "somewhere" or demand a justificatory foundation in some conception of the good life – precisely what the a-cultural, liberal idea of law seeks to avoid. If it is to remain faithful to the conventional account, the law's response to these objections must take a disappointing, anaemic form, turning to language of procedural fairness, proportionality, and balancing. Confronted with substantive claims about justice and ethics, the law "is quite defenceless ... it has only proceduralism to fall back on, and thus cannot deliver compelling judgments about, or even interpret the meanings of, a polity's thorniest ethical or political dilemmas."[37] The a-cultural account not only opens up gaping vulnerabilities in the law to charges of cultural partisanship; fealty to it strips the law of the resources necessary to defend the normative judgments made by the social institution.

One might reply that, in modern Canadian constitutionalism, there is such a resource: appeal can be made to constitutional rights and that set of "*Charter* values" that are said to animate and regulate the

---

36 See Brown, *supra* note 11 at 94. Although concerned more broadly with liberalism's normative emptying of the public sphere, Brown explains that "[t]he commitment of liberalism to a public sphere uncontaminated by nonliberal moral discourses, whether explicitly religious or not, paradoxically makes it vulnerable to challenges to its imbrication with norm-based inequalities as well as to claims of fundamentalist or essentialist identity-based social movements."

37 *Ibid* at 93.

exercise of public power in Canada.[38] But this is really no response at all. The Supreme Court of Canada has offered various lists of the "*Charter* values," including "human dignity, equality, liberty, respect for the autonomy of the person and the enhancement of democracy."[39] But to appeal to the good of equality or the value of human dignity is to invite a debate about the demands of and basis for these principles, not to invoke a principle with a stable or settled content. As George Grant put it, "[W]hat is it about human beings that makes liberty and equality their due? ... why is justice that which we are fitted for, when it is not convenient? Why is it our good?"[40] Subject to the conceits of cultural neutrality, law has difficulty supplying answers to such questions.

The *AC* blood transfusion case is, again, exemplary. As incomprehensible as it might be to those outside her world view, AC had a thick story about the source of her human dignity and the value of her existence, with concrete implications for the most difficult choices to be made in her life. Simmering under the surface of the case, of course, is a substantive disagreement: standing against AC's view is a value-laden claim that the preservation of life and flourishing in this world is of ultimate good, a claim that is stitched deeply into the culture of the liberal rule of law.[41] And yet the legal answer to this conflict posed by the case? The Court responds – as it must, in fidelity to the conventional narrative – that what is really at stake here is a generalized claim about decisional autonomy calibrated to developmental maturity and that what we need here is a doctrinal fix: her world view should go into the "mix" as part of the decision about the best interests of the child.

The gap between the reality exposed in this book and the conventional account runs the risk not only of alienating religious groups, but also of enfeebling the constitutional rule of law. It exposes the law to attack as hypocritical in holding itself out as above culture but acting

---

38  *R v Salituro*, [1991] 3 SCR 654 at 675; see *Health Services and Support-Facilities Subsector Bargaining Assn v British Columbia*, 2007 SCC 27 at para 81, [2007] 2 SCR 391 [*Health Services*], for a list of *Charter* values. See also *R v Mabior*, 2012 SCC 47, [2012] 2 SCR 584, in which the *Charter* values of "equality, autonomy, liberty, privacy and human dignity" (para 22) are used to interpret the legislation in issue.

39  *Health Services, supra* note 38 at para 81. See also *Wilson Colony, supra* note 21 at para 88.

40  Grant, *supra* note 1 at 86.

41  See Robert A Burt, *Death Is That Man Taking Names: Intersections of American Medicine, Law, and Culture* (Berkeley: University of California Press, 2002).

in a thoroughly cultural fashion while prohibiting use of the normative resources needed to meet these charges. To embrace my account of the relationship between law and religion would reduce this vulnerability by acceding to the reality of history, power, and culture, thereby repoliticizing law's engagement with religion. Again, repoliticizing in this fashion has risks and poses struggles. In particular, this way of seeing matters raises the hard issue of why it is that law's culture enjoys a certain priority. Once law and religion are levelled as both cultural forms, what justifies the privilege and violence of the culture of Canadian constitutionalism? Though challenging, this question gets us closer to the heart of what is so difficult about the interaction of law and religion.

## The Creation of Proxy Debates

A final malign effect of the conventional story about the nature of constitutional law and its encounter with religion is the manner in which it engenders proxy debates. This is yet another blow that public life suffers from the depoliticization of law's engagement with religion, a blow that denies nobility to the lie of the prevailing account of law's role in the management of religious difference.

The conventional account places an obligation on judges to talk about contested legal and policy issues in terms divested of the kinds of symbolic and normative commitments that are always fundamentally at play in the constitutional rule of law. Law must present itself as starting from outside a particular framework of understanding – a particular culture. A strong reciprocal demand is placed on those who come before the law to match this form of discourse. To engage with the law, the private citizen must speak like the law, also divesting himself or herself of these encumbrances of interest before entering the public domain of reason. The truth of this is clear when one watches the unrepresented litigant in a Canadian courtroom. Unschooled in this game, this individual invariably draws the personal into the field of legal debate in a way that is intensely awkward and somehow embarrassing.

As a result, what we appear to be debating is often not at all what is really at issue. This is what I mean by "proxy debates": a form of sanitized legal discourse relieved of the fraught reality of cultural and normative difference. To the extent that transparency about our animating concerns is a minimal prerequisite for respectful and meaningful engagement in a democracy, these kinds of proxy debates seem antithetical to the internal aspirations of our political order.

Perhaps the clearest example of the emergence of this kind of proxy debate can be found in contemporary Canadian criminal law and criminal law policy. In recent years, the harm principle has become the lodestar for discussion about the proper limits of the criminal law. The question of the legalization of marijuana was debated and ultimately decided on the basis of whether it causes harm.[42] The harm principle has dethroned the older "community standards of tolerance" test in matters of criminal obscenity and indecency.[43] That the harm principle has assumed such a prominent position in contemporary Canadian criminal law is telling. Drawn from Mill, the harm principle is inextricable from the liberal contractarian theory of the state.

Yet the harm principle is essentially unstable and debate about it decides little of interest. As Bernard Harcourt has convincingly argued, what "counts" as harm depends upon one's normative system.[44] The intelligibility and plausibility of any particular claims about harm turns on one's broader framework of understanding.[45] As such, the harm principle veils cultural conflict; it holds off normative and interpretive questions by burying them under the second-order issue of what qualifies as harm.[46] In short, "harm" serves as the core concept in a proxy debate whose function it is to help cleanse the sphere of public policy of substantive moral claims.

The role of proxy debates about harm as a technology of depoliticization is clear in a contemporary example that straddles the domains of criminal law and religious freedom. When the constitutionality of the criminalization of polygamy arose in Canada, much of the public

---

42  *R v Malmo-Levine; R v Caine*, 2003 SCC 74, [2003] 3 SCR 571. Judgments about harm were also at the heart of the Supreme Court's decision regarding the constitutionality of criminal laws prohibiting sex work. See *Canada (Attorney General) v Bedford*, 2013 SCC 72, [2013] 3 SCR 1101.

43  See *R v Labaye*, 2005 SCC 80, [2005] 3 SCR 728.

44  Bernard E Harcourt, "The Collapse of the Harm Principle" (1999) 90:1 J Crim L & Criminology 109.

45  See Dan M Kahan et al, "Fear of Democracy: A Cultural Evaluation of Sunstein on Risk" (2006) 119:4 Harv L Rev 1071.

46  Another way of characterizing this same point would be to say that reliance on the harm principle nevertheless leaves open the question of the *magnitude* or *seriousness* of harm necessary to warrant criminal sanction. See Alan Brudner, *The Unity of the Common Law: Studies in Hegelian Jurisprudence* (Berkeley: University of California Press, 1995) at 211. Brudner's position is that "disrespect for another's freedom ... and not the infliction of harm is the gravamen of crime."

debate and legal analysis has clustered around the question of harm.[47] With the discursive focus on harm, the historical links between Christianity and this criminal law are skated over. The cultural dimensions and meaning of the practice in question are, equally, bracketed in favour of a debate about whether polygamy is harmful. Law is excised from history, power, and culture. The claim is, of course, not that one should ignore harms in legal decision-making. If a practice causes harm, surely that ought to matter to the law. The problem is that deciding the question of harm leaves the cultural conflict under the surface untouched. It is like debating the location of the wall between Israel and the West Bank. It is not that the result is irrelevant or that the issue is unimportant. But no matter how it is decided, it leaves the essential conflict untouched.

The harm principle is just a particularly cogent example of a form of proxy debate. There are others. Proportionality review – a modern mainstay and defining feature of the rationalist presentation of the rule of law, not to mention the backbone of Canadian constitutional analysis – is another powerful proxy debate. This is the proxy debate that governed the *Wilson Colony* case. There were subtexts surrounding "risk" and "harm," generated by the government's stated need for a face-recognition system, tapping into (and part of the generation of) public security concerns. But the larger "proxy" was the section 1 proportionality test as a whole. As I showed in chapter 3, the analysis of religious freedom in Canada is now dominated by the analysis under section 1 of the *Charter*, which translates substantive rights claims into the dominant idiom of liberal constitutionalism: proportionality. Rather than directly debating the political and ethical obligations to a community that lived by non-liberal, collectivist, and religiously inspired ideals, everything turned on proportionality. Cast in the legal idiom, we are no longer talking about the issues at stake to the litigants or, as I argued in chapter 3, the tacit norms of the legal and political system

---

47 The leading case on the constitutionality of the crime of polygamy, the *Reference re: Section 293 of the Criminal Code of Canada*, 2011 BCSC 1588, focused precisely on the question of harm. I have offered critical analyses of the role of harm arguments in debates about polygamy in Benjamin L Berger, "Moral Judgment, Criminal Law, and the Constitutional Protection of Religion" (2008) 40 SCLR (2d) 514; and Benjamin L Berger, "Polygamy and the Predicament of Contemporary Criminal Law" in Gillian Calder & Lori G Beaman, eds, *Polygamy's Rights and Wrongs* (Vancouver: UBC Press, 2013) 69.

that are the unacknowledged backbone of a proportionality analysis. Of course this is the very genius of constitutional law: the translation of a hard political question raised by social and political interests into a legal debate about whether a governmental measure is rational, well-tailored, and proportionate in its impacts. The result, however, is that the debate does not engage deeply with what is truly at stake on either side. We are left with an answer in the given case but with no more clarity about the political issues that gave rise to the question.

As *AC* shows, the "best interests of the child" is another species of proxy debate. The case was resolved on the basis that the "best interests of the child" required consideration of her wishes (here, religiously based wishes but just as plausibly any sincere wish) commensurate with her degree of maturity. But AC's claim was that the impact on her of having a blood transfusion was immeasurably greater than even the worst-case scenario should she refuse the transfusion. But of course the culture of the constitutional rule of law is unable to give credence or effect to the ontological and metaphysical commitments that generate that view. Just as AC is committed to her culture and what it entails for life in this world, so too is the culture of Canadian constitutionalism, though its governing conceits prevent it from engaging at that level. And so Justice Binnie, dissenting in this case and demonstrating notable honesty about the shape of the issue, was quite right when he explained that the fundamental challenge of the *AC* case was that this child was asking for the right "to make a choice that most of us would think is a serious mistake."[48] Given her status as a child, the law has a foothold to continue to impose its sense of the value of the human being and its hope that, with time, reason will lead AC out of these beliefs. There is a metaphysical disagreement at the heart of this case, one that the language of "best interests of the child" effaces. The best interests of the child are supremely important, of course. But what was at stake in this case was really a substantive dispute about what counted as a genuine and cognizable "interest" for this child. Ultimately, the law simply cannot contemplate the possibility that AC might be correct in her views. Much like "harm," "best interests of the child" works in this case as a normative placeholder that offers a safe ground for resolving the issue, one that allows escape from the enormously challenging cultural conflict raised by the case.

---

48  *AC, supra* note 22 at para 162.

In short, when the public story puts law outside of culture, proxy debates are the result. These kinds of proxy debates become a normative shell game, surreptitiously shifting around the more perplexing and fundamental questions raised by the interaction of law and religion, and engendering an evasive form of policy debate.

Perhaps proxy debates nevertheless serve an important function: to reduce cultural conflict in the public sphere. But all of the evidence suggests that covering the conflict with proxy debates has not soothed irritation around questions of religious difference. Quite the contrary, it has left these issues simmering, gathering heat under the surface. What's more, significant social energy is spent contesting issues in a discursive mode that never really confronts the underlying tensions. This diversion of deliberative energies can impoverish public life. Brown writes that tolerance discourse, which I identified as a core feature of the conventional story, "forces the displacement of religious belief and ethical conviction into rhetorically strategic political claims, giving political debate about value-laden policy a deeply disingenuous character and intensifying the rationalization of political life that Weber forecast even as he rooted it in other causes."[49] This kind of disingenuous debate is not only highly ineffective; it displaces other possible meaningful forms of public debate and seems at odds with the principles and practices that should guide a deliberative democracy.

Climbing the front steps of the Supreme Court of Canada building in Ottawa, one is flanked by two statues. On the right stands a tall black figure holding a sword: Iusticia. To the left is a woman holding a book, looking upwards: Veritas. There is a certain wisdom reflected in this suggestive splitting of justice and truth on the steps of the institutional metonym for the culture of law's rule in Canada. Neither in the personal realm nor in matters of politics do the just and the true, the good and the accurate, invariably coincide. We are justified, sometimes, in living by noble lies. In the case of our public story about law's encounter with religion, however, the story by which we are living does not lend itself to even the goods to which Canadian constitutionalism internally aspires.

---

49 Brown, *supra* note 11 at 40.

The pernicious effects of holding on to the conventional public story all flow from a misfit between appearance and reality: the appearance peddled by the conventional account and the reality that I have exposed in this work. Tacit in my discussion of the ignoble nature of the "lie" of the conventional account of law's relationship with religion has been an assumption about the political virtue of transparency. Nevertheless, in arguing for the investment of the public story with the messy cultural realities, I am not sanguine about the good of transparency in public life. In showing a sometimes disturbingly fraught reality, transparency has the potential to breed conflict and sharpen difference. Accordingly, I have not leaned on an abstract claim for transparency as a virtue. Rather, I have delineated a series of harms arising from the opaqueness of the story that guides public consideration of law and religion in Canada. Exposing the cultural nature of the rule of law and its encounter with religion repoliticizes our public account of the interaction of law and religion in a way that could palliate these harms. This is not to suggest that the results in any given case would or necessarily should be different. Nor is it a step towards the reformation of law's culture. Mine is a claim based on seeing the way in which the conceit of law's autonomy from culture has structured the interaction of constitutional law and religion, and that this prevailing account has not served us well.

## Adjudicative Virtues in Cross-Cultural Encounter

Any retelling of the public story about the nature of the constitutional rule of law and its essential relationship to issues of social policy has implications for conceiving of the role of those who act within and are responsible for the culture of law's rule. Having argued for a new way of describing Canadian constitutionalism's interaction with religious difference, I want now to make a move sympathetic in form to Alexander Bickel's appeal to the passive virtues – the "various devices, methods, concepts, doctrines and techniques" of "not doing"[50] that he argued could reconcile the Supreme Court's role as the authoritative speaker of constitutional principles with his story about the inter-branch challenges posed by judicial review. A new account of the relationship

50 Alexander M Bickel, *The Least Dangerous Branch: The Supreme Court at the Bar of Politics*, 2nd ed (New Haven, Conn: Yale University Press, 1986) at 169.

between constitutional law and religious difference will similarly affect our understanding of the behaviour of judges. What are the virtues of adjudication in a repoliticized story about religion and Canadian constitutionalism, one that seeks to come to terms with religious pluralism, but in a manner that takes to heart the lessons of my account? The answer lies in a particular ethos suited to the adjudication of religious claims, and an intimately related adjudicative practice.

## The Ethos of Adjudicating Religion

Having provided a fresh account of the political and structural challenges of judicial review in the American constitutional system, Alexander Bickel turned his attention to the question of what kind of attitudes and postures an appreciation of that story would properly instil in a judge working within that world. We can similarly reflect on the kind of adjudicative ethos that would be well calibrated to – that ought to be inspired by – the account of law's relationship to religion that I have offered in these pages. To see the cultural nature of the constitutional rule of law and its interaction with religion invites an adjudicative sentiment when faced with the challenges of adjudicating religious claims, a posture towards both religion and law itself. This sentiment, or ethos, is really twofold. Clearly seeing the engagement of law and religion as the meeting of culturally particular and meaningful ways of framing experience demands from the adjudicator a kind of *fidelity* to the culture of the constitutional rule of law. Equally, however, it should inspire a kind of *humility*. This twofold sentiment of fidelity and humility is, I suggest, the virtuous ethos for adjudication. These are ethical virtues that seem, on first blush, to oppose one another, but whose value arises precisely out of the tension between them.

By "fidelity" I mean to capture the sense that the judge in a liberal constitutional order is justified in claiming and expressing a certain commitment to the language, framing assumptions, and structural values expressed in the culture of Canadian constitutionalism. The judge must be, in Bickel's terms, "defender of the faith." Like Bickel, I do not mean for this to sound in the register of crusades and inquisitions. The point, rather, is that a judge who understands the cultural nature of the constitutional rule of law appreciates a central lesson of this account: that each act of judgment necessarily participates in and draws integrity from a unique and rich web of meanings and ways of framing experience. To internalize the idea that the constitutional rule of law

does not sit above the world of culture, but is rather an active participant in that realm, does not call for a detached relativism on the part
of adjudicators. Quite the contrary. Every cultural form has its peculiar
gifts, and the judge has a special role in cultivating and caring for the
public gifts of a liberal constitutional culture, of which there are many.
It is to the internalization of that ethic of care and commitment that the
virtue of fidelity points.

The reticence in constitutional adjudication to speak openly about
the informing commitments, projects, and ways of being that are valued and pursued in the constitutional rule of law is an artefact of the
conceit of law's autonomy from culture. As I have explained in the first
part of this chapter, in thrall to that conceit, there is a tendency to view
the expression of commitment to certain values, visions of a just society, and framing assumptions as somehow embarrassing or disloyal.
Freed from that conceit, the judge's role in articulating – for scrutiny
and, perhaps, for political contestation – and applying those shaping
commitments is far more clear. In the hands of some, the call for state
neutrality can expand to suggest that any position-taking on the part
of the judges executing their duties, any pursuit of a vision of a good
society, is a mischief. Although the principle of state neutrality counsels even-handedness in the treatment of religion (and non-religion), it
does not go so far as to require agnosticism about the value, principles,
and needs of a public life constituted by the culture of Canadian constitutionalism.[51] To claim otherwise is to feed the misleading conceit

---

51 I discuss this understanding of state neutrality in Benjamin L Berger, "Religious
   Diversity, Education, and the 'Crisis' in State Neutrality" (2013) 29:1 CJLS 103. See
   also Richard Moon, "Freedom of Religion under the Charter of Rights: The Limits of
   State Neutrality" (2012) 45 UBC L Rev 497. For the Supreme Court's most extensive
   discussion of its understanding of the nature and demands of state neutrality, see
   *Mouvement laïque québécois v Saguenay (City)*, 2015 SCC 16, released while this volume
   was in final production. The case concerned a discernibly Christian public prayer
   recited at the opening of municipal council meetings. Justice Gascon, writing for the
   Court, found that the prayer breached the state's duty of neutrality, understood as
   the requirement "that the state neither favour nor hinder any particular belief" (para
   72). The City of Saguenay had thereby interfered with the appellant's freedom of
   conscience and religion. Resonant with themes explored in this volume, Justice Gascon explained that adherence to this principle of state neutrality "preserves a neutral
   public space that is free of discrimination and in which true freedom to believe or
   not to believe is enjoyed by everyone equally," and linked this neutrality of the public space to "the multicultural nature of Canadian society" (para 74).

upon which the conventional account of law's relationship to religion is based.

As such, for those charged with adjudicating the claims of religion within the courts, the manifestation of commitment to the culture of Canadian constitutionalism is both appropriate and necessary. Each act of judgment is a performance of the culture of the constitutional rule of law. Met with the challenges of intercultural judgment, one role of the judge is to manifest fidelity to the terms, projects, and goods of Canadian constitutionalism. Constitutional judgment must reflect and nurture a certain commitment to the web of meanings and ways of being that inhere in that culture.

Some might worry that this vision of an ethic of fidelity to the culture of Canadian constitutionalism looks like taking Charles Taylor's felicitous observation that "liberalism is also a fighting creed"[52] and translating it into a troublingly literal and institutional form. If that were the only component of the ethos inspired by internalizing the cultural nature of the relationship between law and religion, that concern would be well founded. Unchecked, the posture of fidelity that I have described could produce a dangerous form of institutional arrogance and insensitivity. There is, however, a second adjudicative sentiment that arises from internalizing this cultural account, a sentiment that balances this fidelity to the culture of law's rule.

To understand Canadian constitutionalism as a cultural form also means seeing that the constitutional rule of law is always in competition with other cultures, other compelling and rich ways of generating meaning and giving structure to experience.[53] It means viewing law as a critical but by no means exclusive site of cultural allegiance within Canadian society. Those who come before the bar of the law are no less touched and informed by their meaning-giving frameworks than the judge. For each good or principle that presents itself to the judge as utterly natural or incomparably valuable within the framework of law's culture, there is the possibility for an alternate symbol, good, or ritual without which the world seems equally unintelligible to the committed

---

52 Charles Taylor, "The Politics of Recognition" in *Philosophical Arguments* (Cambridge, Mass: Harvard University Press, 1995) 225 at 249 [Taylor, "Politics of Recognition"].

53 See Kahn, *The Cultural Study of Law, supra* note 9 at 120: "The rule of law is a world of meaning that is always maintained against alternative forms of meaning ... These alternatives are just as historically contingent as the rule of law. Despite their contingency, they too are constitutive of the possibilities of meaning in our common life."

actor in another culture.[54] In this way, having "levelled" both law and religion as cultural forms, this account seizes the judge with an appreciation of the ways in which law and religion can serve as homologous sources of meaning and the difficulty that law may have in hearing and understanding the nature and gravamen of religious claims. Recognizing this induces a kind of humility. That humility arises from an appreciation of the role that religious culture can play in identity, belonging, and the narration of a meaningful and authentic story about one's life. At the same time, this ethic is inspired by an awareness of the limits of adjudication, limits exposed by a cultural account of the interaction of law and religion.[55] As discussed in this chapter, those limits include the cultural limits of legal toleration, as well as institutional, epistemological, and remedial limits associated with approaching issues of religious difference through constitutional adjudication. Essential though their role may be, courts are never the only – and rarely the best – institutional and social settings for appreciating and attending to the richness of the interests, subtleties of power, and need for creative solutions raised by issues of religious identity, belonging, and difference.

The resulting ethos of humility is triune: a humility about the potential universality of law's culture, about the capacity of law to understand other cultural forms, and about the ultimate contingency of the privilege enjoyed by law's culture. This attitude of humility is related to the sentiment that Cover hoped would install itself in the judge who saw that the act of adjudication involves violence to other rich worlds of meaning.[56] As Judith Resnik explains, Cover "wanted the state's actors (here, its judges and, derivatively, commentators on their work)

---

54  As Charles Taylor explains in "Understanding and Ethnocentricity," *supra* note 2 at 129, "We are always in danger of seeing our ways of acting and thinking as the only conceivable ones. That is exactly what ethnocentricity consists in. Understanding other societies ought to wrench us out of this; it ought to alter our self-understandings."

55  In her insightful work on the assessment of identity claims, Avigail Eisenberg makes a sympathetic call for the importance of "institutional humility," which she defines as "the capacity of public decision makers to detect the errors of their decisions and the biases in their procedures caused by employing criteria that favour the identities, including the histories and values, of (usually) dominant groups over all others." Avigail Eisenberg, *Reasons of Identity: A Normative Guide to the Political & Legal Assessment of Identity Claims* (Oxford: Oxford University Press, 2009) at 25.

56  See Robert M Cover, "The Supreme Court 1982 Term – Foreword: *Nomos* and Narrative" (1983) 97 Harv L Rev 4.

to be uncomfortable in their knowledge of their own power, respectful of the legitimacy of competing legal systems, and aware of the possibility that multiple meanings and divergent practices ought sometimes to be tolerated, even if painfully so."[57]

Justice Binnie's dissenting opinion in *AC* is exemplary of this mix of fidelity and humility that I suggest is demanded by the adjudication of religious freedom and equality. His reasons in that case point towards the ethics of adjudication suitable to an understanding of law's engagement with religious difference as, at core, cultural.

The first words of his judgment are, simply, "This is a disturbing case."[58] Elaborating, Justice Binnie explains that AC "claims the right to make a choice that most of us would think is a serious mistake, namely to refuse a potentially lifesaving blood transfusion. Her objection, of course, is based on her religious beliefs."[59] The tension in his judgment is palpable: "The *Charter* is not just about the freedom to make what most members of society would regard as the wise and correct choice. If that were the case, the *Charter* would be superfluous. The *Charter*, A.C. argues, gives her the freedom – in this case religious freedom – to refuse forced medical treatment, even where her life or death hangs in the balance."[60] He goes on to acknowledge the foreignness – indeed, the apparent folly – for many of the particular religious beliefs that the Court is being asked to protect. Justice Binnie recognizes what I have argued is at the heart of the difficulty of cases involving religious difference: "Individuals who do not subscribe to the beliefs of Jehovah's Witnesses find it difficult to understand their objection to the potentially lifesaving effects of a blood transfusion."[61] Such is the chasm of cultural understanding that the constitutional protection of religion asks that we venture across. "It is entirely understandable that judges, as in this case, would instinctively give priority to the sanctity of life,"[62] Justice Binnie concedes. "Religious convictions may change. Death is irreversible. Even where death is avoided, damage to internal organs caused by loss

---

57  Judith Resnik, "Living Their Legal Commitments: Paideic Communities, Courts, and Robert Cover" (2005) 17 Yale JL & Human 17 at 25. I address below my sense of the possible shape of this "toleration."
58  *AC, supra* note 22 at para 162.
59  *Ibid.*
60  *Ibid* at para 163.
61  *Ibid* at para 191.
62  *Ibid.*

of blood may have serious and long lasting effects."[63] Yet he also draws to the surface a familiar value that may be of assistance in understanding the stakes of this decision to refuse a blood transfusion, a decision that some would view as incomprehensibly and tragically wrong: "[S]trong as is society's belief in the sanctity of life, it is equally fundamental that every competent individual is entitled to autonomy to choose or not to choose medical treatment."[64]

Having laid bare the difficulty and stakes of the adjudicative task presented in the case, Justice Binnie makes an obvious effort to go some distance to understanding what is involved in this decision from the perspective of the religious claimant. When he turns to his analysis of freedom of religion, he dedicates a paragraph to the following: "Jehovah's Witnesses believe that blood represents life and that respect for this gift from God requires the faithful to abstain from accepting blood to sustain life. They say that the Bible's prohibition applies equally to eating, drinking and transfusing blood and is not lessened in times of emergency. They believe that observance of this principle is an element of their personal responsibility before God. In *Malette*, the Ontario Court of Appeal recognized that '[i]f [Mrs Malette's] refusal involves a risk of death, then according to her belief, her death would be necessary to ensure her spiritual life.'"[65] Having sought to understand and display the shape of the commitment from the perspective of the religious claimant, Justice Binnie captures the essence of the adjudicative challenge when he addresses section 7. He notes, "The Court has ... long preached the values of individual autonomy. In this case, we are called on to live up to the s. 7 promise in circumstances where we instinctively recoil from the choice made by A.C. because of our belief (religious or otherwise) in the sanctity of life."[66]

In the end, Justice Binnie concludes that "A.C. has demonstrated that the deleterious effects are dominant"[67] and would have found the legislation to be unconstitutional. Though his decision would have resulted in the staying of law's hand in this matter of religious freedom, it is not the conclusion that he reaches that commends this judgment as much as the virtues displayed in his analysis. The palpable ethical tension

---

63  *Ibid*.
64  *Ibid* at para 192.
65  *Ibid* at para 213.
66  *Ibid* at para 219.
67  *Ibid* at para 237.

in his judgment arises from the fusion of fidelity and humility that I have discussed. Justice Binnie speaks clearly and powerfully about the constitutional commitments at play in this case: the sanctity of life and the sacrality of individual autonomy. In so doing he affirms the principles, symbols, and commitments that matter most to the culture of law's rule, as well as its authority. Yet his overt attempt to understand the meaning of this moment for AC from within her religious horizon and his clear articulation of the nature of the challenge that this poses for doing justice in this case reflects humility about law. This humility is multilayered, just as I have described it: it is a humility about the universality of law's culture, about the capacity of law to understand other cultural forms, and about the exercise of law's coercive power.

One could have found the limit in *AC* to be justified and still have displayed all of these virtues. Had this been the result, it would have been with the stakes and commitments for all on full display. Having engaged in this hard work of cross-cultural engagement, the matter becomes far more difficult, far more fraught; however, even for those who would disagree with the result, the difficult, contestable work of judgment in cases involving religious difference would have been manifest.

The challenges posed by – and, hence, the virtues necessary for – politics in a time of deep pluralism are unique. In his provocative book *Pluralism*,[68] William Connolly asks what interpersonal ethics are needed to live within this "[m]ultidimensional pluralism," whereby "the expansion of diversity in one domain ventilates life in others as well."[69] The essence of Connolly's answer is a call for a personal sensibility appropriate to the multidimensional pluralism that he sees as characterizing our modern condition. He calls this sensibility a "bicameral orientation to political life."[70] It is bicameral in the sense that it holds together a commitment to one's own "faith, doctrine, creed, ideology or philosophy" with an openness to others. One must "appreciate how [one's culture] appears opaque and profoundly contestable to many who do not participate in it."[71] I have outlined an adjudicative ethos that is similarly bicameral. Both fidelity and humility are sentiments

---

68  William E Connolly, *Pluralism* (Durham, NC: Duke University Press, 2005).
69  *Ibid* at 6.
70  *Ibid* at 4.
71  *Ibid*.

that should arise from a judicial internalization of an account of the constitutional rule of law and its interaction with religion that takes seriously the cultural nature of each. The presence of both sentiments means that neither aspect of this ethos of adjudication is permitted to run to its natural extreme. Humility checks the risk that fidelity will turn to unreflective universalism. Fidelity staves off a debilitating relativism of excess humility. The influence of this bicameral ethos could be deep. For present purposes, most important is its role in spawning and animating the practical adjudicative virtue to which I now turn, the active cultivation of indifference.

## The Cultivation of Indifference

Examined in the light of Bernard Williams's observation that the basic problem of tolerance is that "[t]oleration … is required only for the intolerable,"[72] in chapter 3 the practices of legal tolerance showed themselves to be a kind of "tolerance as indifference" characterized by two zones of relevance for religion: those manifestations of religious culture that do not really (either on their face or on critical reflection) matter to the law and those that do, indeed, matter. The former enjoy legal "tolerance" and the latter are intolerable, trumped by law in an enforcement of its own meanings and way of life. Crucially, however, whatever the result in a given case, both zones involved the use of law's culture as the controlling frame of reference. As such, both involve the kind of insistence upon and spreading of law's cultural framework, a feature of legal tolerance that gives it a distinctively colonial or assimilationist flavour. The indifference upon which tolerance depends is indifference with an edge.

What does this understanding of legal tolerance mean for the judge faced with adjudicating claims born of strong religious difference? It leaves the judge in command of a meaningful adjudicative virtue: the cultivation of indifference. The virtue of this adjudicative practice does not lie in offering a technique for juridically solving the cultural tensions between law and religion. That is the misleading aspiration of the conventional account of legal multiculturalism. The virtue of the cultivation of indifference lies in seeking to expand the meaningful margin

---

72 Bernard Williams, "Tolerating the Intolerable" in Susan Mendus, ed, *The Politics of Toleration in Modern Life* (Durham, NC: Duke University Press, 2000) 65 at 65.

for difference created when, while giving due regard to the ineradicable influence of law's culture on the adjudicative process, the judge nevertheless stays the violent hand of the law. In exploring this concept as it applies in the interaction of law and religion, I am disturbing the negative connotation that the term *indifference* commonly carries. As I argued in chapter 3, the seemingly modest declaration that a particular religious expression is the subject of legal indifference and, hence, "not intolerable" is a kind of political intervention the significance of which it would be a mistake to ignore.

The hope of cultivating indifference lies in the possibility that those cultural manifestations one initially sees as foreign, objectionable, or intolerable might, with effort and reflection, be understood as untroubling to the law. As such, the judge's central task is simply to discharge his or her traditionally understood responsibility: to interpret. This interpretation occurs as all interpretation does: by confronting what is unfamiliar and seeking to understand it within a familiar conceptual framework, often through analogy and metaphor. Faced with a complex and homologous culture and a claim to religious freedom, the judge critically assesses whether a given religious practice or commitment ought really to matter to the law. Exploring and testing the geography of legal indifference in this way, the judge has no choice but to work with law's own categories (such as the private or public), its own values (like autonomy and choice), and its own framing intuitions. But he or she can ask whether, within that frame, the controverted religious practice can be understood – interpreted – in a way that may be able to attract the liberty that comes with legal indifference.

There are certain similarities between my conception of the analytic process involved in the adjudicative cultivation of indifference and Taylor's notion of a "language of perspicuous contrast."[73] Taylor argues that a language of perspicuous contrast "would be a language in which we could formulate both their way of life and ours as alternative possibilities in relation to some human constants at work in both."[74] I share this call for the virtue of cultural perspicuity in judgment. But there is a key difference between Taylor's approach and my conception of the adjudicative cultivation of indifference. Taylor insists that a language of perspicuous contrast must not be "our language of understanding,

---

73 Taylor, "Understanding and Ethnocentricity," *supra* note 2.
74 *Ibid* at 125.

or theirs."[75] This demand is an artefact of Taylor's concern with the forms and processes of understanding appropriate to the social scientist, concerned with generating social and political theories. But our judges are not social scientists, nor should we want them to become so. The judge is, as I have explained, a faithful speaker of the culture of law's rule. As any layperson encountering law's rule understands, legal language, rich with symbols and metaphor, is fundamental to the culture of law. To impose upon the judge the demand to adopt as authoritative, or even as heuristically useful, a language outside of law is to ask the judge to stand outside law's rule. This is one of the conundrums of cross-cultural adjudication: it demands engaging with and seeking to interpret the cultural other but necessarily from within, and in a manner intelligible to, the culture of law.

One possible result of this interpretive effort is that what once appeared quite foreign is now seen as actually sympathetic to the practices, values, and symbols with which law frames experience. In such instances, the religious expression at issue will not bother the law, but this is because the interpretation really yields a kind of translation – a strong form of understanding whereby the judge is able to re-describe the practice or commitment in terms that make it consistent with or familiar to the culture of the law.[76] One can find examples of this interpretation-as-translation in certain areas of Indigenous legal relations in Canada. John Borrows has persuasively shown the manner in which translation, close listening, and conceptual agility can help to make Indigenous legal practices and concepts comprehensible and acceptable to non-Indigenous Canadian law.[77] One can see this tangibly in Canadian law's reluctant but progressive acceptance of oral histories – sometimes mythically cast and creatively presented – as cognizable forms of evidence before courts. On first blush, these forms

---

75 *Ibid.*
76 Spinosa and Dreyfus refer to this kind of understanding as "minimal intelligibility," whereby someone in a given culture is able to translate an "instance of a given type in the other's language into an instance of a type in their own." They refer to this as the ability to "follow up the other culture's projections with ad hoc translations." Charles Spinosa & Hubert L Dreyfus, "Two Kinds of Antiessentialism and Their Consequences" (1996) 22:4 Critical Inquiry 735 at 750–1.
77 John Borrows, "With or Without You: First Nations Law (in Canada)" (1996) 41:2 McGill LJ 629. See also John Borrows, "Listening for a Change: The Courts and Oral Tradition" (2001) 39:1 Osgoode Hall LJ 1.

of knowledge simply seem to be intolerable hearsay and of marginal relevance. But better understood, they turn out to look no less reliable or relevant than the written accounts of fur-traders upon which the law has more readily relied. Such oral histories are now admissible.[78]

In the realm of law and religion, an example of achieving intelligibility through translation can be found in the Supreme Court of Canada case *Bruker v Marcovitz*.[79] The Court was faced with the task of deciding whether it ought to award damages for failure to fulfil a commitment to obtain a document securing a Jewish religious divorce, a *ghet*. The husband had undertaken, as part of a divorce agreement, to go to the rabbinic authorities to obtain a *ghet* for his wife, without which, according to the Jewish law to which they both claimed to adhere, she would not be able to remarry, nor to have children that would be recognized as "legitimate" in Jewish law. Over a fifteen-year period, until she was almost forty-seven years old, he refused to provide the *ghet*. Ms Bruker claimed breach of contract under Quebec's *Civil Code*, but Mr Marcovitz argued that this was a religious matter, non-cognizable within Quebec law, and that he was further protected by his freedom of religion. Although the Court of Appeal of Quebec concluded that the religious nature of the commitment meant that it was not enforceable by the courts, the Supreme Court of Canada ruled that the wife was entitled to damages. Despite the apparent chasm between civil and Jewish marriage law, the majority of the Court found that the *ghet* could be understood as simply a form of contract, entirely comprehensible and familiar to, and hence justiciable within, the culture of law's rule. The *ghet* was, in effect, interpreted as an ordinary contract, consistent with and expressive of the value put on autonomy and choice within the rule of law. It was translated into a form in which the religious content of the practice could be the subject of indifference.

---

78 *Delgamuukw v British Columbia*, [1997] 3 SCR 1010. And yet one also sees the swiftness and force with which the epistemological and cultural assumptions of the law are reintroduced. In *Mitchell v MNR*, 2001 SCC 33 at para 38, [2001] 1 SCR 911, the Court added a crucial caveat to this expanded regard for the forms of evidence appropriate for Aboriginal rights, title, and treaty claims: "While evidence adduced in support of aboriginal claims must not be undervalued, neither should it be interpreted or weighed in a manner that fundamentally contravenes the principles of evidence law, which, as they relate to the valuing of evidence, are often synonymous with the 'general principles of common sense.'"

79 *Bruker, supra* note 23.

Such translation is one possible result of working to make sense of the religious other within the terms precious to law's rule. It is, however, more than the cultivation of difference demands. The tolerance of indifference does not require this kind of comfort and familiarity. The process of interpretation – of testing the religious expression against those cultural commitments essential to the Canadian constitutional rule of law – may simply yield the conclusion that, on reflection, what appeared objectionable does not trouble or challenge the law's constitutive commitments, intuitions, or practices. This adjudicative virtue can be realized when the judge must furrow his or her brow in non-comprehension of the religious culture but is, nevertheless, able to turn an unconcerned shoulder, satisfied that the practice or commitment at stake simply does not offend the culture of Canadian constitutionalism.[80] This is the essence of the cultivation of indifference. The judge who succeeds in offering up an interpretation of the religious commitment or practice in question that shows it to be, in this sense, untroubling and the possible subject of indifference has expanded the margins of legal tolerance. That judge has thereby stayed the culturally forceful hand of the law.

Halberstam's response to the paradox of tolerance – that at the moment we begin to care and, hence, when tolerance is demanded, it becomes impossible – is that our goal should therefore be "maintaining an openness in perspective which refuses to elevate our transitory tastes and beliefs into deep-seated convictions for whose sake we are prepared to violate the freedom of others."[81] The assumption at play in my description of the cultivation of indifference as an adjudicative virtue is that, inasmuch as the judge is responsible for giving voice and

---

80  There are certain apparent affinities between this conception of the cultivation of indifference and the idea of *modus vivendi* liberalism developed most thoroughly by John Gray in *Two Faces of Liberalism* (New York: New Press, 2000). Both are attempts to understand tolerance in a way that allows for value- and cultural-pluralism in light of the potential incommensurability of cultures. Gray also shares my concern with the depoliticizing effect of liberal legalism and is similarly sceptical of resolving these cultural conflicts once and for all (137). But there are fundamental differences between the two concepts that lead us in very different directions – differences that stem from our differing conceptions of and concern with law's nature and role. Gray's is a conception of the challenges of pluralism that extricates law's culture from the equation.

81  Joshua Halberstam, "The Paradox of Tolerance" (1982–83) 14:2 Philosophical Forum 190 at 206.

force to the culture of law's rule, he or she also has a crucial role to play in maintaining this kind of openness. This is the practical expression of that ethical mix of fidelity and humility.

Halberstam's conclusion brings to mind the famous Hart-Devlin debate about the proper limits of the criminal law.[82] Although this debate was concerned specifically with the use of the criminal law to enforce morality, one way of understanding the cultivation of indifference is by setting it against this conversation about the nature of tolerance and the role of law in matters of social cohesion. The cultivation of indifference draws certain sensibilities from both Devlin and Hart. It takes seriously Devlin's argument about the normatively constitutive force of the law and, in certain respects, his conception that "the work of the courts is to be the guarding of a heritage."[83] But in suggesting that the role of the judge is to explore the ways in which the law need not concern itself with much of what initially appears offensive or objectionable to this cultural system, it rejects Devlin's tacit sense of the fragility of society and his resultantly immodest approach to the infliction of law's force.[84] In this respect, the cultivation of indifference is a conception of the judicial role in matters of cross-cultural encounter that shares much more with Hart's sentiment that we should be

---

82  See Patrick Devlin, "Morals and the Criminal Law" in *The Enforcement of Morals* (London: Oxford University Press, 1965) 1; HLA Hart, "Immorality and Treason" in Richard A Wasserstrom, ed, *Morality and the Law* (Belmont, Cal: Wadsworth, 1971) 48 [Hart, "Immorality and Treason"]; Hart, *Law, Liberty, and Morality* (London: Oxford University Press, 1963) [Hart, *Law, Liberty, and Morality*]. In fact, Halberstam's conclusion follows a short reflection on the Hart-Devlin debate.

83  Patrick Devlin, "Democracy and Morality" in Devlin, *supra* note 82, 86 at 89.

84  Devlin, *supra* note 82 at 17, famously argues that "no society can do without intolerance, indignation, and disgust; they are the forces behind the moral law" and that the law, therefore, has warrant to enforce the society's political, ethical, and moral judgments. "Societies disintegrate from within more frequently than they are broken up by external pressures. There is disintegration when no common morality is observed and history shows that the loosening of moral bonds is often the first stage of disintegration, so that society is justified in taking the same steps to preserve its moral code as it does to preserve its government and other essential institutions" (13). In *Law, Liberty and Morality*, *supra* note 82 at 50, Hart directly challenges the "factual" premise of social disintegration upon which Devlin leans, stating, "No reputable historian has maintained this thesis, and there is indeed much evidence against it." He argues that such a claim of the threat of social disintegration masquerades as factual assertion when, in truth, it is more akin to "an *a priori* assumption, and sometimes a necessary truth and a very odd one."

cautious about raising our instinctive objections to the level of legal offence. The essence of Hart's rejoinder to Devlin is a call to "summon all the resources of our reason, sympathetic understanding, as well as critical intelligence"[85] and to ask ourselves, "Is it really true that failure to translate this item of general morality into criminal law will jeopardize the whole fabric of morality and so of society?"[86] For Hart, far fewer instances of difference actually shake the foundations of society than is often feared. Hart offers a more plastic conception of society, and our overwhelming experience has been that he was correct.

A number of Canadian cases that engage religious freedom are reflective of the kind of interpretive effort yielding parsimonious withdrawal that I have described as the core of the cultivation of indifference. *Trinity Western University*[87] is one such example. Viewed through the lens of the anti-discrimination values dear to the culture of Canadian constitutionalism, the religious code of conduct at issue in *TWU* seems insufferable. Yet when the Court characterizes the code of conduct as a matter of belief, rather than conduct, it takes on a private character that attracts the Court's forbearance. By contrast, in *Chamberlain*[88] the decision of the local school board to prohibit the use of materials depicting same-sex parented families in a kindergarten/grade one class on the basis of the religious views of parents in the community could not be digested within the essential commitments of the law. A similar interpretive struggle to make sense of the religious practice within the commitments of the rule of law, whether successful or not, can be found in a host of Canadian cases: *Amselem*,[89] *Multani*,[90] *Ross*.[91] In all such cases, the judge must embrace, but then explore and manipulate, the symbols and understandings of Canadian constitutionalism in a positive effort to find an interpretation that can expand the margins of indifference.

The contrast between the majority and dissent in *Wilson Colony* is a study in the practices involved in this cultivation of indifference. The majority was unable to find a way to reconcile this Hutterite community's mode of life and religious beliefs with the exigencies of the

---

85  Hart, "Immorality and Treason," *supra* note 82 at 54.
86  *Ibid* at 52.
87  *TWU*, *supra* note 24.
88  *Chamberlain v Surrey School District No 36*, 2002 SCC 86, [2002] 4 SCR 710.
89  *Amselem*, *supra* note 26.
90  *Multani v Commission scolaire Marguerite-Bourgeoys*, 2006 SCC 6, [2006] 1 SCR 256.
91  *Ross v New Brunswick School District No 15*, [1996] 1 SCR 825.

administrative state. Yet the chief objection to the majority judgment is that it failed to seriously engage with the significance of the prohibition on photographs and the impact that an inability to drive would have on the communal and autonomous life of the Wilson Colony. The controlling concept in the majority judgment is "meaningful choice to practice one's religion." An impoverished engagement with the potential impact of the government's universal photo requirement allowed the majority to conclude that the community retained a meaningful choice regarding its religious practices. That being so, the impact of an exemption on the regulatory scheme was intolerable. Although Justice Abella dissented, she importantly did not dispute the governing principle; the liberal political cultural commitment to meaningful choice is as important to her reasons as it is for the majority. Her closer engagement with the nature of the community, however, led her to conclude that the interference with this community struck at the heart of the law's concern with religion, depriving community members of their ability to choose their form of the good life free from government interference. In this way she worked with the categories precious to the law to condition her understanding of the case and the otherwise quite marginal and foreign belief and way of life appearing before the Court. With this in place, her assessment of the impact of an exemption on the government regime provides a sterling example of the cultivation of indifference: "Hundreds of thousands of Albertans have no driver's licence and their photographs, therefore, are not available in the facial recognition database, to help minimize identity theft. It is not clear to me how having approximately 250 additional Hutterites' photographs in the database will be of any significance in enhancing the government's objective, compared to the seriousness of the intrusion into the Hutterites' religious autonomy."[92] The community is so small, the colony so insular, the exemptions so few, the risk of a slippery slope so remote, that the practice should be accommodated. In sum, the religious beliefs and practices in question are not in meaningful conflict with the values and purposes of law's rule.

The *NS* decision is another case that is profitably analysed in terms of the mandate to cultivate indifference.[93] The religiously motivated request of a witness to wear a face covering, the niqab, while giving

---

92 *Wilson Colony, supra* note 21 at para 174.
93 *R v NS*, 2012 SCC 72, [2012] 3 SCR 726.

testimony in criminal proceedings is obviously foreign to and disruptive of "the long-standing assumptions of the common law regarding the importance of a witness's facial expressions to cross-examination and credibility assessment."[94] Cast in these terms, the religious liberty claim in this case seemed to collide directly with one of the most justifiably cherished commitments within the constitutional rule of law, the right to a fair trial. For the majority of the Court, the weight of tradition was such that, without strongly negating evidence, the common law assumption "that the ability to see a witness's face is an important feature of a fair trial" could not "be disregarded lightly."[95] As I suggested in chapter 3, the majority's embrace of the balancing approach to determine whether, in a given case, the religious practice could nevertheless be accommodated amounted to a kind of toleration of indifference: in practical effect, given the evidence put before the Court in this case, the niqab would be permitted only when it was uncontested or truly peripheral. Justice LeBel's decision would not go even that far: this expression of religious conscience was simply incommensurable with "[a] system of open and independent courts," which is "a core component of a democratic state, ruled by law."[96] In the terms that I am suggesting, his decision failed to show the openness and appetite for self-critical testing that the ethos of humility adds to the judge's fidelity to constitutional culture.

By contrast, Justice Abella's decision went beyond the majority's approach, not just embracing a toleration of indifference, but seeking to find creative ways to cultivate and expand it. As one looks to the exceptions already stitched into the fabric of the legal system and tests the challenge of the niqab against the complexity of these practices within the constitutional rule of law, the intolerability of the niqab, even in cases in which the evidence is contested and significant, seems far less obvious and categorical. This is not an abdication of commitment to the culture of law's rule; it is the kind of creative and searching testing of received wisdom called for by the bicameral ethos appropriate to cross-cultural adjudication. To exploit an analogy not fully explored in Justice Abella's reasons, if it is the case (and it is) that our doctrines of hearsay mean that we will forgo any appearance of the witness – all of

---

94  *Ibid* at para 22.
95  *Ibid* at para 21.
96  *Ibid* at para 74.

the safeguards associated with observation and cross-examination – if the conditions of reliability and necessity are met, is it possible that "a democratic state, ruled by law" could more comfortably accede to the far lesser procedural and epistemological losses represented by the niqab? One need not ultimately endorse Justice Abella's outcome to see the virtues of engaging in the exercise of trying to cultivate indifference.

The comparison of *TWU* and *Chamberlain* and the examples of *Wilson Colony* and *NS* underscore the importance of appreciating that this process of the cultivation or refinement of indifference is about the expansion of the limits of legal tolerance, not their elimination. The judge who internalizes this account must slough off any pretence of the progressive working out of a constitutional détente with religion. Understanding the interaction of religion and constitutional law in the way that I have urged opens up the possibility of a cross-cultural understanding that could yield toleration, but it also underscores the brute fact of certain irreducible conflicts, certain points of incommensurability. The processes involved in the cultivation of indifference are attempts to determine which of these two situations the judge is facing.

My account thus insists on recognizing that constitutional law is a cultural form, rich with meaningful and meaning-giving commitments; however, in so doing it opens up a way of thinking about the judge as being well-placed as a creative interpreter of the culture of law's rule, resisting a too-capacious sense of the need to enforce those convictions. Even if intolerance is inevitably found within the practices of constitutionalism, "by restricting the 'extent' of our convictions as well as their sheer number, we can avoid unwarranted intolerance."[97] Here one sees the influence of the bicameral ethos that I described above. The attitude of humility tempers the recognition that fidelity ultimately limits the margins of toleration. The limits of tolerance posed by Williams's and Halberstam's paradox persist because the judge as committed actor ultimately remains duly faithful to the culture of law's rule.[98]

97  Halberstam, *supra* note 81 at 199.
98  In his work, Cover reflected a sense of the need for judicial self-awareness about the violence of law. Resnik, *supra* note 57 at 25, explaining that, for Cover, "[t]he imposition of imperial law ought not, however, be done innocently, unaware of its impact on other forms of law and therefore disrespectful of the validity of those other sources of lawmaking."

Inspired by the bicameral ethos of fidelity and humility, the cultivation of indifference helps to palliate the political harms inflicted by the conventional story about law's encounter with religion. The cultural perspicuity involved in the analytic processes of the cultivation of indifference, as well as in the faithful declaration of those points of incommensurability, resists the tendency to engage in proxy debates. Whether interpreting his or her way to a conclusion of indifference or exposing the way in which the practice in question truly *matters* to the law and, hence, cannot be tolerated, the judge points to where our attention and energies ought to be directed: at the issue of cultural difference. In so doing, if the judge finds that the religious claimant must lose before the bar of the law, the judge does so while gesturing to a reason other than the inability of the individual to participate in a rational community. If the result favours the religious actor, it does so with religious culture having been engaged with, rather than disregarded. This avoids the radical alienation that I argued arises from adjudication tied up in the conceit of law's autonomy from culture. More honest in its presentation of the law, this process also helps to relieve the unique vulnerability that was created by the conventional account. As the perspicuous process of working with and exploring the commitments of the constitutional rule of law takes place, not only does it become far more difficult to level the reactionary charge of hypocrisy against the law, but it also generates resources for meeting objections about the substantive effects of law's rule – objections that are, at core, really objections about power and cultural difference.

Internalizing the cultural account and seeing the judge's central role in constitutional adjudication as the cultivation of indifference also speaks to the tethering of issues of religious difference to the judicial process. The cultivation of indifference is, in its assumptions and processes, overt about the cultural limits of legal toleration. Adjudication is a process for attempting to interpret another culture in a manner that might allow us to see it as acceptable within the culture of law's rule. The chief symptom of this feature of adjudication is cultural dominance that persists in the interpretive effort that I have described, even when indifference is achieved. The law may view the marriage contract at stake in *Bruker* as a simple contract, but this may not be how the parties understand it at all. Whatever good is achieved by this translation, it also involves the imposition of law's cultural understandings. Even in a case like *TWU*, a case that shows the relatively modest attitude necessary in the cultivation of indifference, the school will enjoy the effects of law's parsimonious withdrawal only because, on critical reflection, law's own meaning-giving framework permits it. Adjudication cannot step beyond law's commitments or, itself, radically transform the culture of Canadian constitutionalism.

And this gestures to another set of possibilities. Perhaps you will be able to explain the ways in which your religious practice ought not to matter to the rule of law; maybe you will even feel culturally understood and respected. But if not, you have simply reached the cultural limits of legal tolerance; you have not exhausted the possibilities of cross-cultural justice. As Wendy Brown writes, coming to terms with the limits of tolerance "suggests alternative political possibilities that might affirm and productively exploit rather than disavow liberalism's culturalism."[99] Energy and attention could be redirected to the agonistic realm of politics or the institutions of civil society, each offering their own modes and limits of cross-cultural interaction.[100] Or perhaps we will be provoked to reimagine the shape of our practices of constitutionalism.[101] In this way, understanding the cultivation of indifference as a core adjudicative virtue in the interaction of religion and the constitutional rule of law may help to loosen the grip of the courts on the question of religious difference in Canadian society. This reflects the overarching effect of internalizing my account: to repoliticize the encounter between law and religion.

### Conclusion: Understanding and Self-Deception

Dilthey's thinking about the nature of understanding and how we make sense of ourselves and of our lives raises the problem of self-deception. In continually narrating the story of our lives, we are sometimes led to tell stories that comfort and serve us, even if they are not accurate. This is not the product of design but, rather, happens because we are opaque to ourselves, no less in political, social, and legal respects than in personal ways. This opacity presents an opportunity in which to tell a story about ourselves that, although based in lived experience, is also shaped or distorted by aspiration and fantasy. To be in thrall to such

---

99   Brown, *supra* note 11 at 174.

100  On the possibilities for the political as a realm of agonistic respect more appropriate than liberal toleration to the realities and challenges of pluralism, see Connolly, *supra* note 68.

101  See e.g. James Tully and the discussion of his work in chapter 3.

a story is what it means to be self-deceived. Such stories are natural enough and sometimes they are even self-protective. But the danger of self-deceptions is that they can misdirect our actions in ways that produce real harms in our lives and that, yet further, prevent us from seeing what we need to do to treat these ills.

Recall that, for Dilthey, the process of social understanding mirrors that of understanding in the individual. If so, the manner in which we narrate and, hence, understand our public lives is equally amenable to the perils of self-deception. Indeed, this is one way of understanding the most cogent modern critiques of liberalism.[102] Whatever good lies in the prevailing vision of the liberal political order, this picture also deeply self-deceives. The features of political life are not adequately captured in the story of political liberalism.

The conventional account of the relationship between law and religion is another public self-deception, one that is politically damaging and should be corrected by enriching and retelling our stories about law and religion. At its best, the exposure of self-deceptions opens up new possibilities and modes of action. As Charles Taylor makes clear in one of the epigraphs to this chapter, even as a theory serves us as an explanatory device, "we have to be alive to the way that understanding shapes practice, disrupts or facilitates it."[103] The account that I have provided in this book has not yielded an argument for how to structurally reconfigure Canadian constitutionalism, nor has it offered a doctrinal prescription to resolve the tensions found in this part of contemporary public life. The reconfiguration urged here is in the stories that we tell about the interaction of law and religion, and in the attitudes, postures, and sensibilities incumbent on such a shift. This work has thus heeded a different call: the idea that "what is demanded of a theoretical account is that it make the agent's doings clearer than they were to him. And this may easily involve challenging what he sees/saw as the normal language of self-description."[104] And so it is with the story of the interaction of law and religion, from which a more refined self-description opens up new and clearer ways of thinking about the ethics and practices of the adjudication of religion within the culture of Canadian constitutionalism.

---

102  See e.g. Paul W Kahn, *Putting Liberalism in its Place* (Princeton, NJ: Princeton University Press, 2005); Brown, *supra* note 11.
103  Taylor, "Understanding and Ethnocentricity," *supra* note 2 at 116.
104  *Ibid* at 118.

# Conclusion: Religion and Constitutionalism beyond the Mystification of Law

In the preface to his 1947 essay reflecting on the Moscow trials of the 1930s and the communism of which they were a part, Maurice Merleau-Ponty insisted on the need to push beyond official accounts and declared principles when seeking to assess the nature and justness of a society. He explained that "[w]hatever one's philosophical or even theological position, a society is not the temple of value-idols that figure on the front of its monuments or in its constitutional scrolls; the value of a society is the value it places upon man's relation to man."[1] True to his phenomenological commitments, Merleau-Ponty lamented that, met with the challenges of understanding, people too often "prefer to forget experience, to drop culture there and solemnly formulate as venerable truths the tired sayings which answer their weariness."[2] Resisting that tendency, he argued, was the methodological genius of Marx's critique of liberalism, quite apart from the merits of where that critique led him: "In refusing to judge liberalism in terms of the ideas it espouses and inscribes in constitutions and in demanding that these ideas be compared with the prevailing relations between men in a liberal state, Marx is not simply speaking in the name of a debatable materialist philosophy – he is providing a formula for the concrete study of society which cannot be refuted by idealist arguments."[3] Decrying the "mystification" that inheres in liberalism's insistence on analysis that begins with the purity of principle, Merleau-Ponty insisted that "[i]t is

---

1 Maurice Merleau-Ponty, *Humanism and Terror: An Essay on the Communist Problem*, translated by John O'Neill (Boston: Beacon Press, 1969) at xiv.
2 *Ibid* at xlii.
3 *Ibid* at xiv.

not just a question of knowing what the liberals have in mind but what in reality is done by the liberal state within and beyond its frontiers."[4] Instead, "[t]o understand and judge a society, one has to penetrate its basic structure to the human bond upon which it is built; this undoubtedly depends upon legal relations, but also upon forms of labor, ways of loving, living, and dying."[5]

A mid-twentieth-century essay on communism seems a curious touchstone for the conclusion to a book on the relationship between law and religion in Canada. Yet Merleau-Ponty's admonition to take up experience and culture in seeking to understand social relations echoes the approach adopted in this volume and the phenomenological turn in the study of law and religion that I urged in chapter 1. At the heart of this book is the desire to disturb the tired sayings that present in the guise of venerable truths around the relationship between religion and the constitutional rule of law in contemporary Canada. I have argued in these pages that the notions of legal multiculturalism and rights-based tolerance and accommodation that we find in our "constitutional scrolls," and that serve as our political monuments, have become the kind of value-idols that Merleau-Ponty warned will distract us from the issue that ought to call for our understanding: the character of prevailing social relations. My means of penetrating these stories has been to take up and exploit the category of culture, exploring the ways in which it can be heuristically useful to understand the essential character of the interaction of law and religion in cross-cultural terms. The messiness of culture is precisely that from which the conventional account seeks to redeem law. It is the conceit of law's autonomy from culture (and the political and historical story that it reflects) that sedates and rationalizes an interaction that has excited passions for the full arc of the history of the development of the modern legal and political order, and in Canada since well before the *Brassard v Langevin* case with which this book began.

Yet we are not redeemed from culture; we are insistently and inexorably shaped by it – perhaps always in ways that partially elude us.[6] The same is true of the culture of law's rule, which shapes the experience of social phenomena by setting them within the frame of law's informing intuitions, commitments, and rituals. Our public and private

---

4  *Ibid.*
5  *Ibid.*
6  See Judith Butler, *Giving an Account of Oneself* (New York: Fordham University Press, 2005).

lives are not wholly determined by this culture, but we are never free of its influence.[7] In the interaction of law and religion, that influence is seen in the way that law renders religion, reforming and fitting religion within the contours of its own cultural mould, leaving behind as trimmings the liberally unruly dimensions of religion-as-lived. That influence is felt in the practices of toleration, which are revealed as less pacific and more ambitious than prevailing orthodoxies would have it. And with our hands on this account of the character of law's relationship with religion – with law relocated from a managerial force above the cultural fray to itself an active participant in the realm of culture – I have argued that we are led to difficult questions not only about the public stories that we should tell, but specifically about the ethics and practices of adjudication, with the virtues of fidelity, humility, and the cultivation of indifference offering themselves as responses to the durably fraught experience of religious difference within the culture of Canadian constitutionalism.

The puzzle in this story is the durability of accounts based on law's autonomy from culture despite their descriptive inadequacy – despite the social experience of law's encounter with religion that they callously disregard. In *The Illusion of Free Markets*, Bernard Harcourt reflects on the persistence of the rhetoric of "free markets" and a commitment to the "idea of a natural order in the economic domain," despite the fictions that it perpetuates and the pathologies that it engenders.[8] Harcourt suggests that the answer might lie in the capacity of these ideas – however illusory – to allow us to see order rather than complexity. These rhetorical tropes offer the prospect of equilibrium. While in fact enabling increased regulation, they induce an appealing "sensation of liberation."[9] The result is that "faith in natural order and efficient markets" masks the only important question, which is the distributional justice of existing and alternative regulatory schemes.[10]

---

7  See Talal Asad, *Formations of the Secular: Christianity, Islam, Modernity* (Stanford, Cal: Stanford University Press, 2003) at 199: "Because the modern nation-state seeks to regulate all aspects of individual life – even the most intimate, such as birth and death – no one, whether religious or otherwise, can avoid encountering its ambitious powers. It's not only that the state intervenes directly in the social body for purposes of reform; it's that all social activity requires the consent of the law, and therefore of the nation-state."

8  Bernard E Harcourt, *The Illusion of Free Markets: Punishment and the Myth of Natural Order* (Cambridge, Mass: Harvard University Press, 2011) at 240.

9  *Ibid* at 241.

10  *Ibid* at 242.

Perhaps the persistence of commitment to the autonomy of law in our public understandings of the modern management of cultural difference can be traced to a similar political-emotional need. There is a certain social comfort that comes with the prospect of a legal regime or theoretical framework that can palliate the tensions produced by religious difference. In this, the conventional account of the interaction of religion and Canadian constitutionalism offers relief from an understandable weariness. It is an escape from complexity and from the formidable burdens of cultural understanding, masking the paramount question of how to live once seized with those understandings and with an appreciation for the nature and limits of the culture of law's rule.

## The Path Ahead

This book has primarily looked back, seeking a story of the relationship between law and religion that better captures the experience encoded in Canadian constitutional life and adjudication. Having travelled that path, and with that account now in hand, certain conceptual allegiances and analytic opportunities appear on the horizon for the study of law and religion.

Here in Canada, where so much of the recent history of constitutional theory has been preoccupied with questions of the legitimacy of judicial review and debates between *Charter* advocates and *Charter* sceptics, the essentially conservative nature of both poles in this debate has been exposed and challenged by the study of Indigenous law and Indigenous justice issues. Scholars in this field have begun to clear a different path, one that offers a means of getting at a deeper set of dynamics at play in Canadian constitutional life. The finest Canadian commentators on such issues have shown that the trenchant nature of the issues faced by Indigenous peoples attempting to negotiate (anew) their relationship within Canadian political and legal life is a product not only of barriers of political ideology, but differences of epistemology, ontology, language, and ritual.[11] Stitched into the very fabric of this scholarship

---

11  See e.g. Andrée Boisselle, "Beyond Consent and Disagreement: Why Law's Authority Is Not Just about Will" in Jeremy Webber & Colin M Macleod, eds, *Between Consenting Peoples: Political Community and the Meaning of Consent* (Vancouver: UBC Press, 2010) 207; John Borrows, *Drawing Out Law: A Spirit's Guide* (Toronto: University of Toronto Press, 2010); John Borrows, *Canada's Indigenous Constitution* (Toronto: University of Toronto Press, 2010).

is the insistence that constitutional analysis must grapple with what it means to take culture seriously.

On one hand, this book's sustained effort to expose and explore the way in which the contemporary constitutional rule of law can be profitably understood as itself a cultural form offers something useful to this literature. And yet perhaps more exciting is what Indigenous legal scholarship has to offer a study of law and religion that is sensitive and attentive to the nature and challenges of cross-cultural interaction. There is much in the history and politics of Canada that distinguishes Aboriginal justice issues from the questions raised by the interaction of law and religion. And yet there is also something of a genetic link between these two areas of constitutional reflection. Despite the many differences between the fields, the problem of translation and understanding across framing ontologies, divergent aesthetic intuitions, and ways of life is pivotal to both topics. As suggested in chapter 3, the analysis of constitutionalism and religious difference has much to gain from studying the dynamics of cross-cultural encounter and the cultural force of state law, a study that has long been at the heart of scholarly reflection on Indigenous communities' experiences of Canadian law.

Indigenous legal scholarship also offers a cue to the study of religious difference and the law in its insistent focus on the quality of relationships between and among groups as the controlling question of constitutional law, rather than the distracting question of law's fidelity to its own abstractions.[12] Scholars of Indigenous law and Aboriginal justice have long seen through the conceits of law's autonomy from culture and can lead the way for those committed to a more subtle understanding of what is at stake in the relationship between law and religion. In these ways, there are conceptual allegiances and resonances with Indigenous legal studies from which the future study of law and religion can learn.

This concern with the quality of the relationships that subsist beneath law's stories also suggests ways in which the account offered in this book could contribute to the study of law, religion, and the political in other jurisdictions and as a comparative constitutional matter. This volume has focused on the Canadian setting. In part, that focus is a response to the particularly precious place of the story of legal

---

12  See e.g. Boisselle, *supra* note 11; Val Napoleon, "Living Together: Gitksan Legal Reasoning as a Foundation for Consent" in Webber & Macleod, *supra* note 11, 45.

multiculturalism in Canadians' self-understanding of their political relationship to diversity. The centrality of that account and the associated image of law's role in managing religious difference generated the descriptive problem that fuelled this volume. Yet that focus is also the product of a commitment to a certain approach to comparative constitutional law, one that puts stock in the idea that the path to comparative insight runs through the thick contextualized description of local problems, rather than through jurisdictional tourism.[13] But having now completed the local journey, if one draws back further, away from the Canadian stage, and looks more broadly at the study of law, politics, and religion in other countries and from a comparative perspective, the account in this book suggests certain lessons and directions for further inquiry.

Some of those fruits may come from direct comparison: to the extent that the study of the Canadian setting has yielded insights about the nature of liberal constitutionalism, and the challenges posed by religious diversity in that cultural atmosphere, there is an intuition in this book that one will find similar patterns and dynamics in other liberal constitutional orders. Identifying those resonances and finding points of divergence would be the task of other local studies.

More important than underwriting these direct comparisons, I suspect, is the way that this volume points to the mystification of secularism. Recall Merleau-Ponty's complaint about liberalism's commitment to the purity of principle and his admonition that understanding comes not from "knowing what the liberals have in mind but what in reality is done by the liberal state within and beyond its frontiers."[14] The conceptual core of this book is the demonstration of how very little, indeed, broad invocations of legal principle or policy illuminate the social and political experiences of religious diversity and how they can, in fact, obstruct our view of the human and community bonds and relationships that subsist beneath such claims. If "legal multiculturalism" has that effect in Canada, it is just one expression of a broader habit of hiding the unruly lived experience of religion and modern constitutionalism under the tidy marquee of principle. It usually reads "secularism" and its invocation tells us little of significance.

---

13 It is that approach that informs the series that I co-edit with Andrew Harding, Peter Leyland, Grégoire Webber, and Rosalind Dixon, Hart Publishing's *Constitutional Systems of the World*.

14 Merleau-Ponty, *supra* note 1 at xiv.

Some of the most instructive scholarship in the study of law and religion has been precisely concerned with excavating the social relationships and political experiences that carry on under an official story about secularism. We have learned that despite the rhetorical saturation of *laïcité* in France and its insistence on a politics of common republican identity, unmediated by other associational allegiances, a rich associational life in fact thrives among religious communities in that country[15] and that the expression and negotiation of public religious identity is a far more complicated matter than the orthodox narrative would suggest.[16] Others have argued that the local shape of the secular has more to do with the particularities of political history than the purity of principle.[17] Back in Canada, the 2013–14 debate about a "Charter of Secularism" in Quebec showed the extent to which the "principle" of secularism is – at best – the profoundly unstable starting point for a conversation about the relationships between law, politics, and religion, not a response to the challenges that these relationships produce. Despite the variety of secularisms,[18] there may be academic value in using the concept of secularism as a way of organizing a repertoire of moves available in the project of untethering religion and political authority.[19] But its capacity to hold any stable normative or descriptive content consistently dissolves on close inspection. As a result, when applied to a local context, the idea of the secular conducts

---

15 John R Bowen, *Can Islam Be French? Pluralism and Pragmatism in a Secularist State* (Princeton, NJ: Princeton University Press, 2010).

16 Mayanthi L Fernando, "Reconfiguring Freedom: Muslim Piety and the Limits of Secular Law and Public Discourse in France" (2010) 37:1 American Ethnologist 19.

17 See e.g. Ahmet T Kuru, *Secularism and State Policies toward Religion: The United States, France, and Turkey* (New York: Cambridge University Press, 2009); Elizabeth Shakman Hurd, *The Politics of Secularism in International Relations* (Princeton, NJ: Princeton University Press, 2008).

18 See e.g. Janet R Jakobsen & Ann Pellegrini, eds, *Secularisms* (Durham, NC: Duke University Press, 2008); Michael Warner, Jonathan VanAntwerpen & Craig Calhoun, eds, *Varieties of Secularism in a Secular Age* (Cambridge, Mass: Harvard University Press, 2010); James Q Whitman, "Separating Church and State: The Atlantic Divide" (2008) 34:3 Historical Reflections 86.

19 I explore this idea of secularism as a "repertoire of moves" in Benjamin L Berger, "Belonging to Law: Religious Difference, Secularism, and the Conditions of Civic Inclusion" (2015) 24:1 Soc & Leg Stud 47. Mayanthi Fernando argues that there is a danger in thinking of secularism only in local and particular terms. The risk lies in underestimating "the globalizing power of the behaviors, knowledges, sensibilities, and political arrangements that have come to comprise the secular." Fernando, *supra* note 16 at 31.

(and conduces to) the very conceit of law's autonomy from culture, history, and power that has been the object of critique in this book. In this way, just as the conventional account of the interaction of law and religion does in Canada, invocations of the secular tend to distract from the democratic relationships and lived experiences that ought to be the subject of our concern. I suspect that it is an example of the kind of conceptual ascent whose appeal and popularity is traceable more to its capacity to comfort, through release from messy perplexities of lived experience, than from its philosophical or practical utility. This is the mystification of secularism; this volume suggests that, in pursuit of local understanding, we would do better leaving the concept aside.

Upsetting the conceits of law has thus been not only essential to a richer understanding of the relationship between law and religion in contemporary Canadian constitutionalism; it also offers itself as an important element in the broader comparative study of law and religion. As the mystification of law in matters of religious difference is disrupted, there is, however, another conceit that comes into view, one whose disruption is equally essential to understanding the interaction of law, religion, and the political, and that itself calls for our critical attention. Perhaps the most potent expression of this analytical problem is the emergence of religious freedom advocacy on the international diplomatic stage. The Canadian government's creation of an Office of Religious Freedom, headed by an ambassador of religious freedom, in 2013 – a move that mimicked the U.S. State Department's Office of International Religious Freedom – is an example of a particular way of positioning and framing religion.[20] To be sure, there are concerns about the partisan religious motives that might influence such offices. Of more analytic interest, however, is the way in which the creation of discrete diplomatic offices concerned with religious freedom suggests that religion can be severed or extricated from the web of social and political factors that contribute to a just society. What appear as instances of religious foment or present as complaints about religious oppression are equally likely to be artefacts of economic distress, social injustice, and political disenfranchisement.

These are examples at the international diplomatic level, but a similarly insulated framing of religion can be seen in domestic political and

---

20  For a superb study of this phenomenon, see Elizabeth Shakman Hurd, *Beyond Religious Freedom: The New Global Politics of Religion* (Princeton, NJ: Princeton University Press, 2015).

legal debates. The practical force of constitutional protections invites the neat packaging of complicated social issues into the available categories of legal analysis, extracting religion as the uniquely salient motive, concealing the way that economics, demographic change, and political marginalization are imbricated in issues that are framed simply as matters concerning "religion." And so the touchstone case in the law of religious freedom in Canada, *R v Big M Drug Mart Ltd*,[21] takes up residence in our legal and political imaginations as a case having to do with religion, when Michael Mandel argued persuasively that the case could instead be read as one about economic justice and corporate interest.[22] Similarly, the Parti Québécois' proposed "Charter of Secularism," and the debates it generated, had clear religious freedom contours, but cannot be effectively understood apart from the politics of nationalism and the constitutional history that fuel them. The effect is a different conceit of autonomy; the conceit of law's autonomy from culture is joined by the conceit of religion's autonomy from the other determinants of political and economic freedom and justice.

The idea that the analytic autonomy of religion misleads us is hardly a new insight. In his *Letter Concerning Toleration*, Locke warned of understanding religion and religious tolerance in isolation from other sources and conditions of oppression. Thinking of those who gathered together in conspiracies under the banner of religion, Locke explained that "'tis not Religion that inspires them to it in their Meetings; but their Sufferings and Oppressions that make them willing to ease themselves."[23] Religion offers itself as a category of apparent solidity and self-sufficiency, one that also possesses constitutional significance in modern constitutional democracies. Knowing as we do that religion is, in fact, a highly unstable category that points to a richly dynamic and evolving set of social practices and collective meanings, we also need to trouble this conceit of religion's autonomy.[24] Having cleared our view of the legal mystification, we would learn a great deal from

---

21  [1985] 1 SCR 295.

22  Michael Mandel, *The Charter of Rights and the Legalization of Politics in Canada*, revised ed (Toronto: Thompson Educational, 1994).

23  John Locke, *A Letter Concerning Toleration*, ed by James H Tully (Indianapolis: Hackett, 1983) at 52.

24  See Talal Asad, "The Construction of Religion as an Anthropological Category" in *Genealogies of Religion: Discipline and Reasons of Power in Christianity and Islam* (Baltimore: Johns Hopkins University Press, 1993) 27.

research that tracks the movement of social and economic issues into the language of religious dissent and freedom of religion, tracing the political incentives, both domestically and internationally, of framing and interpreting social critique and conflict in the forms and categories of religious freedom.

## The Priority of Understanding

The ambition of this book has been more modest. Unsatisfied with prevailing stories about law's relationship to religious difference in Canada, I have sought a keener appreciation of the interaction of law and religion in this constitutional setting through sustained reflection on the experiences and dynamics revealed in our constitutional law. In arguing that we think most clearly about this interaction when we approach law as a cultural form, this volume illustrates one of the key meta-lessons in the study of law and religion: that the principal reward of the study of law and religion is a fuller appreciation of the character of law. This is no less true of the study of the contemporary relationship between these rich aspects of social life than it is of historical examination of this interaction in the emergence of modern law.[25]

And if we are to regard the character of this stimulating interaction in the cultural terms that I have suggested, the critical lesson for our legal and political practices is the priority of understanding in pursuit of the just. Merleau-Ponty wrote that "true liberty takes others as they are, tries to understand even those doctrines which are its negation, and never allows itself to judge before understanding. We must fulfil our freedom of thought in the freedom of understanding."[26] That search for understanding – of law, of religion, and of the nature and limits of both – is what must ground our judgments about religious difference and the claims of constitutionalism.

---

25  See e.g. Harold Berman, *The Interaction of Law and Religion* (Nashville: Abingdon Press, 1974); James Q Whitman, *The Origins of Reasonable Doubt: Theological Roots of the Criminal Trial* (New Haven, Conn: Yale University Press, 2008).

26  Merleau-Ponty, *supra* note 1 at xxiv–xxv.

# Bibliography

Anderson, Gavin W. "Social Democracy and the Limits of Rights Constitutionalism." *Canadian Journal of Law and Jurisprudence* 17 (2004): 31–59.

Asad, Talal. "The Construction of Religion as an Anthropological Category." In *Genealogies of Religion: Discipline and Reasons of Power in Christianity and Islam*, 27–54. Baltimore: Johns Hopkins University Press, 1993.

– *Formations of the Secular: Christianity, Islam, Modernity*. Stanford, Cal: Stanford University Press, 2003.

Bakan, Joel. *Just Words: Constitutional Rights and Social Wrongs*. Toronto: University of Toronto Press, 1997.

Bakht, Natasha. *Arbitration, Religion and Family Law: Private Justice on the Backs of Women*. Ottawa: National Association of Women and the Law, 2005.

Barak, Aharon. *Proportionality: Constitutional Rights and Their Limitations*. Translated by Doron Kalir. Cambridge, UK: Cambridge University Press, 2012.

Beaman, Lori G. *Defining Harm: Religious Freedom and the Limits of the Law*. Vancouver: UBC Press, 2008.

Beatty, David M. *The Ultimate Rule of Law*. Oxford: Oxford University Press, 2004.

Benhabib, Seyla. *The Claims of Culture: Equality and Diversity in the Global Era*. Princeton, NJ: Princeton University Press, 2002.

Berger, Benjamin L. "Belonging to Law: Religious Difference, Secularism, and the Conditions of Civic Inclusion." *Social & Legal Studies* 24, no. 1 (2015): 47–64.

– "Children of Two Logics: A Way into Canadian Constitutional Culture." *International Journal of Constitutional Law* 11, no. 2 (2013): 319–38.

– "Moral Judgment, Criminal Law, and the Constitutional Protection of Religion." *Supreme Court Law Review*, 2nd ser., 40 (2008): 513–52.

– "Polygamy and the Predicament of Contemporary Criminal Law." In *Polygamy's Rights and Wrongs: Perspectives on Harm, Family and Law,* edited by Gillian Calder and Lori G. Beaman, 69–88. Vancouver: UBC Press, 2013.

– "Religious Diversity, Education, and the 'Crisis' in State Neutrality." *Canadian Journal of Law and Society* 29, no. 1 (2013): 103–22.

– "Section 1, Constitutional Reasoning and Cultural Difference: Assessing the Impacts of *Alberta v. Hutterian Brethren of Wilson Colony.*" *Supreme Court Law Review,* 2nd ser., 51 (2010): 25–46.

Berlin, Isaiah. "Two Concepts of Liberty." In *Contemporary Political Philosophy,* edited by Robert E. Goodin and Philip Pettit, 391–417. Oxford: Blackwell, 1997.

Berman, Harold. *The Interaction of Law and Religion.* Nashville: Abingdon Press, 1974.

Bhabha, Homi K. *The Location of Culture.* London: Routledge, 1994.

Bickel, Alexander M. *The Least Dangerous Branch: The Supreme Court at the Bar of Politics.* 2nd ed. New Haven, Conn: Yale University Press, 1986.

Blomley, Nicholas K. "Flowers in the Bathtub: Boundary Crossings at the Public-Private Divide." *Geoforum* 36 (2005): 281–96.

– *Law, Space and the Geographies of Power.* New York: Guilford Press, 1994.

Boisselle, Andrée. "Beyond Consent and Disagreement: Why Law's Authority Is Not Just about Will." In *Between Consenting Peoples: Political Community and the Meaning of Consent,* edited by Jeremy Webber and Colin M. Macleod, 207–29. Vancouver: UBC Press, 2010.

Boorstin, Daniel J. *The Mysterious Science of the Law: An Essay on Blackstone's Commentaries.* Gloucester: Peter Smith, 1973.

Borrows, John. *Canada's Indigenous Constitution.* Toronto: University of Toronto Press, 2010.

– *Drawing Out Law: A Spirit's Guide.* Toronto: University of Toronto Press, 2010.

– "Listening for a Change: The Courts and Oral Tradition." *Osgoode Hall Law Journal* 39, no. 1 (Spring 2001): 1–38.

– *Recovering Canada: The Resurgence of Indigenous Law.* Toronto: University of Toronto Press, 2002.

– "With or without You: First Nations Law (in Canada)." *McGill Law Journal* 41:2 (June 1996): 629–65.

Bouchard, Gérard, and Charles Taylor. *Building the Future, a Time for Reconciliation: Report.* Québec: Commission de consultation sur les pratiques d'accommodement reliées aux différences culturelles, 2008.

Bourdieu, Pierre. *In Other Words: Essays Towards a Reflexive Sociology.* Stanford, Cal: Stanford University Press, 1990.

Bowen, John R. *Can Islam Be French? Pluralism and Pragmatism in a Secularist State*. Princeton, NJ: Princeton University Press, 2010.

Brightman, Robert. "Forget Culture: Replacement, Transcendence, Relexification." *Cultural Anthropology* 10 (1995): 509–46.

Brougham, Lord H. *Historical Sketches of Statesmen Who Flourished in the Time of George III*, vol. 1. London: Richard Griffith, 1855.

Brown, David M. "Neutrality or Privilege? A Comment on Religious Freedom." *Supreme Court Law Review*, 2nd ser., 29 (2005): 221–35.

Brown, Wendy. *Regulating Aversion: Tolerance in the Age of Identity and Empire*. Princeton, NJ: Princeton University Press, 2006.

Brudner, Alan. *Punishment and Freedom: A Liberal Theory of Penal Justice*. New York: Oxford University Press, 2009.

– *The Unity of the Common Law: Studies in Hegelian Jurisprudence*. Berkeley: University of California Press, 1995.

Buckingham, Janet Epp. *Fighting over God: A Legal and Political History of Religious Freedom in Canada*. Montreal and Kingston: McGill-Queen's University Press, 2014.

Burt, Robert A. *Death Is That Man Taking Names: Intersections of American Medicine, Law, and Culture*. Berkeley: University of California Press, 2002.

Bushnell, Ian. *The Captive Court: A Study of the Supreme Court of Canada*. Montreal and Kingston: McGill-Queen's University Press, 1992.

Butler, Judith. *Giving an Account of Oneself*. New York: Fordham University Press, 2005.

Cassirer, Ernst. *An Essay on Man: An Introduction to a Philosophy of Human Culture*. New Haven, Conn: Yale University Press, 1944.

Clifford, James. *The Predicament of Culture*. Cambridge, Mass: Harvard University Press, 1988.

Comaroff, Jean, and John L. Comaroff. *Theory from the South: Or, How Euro-America Is Evolving toward Africa*. Boulder, CO: Paradigm, 2012.

Congregation for the Doctrine of the Faith. *Considerations regarding Proposals to Give Legal Recognition to Unions between Homosexual Persons*. Nairobi: Pauline Publications Africa, 2003.

Connolly, William E. *Identity/Difference: Democratic Negotiations of Political Paradox*. Expanded ed. Minneapolis: University of Minnesota Press, 2002.

– *Pluralism*. Durham, NC: Duke University Press, 2005.

– *Why I Am Not a Secularist*. Minneapolis: University of Minnesota Press, 1999.

Cooper, Davina. *Governing out of Order: Space, Law and the Politics of Belonging*. London: Rivers Oram Press, 1998.

Cover, Robert M. "The Supreme Court 1982 Term – Foreword: *Nomos* and Narrative." *Harvard Law Review* 97 (1983): 4–68.

Dallmayr, Fred. *Beyond Orientalism: Essays on Cross-Cultural Encounter*. Albany, NY: SUNY, 1996.

Dannenmaier, Eric. "Beyond Indigenous Property Rights: Exploring the Emergence of a Distinctive Connection Doctrine." *Washington University Law Review* 86 (2008): 53–110.

Delaney, David. *Territory: A Short Introduction*. Oxford: Blackwell, 2005.

Devlin, Patrick. *The Enforcement of Morals*. London: Oxford University Press, 1965.

Diamond, Stanley. "The Rule of Law versus the Order of Custom." *Social Research* 38 (1971): 42–72.

Dilthey, Wilhelm. *The Formation of the Historical World in the Human Sciences*. Vol. 3 of *Selected Works*, edited by Rudolf A. Makreel and Frithjof Rodi, translated by Rudolf A. Makreel and William H. Oman. Princeton, NJ: Princeton University Press, 2002.

Douglas, Mary. *Purity and Danger: An Analysis of Concepts of Pollution and Taboo*. London: Routledge, 2002.

Douzinas, Costas, Shaun McVeigh, and Ronnie Warrington. "The Alta(e)rs of Law: The Judgement of Legal Aesthetics." *Theory, Culture & Society* 9, no. 4 (November 1992): 93–117.

Douzinas, Costas, and Lynda Neal, eds. *Law and the Image: The Authority of Art and the Aesthetics of Law*. Chicago: University of Chicago Press, 1999.

Durkheim, Emile. *The Elementary Forms of Religious Life*. Translated by Karen E. Fields. New York: Free Press, 1995. First published 1912.

Eisenberg, Avigail. *Reasons of Identity: A Normative Guide to the Political & Legal Assessment of Identity Claims*. Oxford: Oxford University Press, 2009.

– "Rights in the Age of Identity Politics." *Osgoode Hall Law Journal* 50 (2013): 609–36.

Eisgruber, Christopher L., and Lawrence G. Sager. *Religious Freedom and the Constitution*. Cambridge, Mass: Harvard University Press, 2007.

Eliade, Mircea. *Sacred and the Profane: The Nature of Religion*. New York: Harcourt, Brace & World, 1959.

Eliot, T.S. "Burnt Norton." In *Four Quartets*, 3–8. New York: Harcourt, Brace, and Company, 1943.

Esau, Alvin J. "Communal Property and Freedom of Religion: *Lakeside Colony of Hutterian Brethren v. Hofer*." In *Religious Conscience, the State, and the Law*, edited by John McLaren and Harold Coward, 97–116. Albany, NY: SUNY, 1999.

– *The Courts and the Colonies: The Litigation of Hutterite Church Disputes*. Vancouver: UBC Press, 2004.

Fernando, Mayanthi L. "Reconfiguring Freedom: Muslim Piety and the Limits of Secular Law and Public Discourse in France." *American Ethnologist* 37, no. 1 (2010): 19–35.

Ford, Richard T. "Law's Territory (A History of Jurisdiction)." *Michigan Law Review* 97 (1999): 843–930.

Forst, Rainer. "The Limits of Toleration." *Constellations* 11 (2004): 312–25.

Freud, Sigmund. "The Future of an Illusion." Translated by James Strachey. In *Civilization, Society and Religion*, vol. 12, edited by Albert Dickson, 179–241. London: Penguin Books, 1991. First published 1927.

– "Totem and Taboo: Some Points of Agreement between the Mental Lives of Savages and Neurotics." Translated by James Strachey. In *The Origins of Religion*, vol. 13, edited by Albert Dickson, 43–224. London: Penguin Books, 1990. First published 1913.

Geary, Adam. *Law and Aesthetics*. Oxford: Hart, 2001.

Geertz, Clifford. *Available Light: Anthropological Reflections on Philosophical Topics*. Princeton, NJ: Princeton University Press, 2000.

– *The Interpretation of Cultures*. New York: Basic Books, 1973.

Geuss, Raymond. *Philosophy and Real Politics*. Princeton, NJ: Princeton University Press, 2008.

Grant, George. *English-Speaking Justice*. Toronto: House of Anansi Press, 1998. First published 1974.

Gray, John. *Two Faces of Liberalism*. New York: New Press, 2000.

Greenblatt, Stephen. "Culture." In *Critical Terms for Literary Study*, edited by Frank Lentricchia and Thomas McLaughlin, 225–32. Chicago: University of Chicago Press, 1990.

Habermas, Jürgen. *Lifeworld and System: A Critique of Functionalist Reason*. Vol. 2 of *The Theory of Communicative Action*. Translated by Thomas McCarthy. Boston: Beacon Press, 1987.

– "Religion in the Public Sphere." *European Journal of Philosophy* 14, no. 1 (2006): 1–25.

Haefeli, Evan. *New Netherland and the Dutch Origins of American Religious Liberty*. Philadelphia: University of Pennsylvania Press, 2012.

Halberstam, Joshua. "The Paradox of Tolerance." *Philosophical Forum* 14, no. 2 (1982–3): 190–207.

Harcourt, Bernard E. "The Collapse of the Harm Principle." *Journal of Criminal Law & Criminology* 90, no. 1 (Fall 1999): 109–94.

– *The Illusion of Free Markets: Punishment and the Myth of Natural Order*. Cambridge, Mass: Harvard University Press, 2011.

Hart, H.L.A. "Immorality and Treason." In *Morality and the Law*, edited by Richard A. Wasserstrom, 48–54. Belmont, Cal: Wadsworth, 1971.

– *Law, Liberty, and Morality*. London: Oxford University Press, 1963.

Heath, Joseph. "Immigration, Multiculturalism, and the Social Contract." *Canadian Journal of Law & Jurisprudence* 10 (1997): 343–60.

Heidegger, Martin. *Being and Time*. New York: Harper & Row, 1962.

Henderson, James (Sákéj) Youngblood. "Postcolonial Indigenous Legal Consciousness." *Indigenous Law Journal* 1 (2002): 1–56.

Hill, Thomas E., Jr. "Kantian Pluralism." *Ethics* 102, no. 4 (1992): 743–62.

Hurd, Elizabeth Shakman. *Beyond Religious Freedom: The New Global Politics of Religion*. Princeton, NJ: Princeton University Press, 2015.

– *The Politics of Secularism in International Relations*. Princeton, NJ: Princeton University Press, 2008.

Jakobsen, Janet R., and Ann Pellegrini, eds. *Secularisms*. Durham, NC: Duke University Press, 2008.

James, William. *The Varieties of Religious Experience: A Study in Human Nature*. London: Routledge, 2002. First published 1902.

Jedwab, Jack. "To Preserve and Enhance: Canadian Multiculturalism before and after the *Charter*." *Supreme Court Law Review*, 2nd ser., 19 (2003): 309–44.

Kahan, Dan M., John Gastil, Donald Braman, and Paul Slovic. "Fear of Democracy: A Cultural Evaluation of Sunstein on Risk." *Harvard Law Review* 119, no. 4 (February 2006): 1071–109.

Kahn, Paul W. *The Cultural Study of Law: Reconstructing Legal Scholarship*. Chicago: University of Chicago Press, 1999.

– *Finding Ourselves at the Movies: Philosophy for a New Generation*. New York: Columbia University Press, 2013.

– *Political Theology: Four New Chapters on the Concept of Sovereignty*. New York: Columbia University Press, 2011.

– *Putting Liberalism in Its Place*. Princeton, NJ: Princeton University Press, 2005.

– *The Reign of Law: Marbury v. Madison and the Construction of America*. New Haven, Conn: Yale University Press, 1997.

Kant, Immanuel. *Critique of Pure Reason*. Translated by J.M.D. Meiklejohn. New York: Dutton, 1934.

Kelsen, Hans. *General Theory of Law and State*. Translated by Anders Wedberg. New York: Russell & Russell, 1961.

Kennedy, W.P.M., ed. *Statutes, Treaties and Documents of the Canadian Constitution, 1713–1929*. 2nd ed. Toronto: Oxford University Press, 1930.

Korteweg, Anna C., and Jennifer A. Selby, eds. *Debating Sharia: Islam, Gender Politics, and Family Law Arbitration*. Toronto: University of Toronto Press, 2012.

Kronman, Anthony T. "Precedent and Tradition." *Yale Law Journal* 99 (1990): 1029–68.

Krygier, Martin. "Law as Tradition." *Law and Philosophy* 5 (1986): 237–62.

Kuru, Ahmet T. *Secularism and State Policies toward Religion: The United States, France, and Turkey*. New York: Cambridge University Press, 2009.

Kymlicka, Will. "Canadian Multiculturalism in Historical and Comparative Perspective: Is Canada Unique." *Constitutional Forum* 13, no. 1 (2003): 1–8.

– *Multicultural Citizenship: A Liberal Theory of Minority Rights*. Oxford: Clarendon Press, 1995.

Latour, Bruno. *The Making of Law: An Ethnography of the Conseil d'Etat*. Cambridge, UK: Polity Press, 2010.

– *Rejoicing: Or the Torments of Religious Speech*. Translated by Julie Rose. Cambridge, UK: Polity Press, 2002.

Legrand, Pierre. Book Review of *Comparing Legal Cultures*, edited by David Nelken. *Cambridge Law Journal* 56 (1997): 646–9.

Lessard, Hester. "*Charter* Gridlock: Equality Formalism and Marriage Fundamentalism." In *Diminishing Returns: Inequality and the Canadian Charter of Rights and Freedoms*, edited by Sheila McIntyre and Sandra Rodgers, 291–316. Markham, Ont: LexisNexis, 2006.

– "Mothers, Fathers, and Naming: Reflections on the *Law* Equality Framework and *Trociuk* v. *British Columbia (Attorney General)*." *Canadian Journal of Women and the Law* 16 (2004): 165–211.

Levine, Philip. *Not This Pig: Poems*. Middletown, Conn: Wesleyan University Press, 1968.

Locke, John. *A Letter Concerning Toleration*. Edited by James H. Tully. Indianapolis: Hackett, 1983.

MacDougall, Bruce. "Refusing to Officiate at Same-Sex Civil Marriages." *Saskatchewan Law Review* 69 (2006): 351–73.

Magnet, Joseph Eliot. "Multiculturalism and Collective Rights." *Supreme Court Law Review*, 2nd ser., 27 (2005): 431–97.

Majury, Diana. "Women Are Themselves to Blame: Choice as a Justification for Unequal Treatment." In *Making Equality Rights Real: Securing Substantive Equality under the Charter*, edited by Fay Faraday, Margaret Denike, and M. Kate Stephenson, 209–43. Toronto: Irwin Law, 2006.

Mandel, Michael. *The Charter of Rights and the Legalization of Politics in Canada*. Rev. ed. Toronto: Thompson Educational, 1994.

Masuzawa, Tomoko. "Culture." In *Critical Terms for Religious Studies*, edited by Mark C. Taylor, 70–93. Chicago: University of Chicago Press, 1998.

– *The Invention of World Religions: Or, How European Universalism Was Preserved in the Language of Pluralism*. Chicago: University of Chicago Press, 2005.

Mathen, Carissima. "What Religious Freedom Jurisprudence Reveals about Equality." *Journal of Law & Equality* 6 (2009): 163–200.

Mautner, Menachem. *Law and the Culture of Israel.* Oxford: Oxford University Press, 2011.

McLaren, John. "The Doukhobor Belief in Individual Faith and Conscience and the Demands of the Secular State." In *Religious Conscience, the State, and the Law,* edited by John McLaren and Harold Coward, 117–35. Albany, NY: SUNY, 1999.

McNeil, Kent. "The Vulnerability of Indigenous Land Rights in Australia and Canada." *Osgoode Hall Law Journal* 42 (2004): 271–301.

Merleau-Ponty, Maurice. *Humanism and Terror: An Essay on the Communist Problem.* Translated by John O'Neill. Boston: Beacon Press, 1969.

Minow, Martha. "Putting Up and Putting Down: Tolerance Reconsidered." *Osgoode Hall Law Journal* 28 (1990): 409–48.

Modood, Tariq. *Multiculturalism: A Civic Idea.* Cambridge, UK: Polity Press, 2007.

Moon, Richard. "Accommodation without Compromise: Comment on *Alberta v. Hutterian Brethren of Wilson Colony.*" *Supreme Court Law Review,* 2nd ser., 51 (2010): 95–130.

– *Freedom of Conscience and Religion.* Toronto: Irwin Law, 2014.

– "Freedom of Religion under the Charter of Rights: The Limits of State Neutrality." *UBC Law Review* 45 (2012): 497.

– "Government Support for Religious Practice." In *Law and Religious Pluralism in Canada,* edited by Richard Moon, 217–38. Vancouver: UBC Press, 2008.

– "Religious Commitment and Identity: *Syndicat Northcrest v Amselem.*" *Supreme Court Law Review,* 2nd ser., 29 (2005): 201–20.

Moran, Dermot. "Hilary Putnam and Immanuel Kant: Two 'Internal Realists'?" *Synthèse* 123, no. 1 (2000): 65–104.

Mouffe, Chantal. *The Democratic Paradox.* London: Verso, 2000.

– *On the Political.* New York: Routledge, 2005.

Nadasdy, Paul. "'Property' and Aboriginal Land Claims in the Canadian Subarctic: Some Theoretical Considerations." *American Anthropologist* 104 (2002): 247–61.

Napoleon, Val. "Living Together: Gitksan Legal Reasoning as a Foundation for Consent." In *Between Consenting Peoples: Political Community and the Meaning of Consent,* edited by Jeremy Webber and Colin M. Macleod, 45–76. Vancouver: UBC Press, 2010.

Nussbaum, Martha C. *Political Emotions: Why Love Matters for Justice.* Cambridge, Mass: Belknap Press of Harvard University Press, 2013.

Ogilvie, M.H. *Religious Institutions and the Law in Canada*. 3rd ed. Toronto: Irwin Law, 2010.

Perry, Michael J. "Why Political Reliance on Religiously Grounded Morality Is Not Illegitimate in a Liberal Democracy." *Wake Forest Law Review* 36 (2001): 217–49.

Petter, Andrew. "Legalise This: The *Chartering* of Canadian Politics." In *Contested Constitutionalism: Reflections on the Canadian Charter of Rights and Freedoms*, edited by James Kelly and Chris Manfredi, 33–49. Vancouver: UBC Press, 2009.

Phillips, Adam. *Terrors and Experts*. Cambridge, Mass: Harvard University Press, 1996.

Pitkin, Hanna Fenichel. "The Idea of a Constitution." *Journal of Legal Education* 37 (1987): 167–9.

Posner, Richard A. *The Economics of Justice*. Cambridge, Mass: Harvard University Press, 1981.

Post, Robert C. "Foreword: Fashioning the Legal Constitution; Culture, Courts, and Law." *Harvard Law Review* 117 (2003): 4–112.

Post, Robert C., and Reva B. Siegel. "Legislative Constitutionalism and Section Five Power: Polycentric Interpretation of the Family and Medical Leave Act." *Yale Law Journal* 112 (2003): 1943–2059.

Pothier, Dianne. "Connecting Grounds of Discrimination to Real People's Real Experiences." *Canadian Journal of Women and the Law* 13, no. 1 (2001): 37–73.

Pue, Wesley. "Wrestling with Law: (Geographical) Specificity v. (Legal) Abstraction." *Urban Geography* 11 (1990): 566–85.

Raustiala, Kal. "The Geography of Justice." *Fordham Law Review* 73 (2005): 2501–60.

Rawls, John. *Political Liberalism*. New York: Columbia University Press, 1996.
– *A Theory of Justice*. Rev. ed. Oxford: Oxford University Press, 1999.

Réaume, Denise G. "Legal Multiculturalism from the Bottom Up." In *Canadian Political Philosophy: Contemporary Reflections*, edited by Ronald Beiner and Wayne Norman, 194–206. Oxford: Oxford University Press, 2001.

Resnik, Judith. "Living Their Legal Commitments: Paideic Communities, Courts, and Robert Cover." *Yale Journal of Law & the Humanities* 17 (2005): 17–53.

Rosanvallon, Pierre. *The Demands of Liberty: Civil Society in France since the Revolution*. Translated by Arthur Goldhammer. Cambridge, Mass: Harvard University Press, 2007.

Ryder, Bruce. "The Canadian Conception of Equal Religious Citizenship." In *Law and Religious Pluralism in Canada*, edited by Richard Moon, 87–109. Vancouver: UBC Press, 2008.

- "State Neutrality and Freedom of Conscience and Religion." *Supreme Court Law Review*, 2nd ser., 29 (2005): 169–99.
Sager, Lawrence G. "Justice in Plain Clothes: Reflections on the Thinness of Constitutional Law." *Northwestern University Law Review* 88 (1993): 410–35.
Schlag, Pierre. "The Aesthetics of American Law." *Harvard Law Review* 115, no. 4 (February 2002): 1047–118.
Schneiderman, David. "Property Rights and Regulatory Innovation: Comparing Constitutional Cultures." *International Journal of Constitutional Law* 4, no. 2 (2006): 371–91.
Seljak, David. "Resisting the 'No Man's Land' of Private Religion: The Catholic Church and Public Politics in Quebec." In *Rethinking Church, State, and Modernity: Canada between Europe and America*, edited by David Lyon and Marguerite Van Die, 131–48. Toronto: University of Toronto Press, 2000.
Sen, Amartya. *The Idea of Justice*. Cambridge, Mass: Belknap Press of Harvard University Press, 2009.
Shachar, Ayelet. *Multicultural Jurisdictions: Cultural Differences and Women's Rights*. Cambridge, UK: Cambridge University Press, 2001.
Shavell, Steven. *Foundations of Economic Analysis of Law*. Cambridge, Mass: Belknap Press of Harvard University Press, 2004.
Sheppard, Colleen. "Constitutional Recognition of Diversity in Canada." *Vermont Law Review* 30 (2006): 463–87.
Spinosa, Charles, and Hubert L. Dreyfus. "Two Kinds of Antiessentialism and Their Consequences." *Critical Inquiry* 22, no. 4 (1996): 735–63.
Stump, Roger W. *Geography of Religion: Faith, Place and Space*. Lanham, MD: Rowman & Littlefield, 2008.
Sullivan, Winnifred, Robert Yelle, and Mateo Taussig-Rubbo, eds. *After Secular Law*. Stanford, Cal: Stanford Law Books, 2011.
Sullivan, Winnifred Fallers. *The Impossibility of Religious Freedom*. Princeton, NJ: Princeton University Press, 2005.
Taylor, Charles. *The Malaise of Modernity*. Concord, Ont: House of Anansi Press, 1991.
- "The Politics of Recognition." In *Philosophical Arguments*, 225–56. Cambridge, Mass: Harvard University Press, 1995.
- *Sources of the Self: The Making of the Modern Identity*. Cambridge, UK: Cambridge University Press, 1989.
- "Understanding and Ethnocentricity." In *Philosophy and the Human Sciences: Philosophical Papers 2*, 116–33. Cambridge, UK: Cambridge University Press, 1985.

- *Varieties of Religion Today: William James Revisited*. Cambridge, Mass: Harvard University Press, 2002.

Teubner, Gunther, and Firenze Bremen. "Juridification: Concepts, Aspects, Limits, Solutions." In *Juridification of Social Spheres: A Comparative Analysis in the Areas of Labor, Corporate, Antitrust, and Social Welfare Law*, edited by Gunther Teubner, 3–48. Berlin: De Gruyter, 1987.

Todorov, Tzvetan. *The Conquest of America: The Question of the Other*. Translated by Richard Howard. New York: Harper & Row, 1984.

Tønder, Lars. *Tolerance: A Sensorial Orientation to Politics*. New York: Oxford University Press, 2013.

Tully, James. *Strange Multiplicity: Constitutionalism in an Age of Diversity*. Cambridge, UK: Cambridge University Press, 1995.

Valverde, Mariana. "Jurisdiction and Scale: Legal 'Technicalities' as Resources for Theory." *Social & Legal Studies* 18 (2009): 139–57.

Van Praagh, Shauna. "Identity's Importance: Reflections of – and on – Diversity." *Canadian Bar Review* 80 (2001): 605–19.

Waldron, Mary Anne. *Free to Believe: Rethinking Freedom of Conscience and Religion in Canada*. Toronto: University of Toronto Press, 2013.

Warner, Michael, Jonathan VanAntwerpen, and Craig Calhoun, eds. *Varieties of Secularism in a Secular Age*. Cambridge, Mass: Harvard University Press, 2010.

Weatherston, Martin. *Heidegger's Interpretation of Kant: Categories, Imagination and Temporality*. New York: Palgrave Macmillan, 2002.

Webber, Jeremy. "Multiculturalism and the Limits to Toleration." In *Language, Culture and Values in Canada at the Dawn of the 21st Century*, edited by André Lapierre, Patricia Smart, and Pierre Savard, 269–79. Ottawa: International Council for Canadian Studies and Carleton University Press, 1996.

Weinrib, Ernest J. *The Idea of Private Law*. Rev. ed. Oxford: Oxford University Press, 2012.

Weinrib, Lorraine E. "Ontario's Sharia Law Debate: Law and Politics under the Charter." In *Law and Religious Pluralism in Canada*, edited by Richard Moon, 239–63. Vancouver: UBC Press, 2008.

Whitman, James Q. *The Origins of Reasonable Doubt: Theological Roots of the Criminal Trial*. New Haven, Conn: Yale University Press, 2008.

- "Separating Church and State: The Atlantic Divide." *Historical Reflections* 34, no. 3 (2008): 86–104.

Williams, Bernard. *Ethics and the Limits of Philosophy*. London: Routledge, 2006.

- "Realism and Moralism in Political Theory." In *In the Beginning Was the Deed: Realism and Moralism in Political Argument*, edited by Geoffrey Hawthorn, 1–17. Princeton, NJ: Princeton University Press, 2005.

– "Tolerating the Intolerable." In *The Politics of Toleration in Modern Life*, edited by Susan Mendus, 65–75. Durham, NC: Duke University Press, 2000.

Williams, Raymond. *Culture*. Glasgow: Fontana Paperbacks, 1981.

Woehrling, José. "L'obligation d'accommodement raisonnable et l'adaptation de la société à la diversité religieuse." *McGill Law Journal* 43 (1998): 325–401.

Wolff, Robert Paul. "Beyond Tolerance." In *A Critique of Pure Tolerance*, edited by Robert Paul Wolff, Barrington Moore, Jr, and Herbert Marcuse, 3–52. Boston: Beacon, 1965.

Young, Iris Marion. "Five Faces of Oppression." *Philosophical Forum* 19, no. 4 (1988): 270–90.

# Index

www.ingramcontent.com/pod-product-compliance
Ingram Content Group UK Ltd.
Pitfield, Milton Keynes, MK11 3LW, UK
UKHW032119310125
454513UK00001B/48